Spoilt for Choice

How senior managers select professional advisors

Wienke Seeger

Series in Business and Finance

VERNON PRESS

www.vernonpress.com

In the Americas:
Vernon Press
1000 N West Street,
Suite 1200, Wilmington,
Delaware 19801
United States

In the rest of the world:
Vernon Press
C/Sancti Espiritu 17,
Malaga, 29006
Spain

Series in Business and Finance

Library of Congress Control Number: 2018965331

ISBN: 978-1-62273-637-9

Also available: 978-1-62273-547-1 [Hardback, Premium Color];

978-1-62273-526-6 [Hardback, B&W]; 978-1-62273-590-7 [PDF, E-Book]

Cover design by Vernon Press, using elements designed by Freepik: https://www.freepik.com/free-vector/worldwide-connection-blue-background-illustration-vector_3439367.htm#term=network&page=3&position=1

Table of Contents

Preface

This book is based on a successful PhD research project - a study of how senior executives of large companies interact with, select and appoint professional service advisors.

The author successively charts the research project - from the first initial hunch to the development of a substantive theory and decision-making models - as a personal journey. Written in the less conventional first-person narrative, it reflects the auto-ethnographic (Anderson 2006) stance and the adopted constructivist grounded theory (Charmaz 2006) approach.

Following an explorative inductive approach, the study has generated some new insights, identifying two decision-making processes and with that bringing together two distinct bodies of literature: the client-advisor relationship decision as part of relationship management in the wider marketing debate and the selection decision as part of discussions on operational procurement or organisational sourcing.

Reading the research narrative from start to finish will appeal in particular to readers with an interest in theory development and the practical application of the research methodology. Whereas, readers drawn to the findings and resulting decision-making models might want to focus on the later sections from Chapter Five onwards, after taking note of the introductory comments in Chapter One.

The thesis has been kept on purpose intact with the full narrative - only a few sections have been abridged and some more personal data points altered - to serve as a type of practical case study for constructivist grounded theory (Charmaz 2006), and moreover, to demonstrate the thoroughness and rigour that has gone into the development of the proposed theories and concepts.

Hopefully, the book will also inspire and motivate researchers and practitioners alike to expand and build on the study findings and/or perhaps follow suit and adopt a constructivist grounded theory methodology in a management and business studied context.

Acknowledgements

The academic research project documented in the ensuing chapters of this book has been a personal journey over many years. I would like to acknowledge and thank those individuals who have accompanied and supported me on this journey. Without their encouragement and help, this doctoral thesis would not have been completed.

I would like to express my warmest gratitude to my first supervisor, Dr Sunitha Narendran, and second supervisor, Dr Stephen Gourlay, for encouraging me to find my own path and supporting me unreservedly.

Likewise, I am grateful to my employer and members of the leadership team who supported my academic interests, gave permission to use and analyse client feedback data, and allowed me to take a longer sabbatical to complete the analysis and write-up. I would like to express special thanks to Nick, who acted as my 'professional sponsor', patiently listened to my ideas and my never-ending lists of results and provided feedback.

Most of all I would like to thank my family, my husband and children, for their understanding and patience, putting up with me hiding away in the study to write. Plus, I would like to mention my parents and sister, who instilled in me early on a desire for academic work, and whose encouragement and continuous interest in my research kept me going.

Finally, I would like to dedicate this thesis to my little Norwich Terrier Phoebe, who has been my constant companion and a calming presence throughout this lengthy process. Her reassuring snoring and intermittent requests for a walkie carried me through the ups and downs of this research journey.

List of Figures

List of Tables

Chapter 1

Starting point – impetus and background for the research journey

Understanding and managing client relationships has been a continuous thread throughout my career, which naturally translated into an academic interest. This research project has been a very personal journey over the past four years, adopting a constructivist grounded theory approach in conjunction with auto-ethnographic elements. For that reason, I have opted for a non-traditional and narrative format. In Chapter Two, I elaborate in detail the rationale for choosing this particular methodological approach and narrative format.

As part of the auto-ethnographically driven narrative format, in this manuscript I effectively retrace the research voyage, step by step, as it evolved. In line with grounded theory methods, the literature review of comparable peer-reviewed studies takes place after the analysis and discussion of my empirical findings. However, in order to help me progress the research journey, I consulted general philosophical and methodological literature throughout the project for assistance, which I refer to intermittently. A detailed description of the thesis structure and content can be found at the end of Section 1.1, Introduction and overview.

1.1 Introduction and overview

Before I start to describe the study and results in detail, I would like to provide an overview and some background to the context of the research project.

The overall aim of this research project was to look inductively and systematically inside an academically relatively unexplored black box: the interactions between professional advisors and senior executive clients, with an emphasis on the decision-making process of such senior executives concerning selecting and appointing advisors.

To clarify what is meant by 'senior executive clients', the primary research informants of this study are employees of commercial organisations who have decision-making authority in the selection and appointment of third-party suppliers of professional services. These services include consulting, accountancy, financial and risk advisory and tax-related services (in the ensuing sections of this chapter, I provide an overview of the professional services industry). Initially, the study investigated various client stakeholders involved in the selection and appointment process. However, during the course of the research project and as part of the theoretical sampling activities, I narrowed down the primary informant group to 'C-suite executives', meaning an organisation's senior leadership, or the top management layer from a hierarchical perspective. In my professional experience, these senior leaders are frequently referred to in this way, as many organisations choose titles with acronyms including the letter 'C', such as chief executive officer (CEO), chief financial officer (CFO), chief operations officer (COO), chief risk officer (CRO) and chief information officer (CIO). Some organisations, of course, make use of different terminology and titles, but for this research project, I have adopted the term 'C-suite' to describe the top layer of an organisation's management.

Large organisations, in the context of this study, are commercial entities which are either listed on the UK stock exchange, are in the FTSE250, or are of comparable size regarding the number of employees and disclosed revenue. In summary, the main actors in this study are senior executives clients of large organisations (client organisations), who interact with individual professional advisors (advisors), who in turn are part of a large professional services firm such as one of the Big Four accountancy and advisory firms (advisory firms), described in the following sections of this chapter.

Fortunately, through my professional role for one of the largest professional services firms in the world, I have been in a privileged position to not only interview senior executives as part of my job but also independently observe the wider interactions between executive clients and advisors as well as the surrounding internal debates. Being exposed to these deliberations, combined with some initial observations I made during my first interviews, as well as my own experience to date, gave me the impetus and motivation for my doctoral research project.

When I started to embark on the research, I quickly realised that most of the accessible material tended to focus predominantly on tactical issues and measures. This did not quite produce a cohesive larger picture describing executives' decision-making processes when it comes to selecting and appointing advisors. Consequently, instead of adopting a particular existing theory, I decided to start my research with a blank sheet of paper with the aim of exploring and developing a new model using a systematic and inductive approach, comparing client commentaries while considering different standpoints.

Due to my professional role, I am fully immersed in and a visible member of the research context. I play an active part in both constructing and interpreting the data and am committed to developing a theoretical understanding of the broader social phenomena that I am investigating (Anderson 2006). With that in mind, I have chosen to follow a constructivist approach to grounded theory, as advocated by Kathy Charmaz (2006), combined with analytical auto-ethnographic elements (Anderson 2006). In so doing, I acknowledge and embrace the interaction between the researcher and the researched and not just the data alone (Easterby-Smith 2008). In the following chapter, I will discuss this decision and how these two research methodologies have shaped my research journey; I will also elaborate on why I have not opted to follow a case study approach.

This book, charting the research journey, is arranged over eight chapters. The following flowchart aims to summarise the content of the manuscript:

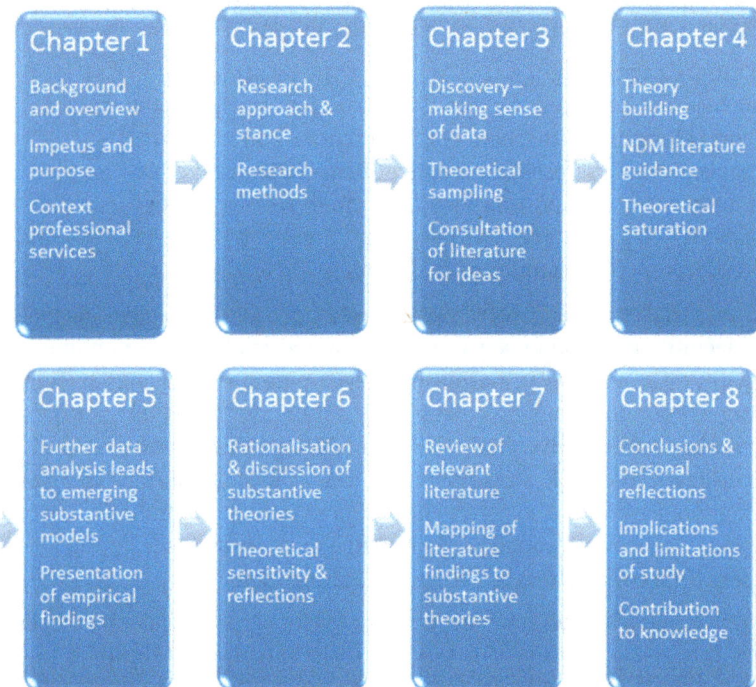

Figure 1.1 – Overview of thesis structure and chapter contents

In **Chapter One**, I offer some background and contextual information underpinning the study and describe in more detail the 'hunch' – the intuitive starting point for the research.

In **Chapter Two**, I discuss the research approach and stance taken and how these are reflected in my research journey and activities, as well as the applied auto-ethnographic framework.

Chapters Three and Four chart the progress from the exploration of the data and observed phenomena to an emerging conceptual framework, advised by naturalistic decision-making theories, and cumulating in theoretical saturation. This is followed by a demonstration and discussion of the empirical findings, resulting in first theories, which are presented in **Chapter Five**.

In **Chapter Six**, the empirical debate concludes with the rationalisation of the emerging theory and the presentation of substantive theoretical models.

In line with the grounded theory methodology, a review of the literature in the field and a critical analysis of the substantive theories follow the data analysis and can be found in **Chapter Seven**.

Lastly, **Chapter Eight** wraps up the research project with a set of final conclusions informed by the literature findings and the substantive theory, alongside a discussion of inferences and implications for client organisations, professional service firms and academia, as well as limitations and opportunities for further research. This last chapter concludes the research journey with a number of reflections and a consideration of the study's contribution to the field.

The actual empirical analysis progressed through three stages: **discovery** – selecting and making sense of the data and exploring the phenomena (Chapter Three); **theory building** – developing an emerging conceptual framework and reaching theoretical saturation (Chapter Four); and **emerging substantive models** – analysing the empirical findings according to theoretical sensitivities to shape a set of substantive theories (Chapters Five and Six). After the empirical analysis, findings from the literature review are added to the research considerations (Chapter Seven) before **final conclusions** are drawn in Chapter Eight.

In summary, and without straying too far into the conclusions, I believe that this research project offers three significant contributions to the knowledge in this field. First of all, the research identifies two decision-making processes that inform the interactions between clients and advisors. These two processes have so far been examined in two, effectively distinct, bodies of literature and theoretical context: the first decision-making process (for the client to develop and maintain a relationship or rapport with an advisor) can be found in the marketing literature as part of the relationship management or marketing debate, and the second decision-making process (for the client to select and appoint an advisor for a particular service or project) has been discussed in operational procurement or organisational sourcing debates. Thus, this study brings these two academic debates together.

Secondly, two substantive theories emerge from the empirical research: a conceptual framework which allows for both decision-making processes to be mapped, as well as a decision-making matrix which provides an understanding as to how the decision-processes might unfold, as the decision-maker considers and balances the four foci of the decision-making matrix as part of the decision-making process.

Lastly, the study also offers noteworthy methodological contributions: The empirical research provides a truly naturalistic account of the interactions between senior executives of large organisations and professional advisors in large professional service firms by adopting an analytic auto-ethnographic (Anderson 2006) constructivist grounded-theory (Charmaz 2006) approach. So far, according to Simone Pettigrew (2000), there has been limited adoption of such an amalgamated research approach and even less in the context of naturalistic decision-making.

1.2 Background and context

The ensuing sections of this first chapter aim to capture the impetus and starting-point of my research journey – what I set out to investigate and why. In conversations with academic peers, I quickly realised that I frequently referred to or made use of numerous concepts and terms used in the field, which I had acquired and become accustomed to by having worked in professional services over the years. Many of these notions are fairly complex, interlinked aspects that determine professional service industry dynamics, and I found myself explaining these fundamental aspects first, especially to those who have not been involved or exposed to this industry, before I could elaborate on my research project. For example, due to their diverse service offering, the four largest professional service firms (also referred to as the 'Big Four' professional services firms) occupy a unique position in this industry. A senior executive might experience 'Big Four' partners in various contexts, such as external audit, corporate finance, risk and regulation debates and management consulting, ranging from strategic advice to hands-on implementation of technologies or even outsourcing. In every context, a different set of competitors appears. For instance, in corporate finance, the 'Big Four' firms compete with 'magic circle' law firms and investment banks, whereas in strategic management consulting, specialised strategy consultancy firms such as McKinsey, Boston Consulting Group or Bain would be the main competitors.

In the subsequent sections, I would like to provide an overview of the research context – the wider landscape in which these 'Big Four' firms are operating. Moreover, the ensuing description of the research context, which is predominantly based on my personal observations and experiences, aims to *'reflect on and convey the current position'* or understanding *'and state of the researcher'*, in line with the auto-ethnographic approach taken (Noy 2003, page 7).

1.2.1 'Big Four' – key players in the professional services industry

The research investigates the dynamics of interactions between senior executives, such as the chief executive and financial officers of large organisations (clients), and advisory partners of equally large professional services firms (advisors). In other words, it seeks to understand the client–advisor set-up. Furthermore, the emphasis of the research is to investigate the implicit decision-making processes that underpin the selection and appointment of advisors.

The so-called 'Big Four' firms, namely Ernst & Young (EY), Klynveld, Peat, Marwick and Goerdeler (KPMG), PricewaterhouseCoopers (PwC) and Deloitte, are often described as a driving force within the wider professional services provider community, which also includes global law firms, strategy houses such as McKinsey and Bain, tech firms such as IBM and EDS, as well as a host of other firms and organisations ranging in size, offerings and specialisations (Boussebaa 2015, Carter, Crawford et al. 2015, Czerniawska 1999, Czerniawska 2006). Furthermore, the competitive landscape for these 'Big Four' firms is constantly shifting and evolving; fairly recently, there has been renewed interest by these four firms in extending their service offering and providing legal services to clients (Attack of the bean- counters; Professional services. 2015). The following statement taken from a Thomson Reuters blog offers an insight:

> *"The 'Big Four' together have more revenue ($120 billion) than all the AmLaw 100 firms combined ($89 billion). Because the accounting / auditing industry is more concentrated, each serves many more corporate clients than any law firm ever could, and their clients are well positioned, in key leadership functions." (Curle 2015)*

In 2014, the 'Big Four' firms generated revenue of over £9 billion in the UK alone (Agnew 2015) while employing over 56,000 individuals; on a global level, the revenue figure increases to US$ 120 billion (Statistica - the Statistics Portal 2015). The traditional core offering of these firms has been external audit services (statutory and non-statutory audit). However, auditing services now only constitute a small portion of the overall revenue data: £2.8 billion out of the £9 billion quoted above (Agnew 2015). The remaining £6.2 billion of revenue is being generated by what is referred to in the industry as 'advisory services', which can be broken down into consulting, financial advisory, tax and enterprise risk (Statistica - the Statistics Portal 2015). Even though the firms are being referred to and branded as one entity, each of them is actually a network of regional firms managed in a partnership structure.

1.2.2 'Big Four' – impact on public issues

Due to their size, general presence and impact on the economy, the 'Big Four' firms garner substantial public interest in the form of public debate and press coverage but also academic interest. In the past two years, over 17,000 academically linked articles and books have made reference to the 'Big Four' firms (source: Google scholar search 'Big Four' firms and professional services). 'Big Four' firms have frequently been linked to the following, at times controversial, debates in the recent past:

- General convergence in the external audit space: In the 1980s, there were eight big accounting firms worldwide; over the following two decades, the number has consolidated via mergers to only four. Naturally, government and regulatory bodies are concerned about the lack of competition and the influence that these firms are able to exert (Boussebaa 2015, Crump 2013, Greenwood et al. 2010, Pong and McMeeking 2007).
- The recent financial crisis and the 'Big Four' firms' involvement or contribution to the crisis, which has led to calls for more oversight and regulation from authorities, and has also resulted in potentially significant fines for the firms (Arnold 2009, Greenwood et al. 2010, Warner 2011).
- The public debate and government hearings around corporate tax 'avoidance' programmes set up by the firms for foreign organisations in particular such as Starbucks and Google (Carter et al. 2015).
- Individual cases of UK-based firms going through either cost-reduction or liquidation programmes involving substantial local redundancies and off-shoring of business units (Boussebaa 2015, Greenwood et al. 2010).

There are numerous other topics that could be mentioned here and elaborated upon at length. Nevertheless, the fundamental concern of all these debates is the tremendous impact that these firms have on global economies and governments as well as individuals' lives. Some scholars like Mehdi Boussebaa (2015) go as far as to compare these firms' sphere of influence to a type of imperialism and colonisation. In his article *'Professional service firms, globalisation and the new imperialism'* published in 2015, Mehdi provides a comprehensively and independently researched view of these firms:

> *"Global professional service firms (GPSFs) have emerged as major international corporate players ... they play a major part in the global expansion and management of capitalism. ... GPSFs also offer specialised services that are crucial for major multinational corporations in running their geographically dispersed operations (Sassen 2001)." (Boussebaa 2015, page 1217)*

Therefore, investigating the dynamics between large client organisations and 'Big Four' advisory firms and how they choose to select and work with each other should be of wider general and academic interest.

1.2.3 'Big Four' – competitive landscape and service offerings

As previously indicated, the 'Big Four' firms operate in a multidimensional competitive landscape. Based on my experiences and observations, these firms not only rival each other but compete against a host of other companies, ranging from small boutique partnerships to Fortune 500 tech firms. Furthermore, due to their wide advisory service offering, these four large firms are able to compete in numerous different domains (consulting, tax, legal, corporate finance) and levels (ranging from strategy to outsourcing). For example, in management consulting, a 'Big Four' firm will compete with strategy houses such as McKinsey, Boston Consulting Group and Bain for short but high-end strategy projects at one level, while at the same time bidding for large-scale, multi-year technology implementations and against tech and outsourcing companies such as IBM, WIPRO, SAP as well as large corporate consultancy firms like Accenture and Cap Gemini, and niche players such as Baringa and CapCo. This, of course, adds a certain complexity for clients engaging with them. For example, a CFO might experience a 'Big Four' firm in the context of a business-critical regulatory project, but then also interact with the firm on tax and structuring matters, or his management team may view the same firm as a potential service provider for a large system implementation. The 'Big Four' firms view and position their wide range of service offerings as their main selling points, meaning that the client or client organisation is able to source various professional services from one partner instead of having to engage with multiple providers.

'Big Four' firms differentiate between audit and non-audit, also referred to as advisory services, whereby many consider external audit services to be the 'bread and butter' or the original offering of the 'Big Four' accounting firms. However, the scope of this research project is limited to advisory services. I consciously decided to exclude audit services because the 'client organisation–audit firm dynamics' are notably different, with the auditor having to follow strict regulatory stipulations, act independently and be accountable to the company board and stakeholders and not to senior management. External audit is defined as a regular examination of the books …

> *"… carried out by an independent third party (the auditor), to ensure that they [the accounts] have been properly maintained, are accurate and comply with established concepts, principles, accounting standards, legal requirements and give a true and fair view of the financial state of the entity". CIMA's Management Accounting Official Terminology (CIMA - Chartered Institute of Management Accountants 2016)*

whereas advisory services are considered to be all other services offered and provided by the professional services firm.

1.2.4 'Big Four' – partnership structure and account management

Drawing on my own professional experiences and a common understanding in the industry (Czerniawska 1999, Czerniawska 2006, Greenwood et al. 2010), another inherent level of complexity lies in the partnership structure of the 'Big Four' firms. They are not corporates such as a multinational Fortune 500 company. Local or regional firms are linked together via global networks and governed by elected groups of partners, often referred to as the 'Executive' and the 'leadership team'. Even within local firms, for example, the 'Big Four UK', there can be various management set-ups and fractions with differing opinions brought together by one elected leadership team. Operating structures vary from firm to firm, local member firm to member firm (the UK is set up differently from, for instance, Germany) and even between service line divisions (for example, tax often has no industry segmentation while the other service lines are organised by industry or sectors). Frequently, one or two senior partners will start their own initiatives, recruiting or diverting staff to work on particular internal and client-facing initiatives. Senior firm internal stakeholders often referred to the different groups as a 'bunch of cottage industries'.

Furthermore, those senior partners who have secured the lead position and therefore 'ownership' of the larger client accounts frequently run and service these accounts like mini operations with the support of a group of other partners under the overall stewardship of the firm's Executive. Depending on the lead partner's management style, he or she will either personally manage the relationships with clients' top management or ask another partner to 'face off', meaning liaise, with a senior client contact. The following two examples taken from the study illustrate the client–advisor account team dynamics:

The account team serving company D is led by a senior consulting partner who specialises in technology. This particular partner manages the account very collaboratively, by rallying a group of experienced partners around him who are willing to dedicate time and effort to develop the account and the relationship with key client stakeholders. Selected partners 'face off' to different client stakeholders either based on technical expertise (for example, an audit partner manages the relationship with the client contact responsible for internal audit) or previous and existing relationships (for example, a partner who is not part of the core account team but has a long-standing personal relationship with the chief operations officer). The lead partner acts as a point of escalation and holds a coordinating function within the account team but also for the client contacts. The account team meets at regular intervals to discuss strategies, longer-term plans and tactical next steps, as well as to exchange information.

The account team serving company B, in contrast, is led by a senior audit partner who specialises in risk and regulation. The partner effectively manages the account on his own, with some operational day-to-day support from a few junior staff. The lead partner 'faces off' to all of the senior stakeholders in the client organisation on a regular basis, and only if an engagement is being discussed does he bring in another partner with the relevant technical and industry experience. This new partner may or may not stay engaged with the client contact after the completion of the project.

These are two very diverse examples of how client organisations are being serviced by professional services lead partners and account teams. It might be helpful, in order to create a common understanding, to point out a number of other initial observations I have made concerning the contact between client and advisor:

- In general, advisors aim to meet with senior client stakeholders on a regular basis. Depending on personal preferences and established patterns, these meetings could be informal over a cup of coffee or lunch or more formal in an office setting. Frequency and content vary and are contingent on circumstances, client needs and advisors' agendas. The main objective from an advisor's point of view is to stay engaged and connect with the client contact, to take note of the clients' issues and challenges, and to bring some new ideas and insights; in other words, they try and build a rapport or relationship.
- The advisor offers this interaction without charging the client for their time and preparation; it is seen as an investment in the account and the client contact by the firm.
- Some client contacts like and value these meetings; others accept them as part of doing business; some individuals try and avoid them or keep them as short as possible.
- All of the above points fall under what is frequently referred to as relationship building, or more precisely business development – to advance and nurture opportunities with clients and client organisations.
- When it comes to actually selecting an advisory firm to provide a service which is formalised in a written contractual agreement between the organisation and the firm, the dynamics are or can be different, meaning different parties and processes might be involved in the decision-making. However, these more or less regular meetings with the client are seen as a platform to 'sell' services.
- The initial contact between advisor and client could either be a function of an existing relationship between the two organisations or individuals – for example, a new finance director joins a company and that company has an existing relationship and maybe a number of ongoing projects with the advisory firm; either he or she will then meet the advisor as part of a regular project meeting or the advisor might ask for an introductory meeting. Alternatively, for example, an advisor and client contact may have worked closely together in the past and stayed in contact; now the advisor has changed to another firm and he or she might approach the client to continue the dialogue under these new circumstances. There are also situations where a client pro-actively contacts an advisory firm for the first time – for example, a company decides to

implement software such as SAP and a firm is listed in publications as the expert in this technology or module. Alternatively, the advisor pro-actively tries to build a rapport by asking someone in his or her network to arrange for an introduction or even 'cold calling' a client for a meeting.

Naturally, this relationship element is central to the client–advisor dynamic and there is always a degree of tension as to who within the advisory firm 'owns' the relationship with the client contact and the overall account. Does the individual partner 'own' the relationships and the account, being ultimately accountable for revenue figures and some internal metrics? Or does the firm as an entity own the relationships and, by assigning the account to the partner, offer him or her the opportunity to engage? This is an interesting debate, which can be viewed from many angles and could warrant further academic investigation.

In conclusion, these diverse and flexible set-ups within the advisory firms offer opportunities for innovation and entrepreneurial activities and provide a personal touch to each account and client relationship. Simultaneously, it creates a rather multifaceted and complex structure, which is at times difficult to grasp as well as hard to operate in for both clients and advisory teams.

1.3 Study based on personal journey

This research journey is closely linked to my professional role, since the study is based on empirical client interview data that I gathered while working for a 'Big Four' firm, and draws on field observations and personal experiences. Considering the research context, I have opted to adopt and combine Kathy Charmaz's (2006) constructivist approach to grounded theory with elements of an analytic-auto-ethnographic research framework as advocated by Leon Anderson (2006). My current and previous experiences, having worked for a number of different professional service firms, played a role in how I viewed and interpreted client commentary (primary data), and has helped me to identify patterns and articulate the resulting substantive theories. In the next chapter – the foundation of my research journey – I will return to this combined approach and elaborate in detail on the philosophical and methodological underpinnings of my research and reflect on my personal, auto-ethnographic involvement.

In the next sections, I provide some background information about how I gathered the data for this study and describe the impetus and my general motivations for embarking on this research journey. The following comments capture the starting point and the context of the research process; thus, they are a reflection on my initial position and state (Noy 2003).

1.3.1 Client feedback – client listening

After having spent over ten years in various management consulting roles, primarily specialising in client relationship management (CRM) projects, I took on a role for one of the 'Big Four' firms to manage their internal client feedback programme, often also referred to as 'client listening'. (Some organisations outsource some or all of their client feedback or listening activities. Hence a distinction is made between internal and external client feedback programmes and activities.) Based on my observations and having networked with peers in the past four years, I am able to conclude that many of the professional services firms and all of the 'Big Four' firms have a type of client feedback operation in place, albeit the focus, structure and type of data gathered vary from firm to firm. Some professional services firms only ask for client feedback on past project experiences; others might follow up after an appointment decision has been made, in the form of a bid debrief, also referred to as a win-loss review. Only a few firms carry out a substantive holistic review of accounts on a regular basis. Feedback can be captured either in the form of an electronic survey, structured telephone interview or fairly unstructured face-to-face interviews. Some firms prefer to capture and translate the findings into quantitative datasets and prepare a type of performance dashboard for senior leadership. Others, like my employer, choose to summarise the findings in strategic reports consisting principally of qualitative data and prose. On an aggregated level, client feedback findings are predominately used by firms for business development activities and to inform strategic initiatives: some findings circle back into quality and risk management and talent or performance management. Again, this varies considerably from firm to firm, and the focus might shift over time with leadership changes.

For this research project, I decided to focus on advisory, non-external audit reviews where I had personally conducted the interviews. The rationale for only including my own interviews can be linked to my adoption of the constructivist grounded theory approach, auto-ethnographic elements and chosen narrative format. As the researcher, I acknowledge that I am part of the process and hence analysing interview data generated by another person removes this element of participation. Having said that, in my observations I do of course record experiences of my team members, be it client interview experiences or internal discussions (Charmaz 2006, Anderson 2006).

1.4 Impetus and motivations

Early on, when I started interviewing senior client executives, I quickly came to realise that some of the client comments did not quite match up with the internal models and corresponding debates that both senior leadership and the partner community were using and referring to. This rather intuitive feeling, of things being not quite consistent between what the clients were communicating and the internal discussions, was effectively the trigger for me. It made me want to step back and try and evaluate this social phenomenon that I was observing, more systematically and from an academic perspective. In the following Section 1.4.1, I summarise my observations, which led me to conclude that there was a degree of disconnect between client comments and the advisor's perspective.

1.4.1 Initial observation turns into 'hunch'

The firm had a number of strategies, models and measures in place with the aim of managing client relationships more successfully. Some of the **initial observations** that I made at that point were the following:

- The actual delivery experience – providing the services to the client – was viewed by the advisors and the advisory firm as a foundation layer, and notions such as responsiveness and quality of service associated with the experience were seen as important but rarely discussed. Often these aspects were referred to as hygiene factors that needed to be in place – a tick in a box – in order to be considered by a client 'to be in the game'.
- Most internal discussions within the advisory firm focused on softer aspects of relationship management, such as offering thought leadership, developing affinity with the client and providing challenges, which were perceived to generate value-add for the client.
- The general assumption, made by the advisor and advisory firm, was that once the relationship management side has been mastered, this would propel the overall relationship between the firm and client organisation to a higher level, resulting in even closer collaboration, which could take the form of joint investments or ventures or innovation partnering, and in

general lead to the advisor being seen as THE trusted advisor to the client and the client organisation. This construct was seen internally as the 'holy grail' – to achieve the ultimate goal of being 'the trusted', and with that of course 'the preferred', advisor.

- Moreover, I noticed a strong emphasis on C-suite relationships from the advisors and advisory firm. As noted above, the C-suite constitutes the chief executive officer, chief finance officer and chief operations officer – the top layer of senior management within an organisation. One measure which was frequently discussed was 'C-suite penetration', in terms of how close the relationship was between the client and the advisor. This was a concept I could never quite warm to, from a content or a terminology point of view. I also noticed that partners were engrossed in trying to score highly in this measure and the firm experimented with a number of different definitions and guidelines.

- In addition, there were other measures such as the 'net promoter score' (NPS) which was based on the question 'Would the client recommend the firm?', and a balance score card was introduced, which included relationship measures.

These were just some of my initial reflections as I grappled to understand and capture this social phenomenon. I started to note down a number of observations to articulate more clearly the impetus and underlying 'hunch' for the study:

Did the advisor or the advisory firm really take note of what the individual client and client organisation expected and wanted from them? I came out of some interviews with a feeling that there was not always a common understanding. Although the advisory firm did take into account client comments from feedback interviews, the partners' and firms' objectives appeared to be more self-serving. For example, one of the senior partners saw his relationship objective as 'to be sticky', i.e. become indispensable to the client. The general assumption, or hypothesis, that most partners subscribed to was that if you had a close or strong relationship with a senior manager, this would translate into higher project revenues.

Consequently, I continued to wonder if this was a realistic reflection of how clients made their decisions regarding who they appointed or would even be willing to interact with, and whether clients consciously signed up to this arrangement.

1.4.2 Approach and research aims

While noting down these initial thoughts and observations, I was contemplating how to approach this research prospect. Instead of validating or testing a particular model or notion, I wanted to start with a clean sheet of paper. I did not feel at ease with some of the underlying firm internal principles and assumptions; therefore, a fresh start unburdened by these views combined with a strong emphasis on the clients' perspective would be a more illuminating way to approach the research matter.

I decided to focus more strongly on the client's perspective and to let the clients speak for themselves in the form of the interview data. I was already well aware of and familiar with the advisory perspective as a result of my ongoing professional responsibilities as a client feedback programme lead. In order not to predispose or precondition my thinking, and in line with a grounded theory approach, I consciously tried to ignore most internal, professional and academic studies in this field during the first, empirical phase of my analysis. Of course, there were unavoidable messages that came to my attention via my day-to-day role in the business, which I then included in my memos; I will return to this aspect in Chapter Two.

> *"… narrative research is a voyage of discovery—a discovery of meanings …"*
> *(Josselson and Lieblich 2003, page 250)*

I set out on my research journey with the aim of inquiring into the social phenomenon of how senior executive clients interact with and consequently select professional advisors. In order to determine a general direction of travel and guide my research endeavour, during the initial discovery phase (described in Chapter Three) I drafted four open research questions, in addition to the research aim. These questions emerged once I started investigating the data, and therefore were informed by the empirical data; they were in line with my chosen combined narrative, auto-ethnographic (Anderson 2006) and constructivist grounded theory approach (Charmaz 2006). The four questions were:

- Why do senior executives engage with and employ professional service firms and their advisors?
- How do senior executives choose to interact with professional service firms and their advisors?
- How do senior executives select and appoint professional service firms and advisors?

- To what extent does the interaction (rapport between manager and advisor or firm) influence or shape the selection of an advisor to deliver a project?

In sum, the focus of the research study evolved from the research aim, which was to investigate the interactions between professional advisors and senior executive clients, with an emphasis on the decision-making process of such senior executives concerning selecting and appointing advisors. A set of research questions were formulated, which then translated into a gradually emerging conceptual framework and resulting theory. Chapters Three and Four will describe in detail how these developments unfolded.

Chapter One has described the background, research setting and impetus for the study and reflects on my state and understanding as the researcher at the start of this process. In Chapter Two, I will elaborate in detail on why and how I adopted the constructivist grounded theory approach combined with auto-ethnographic elements and chose a narrative format, as well as discussing other methods and tools that I used during the research project.

Chapter 2

Foundation – research design, methods and tools

In this chapter, I describe how the study's purpose and context, as discussed in the previous chapter, informed and shaped the research design, meaning the theoretical approaches, methods and tools utilised as part of the research process. After reviewing the literature evaluating different research approaches and discussions with my supervisors, I made an informed decision and adopted a constructivist grounded theory methodology combined with an analytical auto-ethnographic stance.

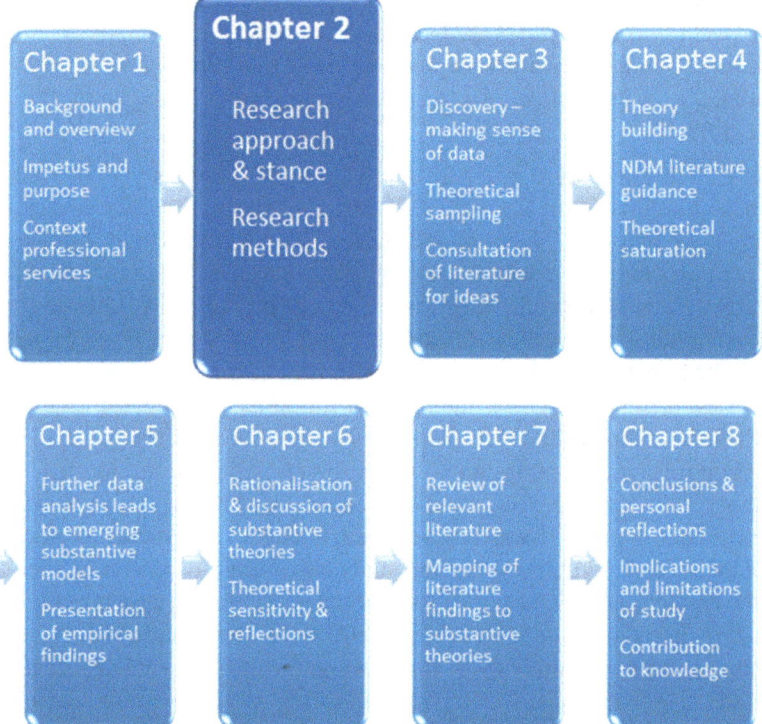

Figure 2.1 – Overview of thesis structure and content of the second chapter

Reflecting on and summarising the starting point of the study, its context and aims, the research encapsulates the following aspects:

- The use of existing and evolving **qualitative data** gathered as part of the client feedback process.
- A focus on **understanding human interactions**, in terms of the rapport between the senior executive and the 'Big Four' advisor, and the selection and appointment of the advisor and advisory firm to deliver a service.
- A clear understanding that the study is primarily **explorative**; it is not intended to test or confirm an existing theory, but to develop a further theory based on the observations and other data points.
- Due to the nature and source of the data, the **sample size is constrained** by the number of interviews and the unstructured style of interviewing.

The four configurations described above are, according to Martyn Denscombe (2010), the hallmark features of grounded theory research *"It (grounded theory) is an approach that emphasises the importance of empirical fieldwork and the need to link any explanations very closely to what happens in practical situations in 'the real world'." (Denscombe 2010, page 107)*

Of course, there were other qualitative research designs which would also have embraced the four aspects mentioned above. I considered a case study approach initially, but once I started reviewing the client interview data more closely, I rejected this approach because I was not able to clearly define what would constitute 'a case'. The literature states that a case should be *"bounded by time or place and inform a problem"* (Hanson et al. 2005, page 241). The multiple relationship layers embedded in the interview data (client, client organisation, advisors, advisory firm), as well as the information from past experiences (with different advisors, different working roles and organisations), made the identification of one case to compare with another case extremely difficult. Furthermore, at the start of the research journey, I was not yet clear enough in my mind as to the precise issues or 'problems' that the study was examining. As I mentioned at the end of Chapter One, I commenced the research with a clear research aim, to investigate the interactions between professional advisors and senior executive clients, with an emphasis on the decision-making process of such senior executives concerning selecting and appointing advisors. But it was only after the first analysis of the data that I was able to draft a set of high-level research questions to guide my subsequent research activities.

2.1 Research purpose and methodologies

The overarching purpose of this study is to reach a nuanced and detailed understanding of the interactions between senior executives and advisors, and the associated decision-making process which leads to the selection and appointment of advisors from large advisory firms such as the 'Big Four' professional service firms. The focus of the research is on observing and comprehending actual or natural behaviours, utilising an auto-ethnographic stance and combining this with a grounded theory epistemology; the approach is reflexive, with care taken to describe and not to prescribe.

This research journey started out with a 'hunch' that client-advisor interactions and the ensuing appointment of advisors were not fully understood, an intuition that came to me as part of my professional role working for one of the 'Big Four' firms. As I mentioned in the introductory first chapter, I made the conscious decision to work inductively, starting with a blank sheet, while my position in the client feedback team provided access to qualitative client data and insights. I examined a number of qualitative research methodologies, such as discourse analysis (Burr 1998, Coyle 1995, Parker 1997, Willig 2003), dimensional analysis (Bowers and Schatzman 2009), content analysis (Krippendorff 2004, Krippendorff 2012) and even linguistic analysis (Pennebaker, King 1999, Pennebaker et al. 2001), as well as a case study research design (Eisenhardt 1989) as discussed in the previous section. Informed by discussions with my supervisors, I adopted a constructivist grounded theory approach and embarked on the research project.

Auto-ethnographic elements were always present as part of the study, primarily since I drew on data and experiences from my work environment. However, during the later stages of the research and in reflection, I recognised the full extent of the auto-ethnographic elements which I had applied intuitively throughout in conjunction with the constructivist grounded theory approach. Recognising the auto-ethnographic elements, and my desire to document personal reflections and thoughts as part of the research process, guided me towards a narrative format for this thesis document. This narrative format allowed me to be the *"visible and active researcher in the text"* (Anderson 2006, page 383), as stipulated in auto-ethnographic research. It also provided the opportunity to demonstrate reflexivity and to retrace my research activities in chronological order, which enabled me to point out how my knowledge and the resulting theory evolved, and what influenced my thinking (literature, personal observations and experiences) and ensuing research actions. I am conscious that the narrative format is not frequently used in academic writing: it is suggested that a third person rhetorical format creates a degree of distance and resulting objectivity and greater credibility (Easterby-Smith 2008). However, for me, on a personal level, the narrative format was an integral part of the described research process, which started with the memo writing. My memos and journal entries were notes written to myself from my own personal perspective and capturing my personal observations and reflections. Therefore, I took guidance from Easterby-Smith's statement that *"constructionist authors often go to great lengths to be reflexive, indicating their engagement with the research setting and influence on the research material; they often write up the research as it actually happened ..."* (Easterby-Smith 2008, page 307).

In the following sections, I elaborate on both methodologies, their epistemological stance and how I utilised them during the research.

As this study is investigating decision-making processes, I have looked at various decision-making theories to help me put my observations and reflections into context theoretically. For example, naturalistic decision-making (NDM) theories offered many helpful frameworks and standpoints to draw on. I have consulted studies and papers of the following authors: Lee Roy Beach, Jennifer Berryman, Mehdi Dastani, Gerd Gigerenzer, Julie Gore, David Jennings, Daniel Kahneman, Gary Klein, Raanan Lipshitz, Peter Meso, Henry Mintzberg, Kathleen Mosier, Judith Orasanu, Jens Rasmussen, Eduardo Salas, Barry Schwartz, Lawrence Shattuck, Herbert Simon, Richard Thaler, Frank Yates and Caroline Zsambok, to name a few. I will return to how NDM informed my research journey in Chapters Three and Four, in which I elaborate on my analysis and theorising activities.

2.1.1 Grounded theory

Kathy Charmaz (2009, page 125) describes the grounded theory as an umbrella term which covers *"several different variants, emphases, and directions – and ways to think about data"* which can also be summarised as *"different starting point and conceptual agendas"*. Furthermore, according to Charmaz the fact that the two creators of grounded theory, Barney Glaser and Anselm Strauss (1967), came from two different philosophical and methodological backgrounds – the University of Chicago's pragmatism and Columbia University's positivism respectively – has put grounded theory on *"somewhat unsteady ontological and epistemological grounds and planted the seeds of divergent directions for the method"* (Charmaz 2009, page 127). From my point of view, this can, of course, also be seen as an enrichment of the theory and might possibly lead to an increased reach of the theory by potentially appealing to academics of both schools of thought (Glaser and Strauss 2009).

Glaser's (2007) starting point is based on the researcher not having any presuppositions of the field and the theory 'emerging' from the data; Strauss (1998), on the other hand, advocated for the researcher to become familiar with the field before applying very structured analytical processes and codes (Seidel and Urquhart 2013). Mark Easterby-Smith describes the Straussian approach to grounded theory as *"mechanical analytical processes to make sense of the data"* (Easterby-Smith 2008, page 101). In the literature, reference is made to two classifications of grounded theory: the 'emergent' grounded theory advocated by Glaser, which implies that the application of *"systematic comparative methods lead[s] researchers to discover theoretical categories"* (Charmaz 2008, page 150) compared to the 'systematic or analytic theory' pursued by Strauss (Strauss and Corbin 1998, 1994), in which *"the investigator focuses on a process, action, or interaction"* (Hanson et al. 2005, page 249). Charmaz (2006, 2008, 2009) refers to both Glaser and Strauss as 'objectivists', denoting that the researcher is to a certain degree removed from the experiences of the researched population. In contrast, Charmaz's (2009) constructivist approach to grounded theory acknowledges that the researcher is part of the research process and therefore embraces the notion of interaction between the researcher and the researched, whereas an objectivist methodology only views the relations between the researcher and the data (Bryant 2003).

2.1.2 Constructivist grounded theory

Constructivist grounded theory is an emergent research methodology (Breckenridge et al. 2012, Mills et al. 2006, Bryant and Charmaz 2007) and it has been applied in a number of empirical studies in recent years (Philp and Martin 2009, Dellve and Wikstroem 2009, Millar et al. 2012, Martin and Barnard 2013, Nyaupane and Poudel 2012). I was first introduced to the constructivist methodology during one of Antony Bryant's grounded theory method seminars (Bryant 2012).[1] The underlying notion that the researcher is very much part of the grounded theory process, and with that is immersed in the research, reflects the circumstances of my own research project and is in line with an analytic auto-ethnographic stance. As part of my professional role, I interview senior executives and make

---

[1] Attended grounded theory seminar given by Antony Bryant and hosted by the University of Reading, March 2012.

sense of their comments, both through my unstructured questioning and by processing the findings into strategic reports for the firm.

In addition, both Charmaz (2006, 2009) and Bryant (2012) stress flexibility in developing codes and concepts in grounded theory. According to them, it is indeed possible to develop codes from the different types of data that include conversations and by other data sources, resulting in the view that *"all is data but data is not all"* (Bryant 2012, slide 73). From this perspective, theories do not emerge from data on their own, as Glaser would argue; it is through the researcher's application of knowledge and in conversations that theories, which are based on the data, develop and get shaped. In the instance of this particular study, I have not only processed client interview data but also included other data such as win-loss review conversations with clients, firm internal reports, observations and reflections as part of my role and discussions. A complete list of all data sources consulted for this study can be found in section 2.4 of this chapter.

Following a constructivist grounded theory method requires the researcher to accept the notion that conducting and writing research are not neutral acts (Charmaz 2009, page 128). Consequently, a key requirement is reflexivity – to contemplate and examine ourselves and the research situations, processes and outputs. Charmaz speaks of *"learning to recognise our standpoints, adopt new perspectives and turn in different directions than those who focus exclusively on the data alone"* (Charmaz 2009, page 128).

In addition, a constructivist approach assumes multiple realities, mutual construction of data through interaction, and that the researcher's values, priorities and actions affect their views (Charmaz, 2006, 2008, 2009). Within the context of this study, I can confirm that the respondents, whether client stakeholders or advisors who briefed me on historic events in the account, frequently had divergent views of a particular situation or even the relationship overall. Furthermore, by asking senior executives questions such as: 'What are your expectations of an advisor in general?' and by paraphrasing responses or completing sentences, I was actively involved in and possibly even subconsciously steering the process as well. A key implication for the constructivist approach to data analysis is to *"seek and represent participants' views and voices as integral to the analysis"*, as well as to acknowledge subjectivities throughout (Charmaz 2009, page 139). Reflecting on the study, a primary motivation for conducting this research analysis was to focus on the client's perspective, to concentrate on client interview transcripts, while placing their views into a wider and theoretical context.

Especially during the initial phases, discovery and theory building, of my study, I put a strong emphasis on the client and client organisation, to make sure that sufficient consideration was given to these pivotal perspectives. Through my professional role, I felt I had ample exposure and understanding of the professional service viewpoints. Later, at the analytical or theorising stage, I cycled back to take on the advisor and advisory firm view in my analysis. Thus, I consciously tried to view the research data from four main standpoints: the senior executive client, the client organisation, the professional advisor and the advisory firm. I also made an effort to reflect on my personal views and how these might have influenced the research in the memos.

And finally, the foremost objective of a constructivist methodology is to *"create a theory that has credibility, originality, resonance and usefulness'* compared to an objectivist approach, which 'aims to create a theory that fits, works, has relevance, and is modifiable' but which might not be as applicable or useful for a wider audience"* (Charmaz 2009, page 139).

One aspect that needs to be highlighted at the outset is my use of client interview quotes. I have intermittently included quotations to underpin key observations and findings, but I have not inserted extensive verbatim passages. This was in accordance with the advice of a number of qualitative researchers (Holloway and Wheeler 1996, Kvale 1987), and also to safeguard the anonymity of the senior executives interviewed.

2.1.3 Grounded theory and ethnography

"Both grounded theory and ethnography have common roots in Chicago School sociology with its pragmatist philosophical foundations." (Charmaz, Mitchell 2001, page 160)

The term ethnography, composed of 'ethno', indicating folk or a group of individuals, and 'graphy' meaning description, involves observing and recording the life and interactions of a particular group, requiring the researcher to immerse themselves or participate to a certain degree in the group's social world (Charmaz 2006, Lee et al. 2005, Pettigrew 2000). *"The hallmark of ethnography is fieldwork; working with people in their natural settings"* (Lee et al. 2005, page 299).

Ethnography and grounded theory share a number of fundamental research principles, most notably a predominately inductive logic, extensive fieldwork and reflexivity (Charmaz 2006, Charmaz and Mitchell 2001, Lee et al. 2005). *"A reflexive stance informs how the researcher conducts his or her research, relates to the research participants, and presents them in written reports."* (Charmaz 2006, page 189). In the following sections, I review each methodology and its features in detail.

The combination of grounded theory and ethnography, at times referred to as *'grounded theory ethnography'* (Charmaz 2006, page 22) is being viewed as an amalgamation of methodologies, which can provide unique insights into behaviours, although it is not frequently found in the published and peer reviewed studies (Charmaz 2006, Pettigrew 2000, Lee et al. 2005). Pettigrew (2000, page 259) concludes that: *"These two methods (grounded theory and ethnography) combined may produce a level of detail and interpretation that is unavailable from other methodologies".*

"Grounded theory ethnography gives priority to the studies phenomenon or process rather than to a description of a setting" (Charmaz 2006, page 22). Consequently, a grounded theory-underpinned research study takes on a more focused and structured approach to fieldwork and concurrent analysis and calls for the comparison of data from the outset and requires the researcher to identify relationships between emerging concepts and categories (Charmaz 2006). According to Charmaz (2006), both theories have the potential to complement and balance each other. Grounded theory's logic of a reiterative and parallel process of data collection and analysis, which requires the researcher to go back in the field to gather more data in order to refine the emerging theory, helps to overcome the following frequently cited ethnographic problems:

> *"1) accusation of uncritically adopting research participants' views, 2) lengthy unfocused forays into the field setting, 3) superficial random data collection and 4) reliance on stock disciplinary categories"* *(Charmaz 2006, page 23).*

On the other hand, the ethnographic approach of the researcher being immersed in the research setting and commonly being a member of the community addresses the grounded theory challenge of relying on statements or interviews provided to an 'external researcher'. *"How people explain their actions to each other (members of the community) may not resemble their statements to an (external) interviewer"* (Charmaz 2006, page 25).

One could argue that a constructivist grounded theory approach has built-in ethnographic elements, since the researcher is encouraged to enter the empirical world and to seek and represent participants' views as part of the analysis (Charmaz 2006, 2009, Charmaz and Mitchell 2001).

2.1.4 Auto-ethnography

Auto-ethnography is a form of ethnography in which the *"writer addresses herself or himself ('auto') as a subject of a larger social or cultural inquiry ('graphy')" (Noy 2003, page 3)*. In the literature, reference is made to two forms of auto-ethnography – analytic and evocative. Evocative auto-ethnography's mode of narrative or storytelling at times moves beyond social science into literature – *"the narrative text refuses to abstract and explain" (Anderson 2006, page 377)*. In other words, evocative auto-ethnographers *"bypass the presentational problem by invoking an epistemology of emotion, moving the reader to feel the feeling of the other" (referring to Denzin 1997, Anderson 2006, page 228)*. Analytic, also termed realist, auto-ethnography:

> *"refers to ethnographic work in which the researcher is (1) a full member in the research group or setting, (2) visible as such a member in the researcher's published texts, and (3) committed to an analytic research agenda focused on improving theoretical understandings of broader social phenomena" (Anderson 2006, page 375)*.

Whilst this research project meets all three characteristics of an analytic auto-ethnographic study (I am a full practising member, or better employee, of a 'Big Four' firm; I am visible in the research document; I am highly committed to a structured and analytic research approach in order to investigate the identified phenomena), I did not embark on the research with an explicit or strong auto-ethnographic agenda. On reflection, I came to realise that I intuitively applied auto-ethnographic elements and elected to use a narrative format guided by the adopted constructivist grounded theory methodology.

The focal point and data source of this study is my professional role as a client feedback manager for one of the 'Big Four' advisory firms. In this particular role, I am one step removed from the client-advisor interactions since I am not an active member of the account team, delivering project or services to the client. The task of the client feedback role is to listen and feed back to the business, to audit or review the relationship and services from the client's perspective. By interviewing senior executives, I am acting on behalf of the advisory firm's leadership and there is a clear mandate to be independent and report the client messages completely objectively. The outcomes of the interviews are strategic review reports, which are meant to be frank and truthful to the client's comments while clearly stating the implications for the firm. However, some of the more harder-hitting messages, such as client requests to remove a partner from an account, are conveyed discretely in one-to-one feedback sessions arranged by senior management. Consequently, my operational role helps me retain an impartial view but with a strong focus on the client and client organisation. Therefore, this research is less about me personally and more about my professional context, as my role removes me somewhat from the ongoing interactions between client and advisor.

Nevertheless, I acknowledge that it is very difficult to conduct an interview and be completely impartial. The prior briefings with the advisors colour one's view of an individual; for example, if a client is being described as 'peculiar' or 'cheery' by the account team that, of course, does create a certain perception, which might or might not be confirmed during the interview. Plus, with some senior executives, there was an instant rapport on a personal level between the individual person and myself, which often led to a very open interview. In other instances, the conversation was more formal or cautious, and this could have been for various reasons beyond a lack of rapport between the client and myself. I reflected on these circumstances and observations in my memos.

In summary, whereas my professional setting and initial 'hunch' led me to adopt the constructivist grounded theory methodology, this theory guided me towards an analytic auto-ethnographic stance while my professional role as a client feedback manager installed a level of objectivity.

2.1.5 Epistemological underpinnings

"Grounded theory has its emphasis on the socially constructed nature of reality' (Goulding 1998), and the aim is to produce interpretations that can explain social phenomena and provide information of value to those engaged in the behaviour under study (Annells 1996, Glaser and Strauss 1967)" (Pettigrew 2000, page 257).

Charmaz's (2006, 2009) constructivist grounded theory approach offers, as discussed in section 2.1.1, an alternative to Glaser's and Strauss' respective 'objectivist' emergent and systematic-analytic approaches. Charmaz's (2009) constructivist approach to grounded theory acknowledges that the researcher is part of the research process, and therefore embraces the notion of interaction between the researcher and the researched, whereas an objectivist methodology only views the relations between the researcher and the data. In addition, *"constructivists view data as constructed rather than discovered, and we see our analysis as interpretive rendering not as objective reports or the only viewpoint on the topic"* (Charmaz 2009, page 129), which calls for a reflective and reflexive stance of the researcher as part of the research process.

Furthermore, Charmaz's constructivist grounded theory approach *"lies squarely in the interpretive tradition"* (Charmaz 2006, page 130) and builds on the initial *"pragmatist underpinnings of grounded theory"* (Charmaz 2009, page 127) while acknowledging that *"any theoretical rendering offers an interpretive portrayal of the studied world, not an exact picture"* (Charmaz 2006, page 10). *"Pragmatist tradition views reality as consisting of fluid, somewhat indeterminate processes. Pragmatism also acknowledges multiple perspectives emerging from people's actions to solve problems in their worlds"* (Charmaz 2006, Charmaz 2009, page 126).

Consequently, by taking on aspects championed by both Strauss, the Chicago School's pragmatism, and Glaser's far more interpretive take on analysing data, Charmaz created a distinctive new approach to grounded theory (Charmaz 2006, 2009). *"The constructivist approach challenges the assumption of creating general abstract theories and leads us to situated knowledges (Haraway 1991) while simultaneously moving grounded theory into interpretive social sciences."* (Charmaz 2009, page 134)

In summary, Charmaz's (2009) constructivist grounded theory is a

"contemporary revision of the Glaser and Strauss (1967) classic grounded theory. It assumes a relativist epistemology, sees knowledge as socially produced and acknowledges multiple standpoints of both the research participants and the grounded theorist. It also takes a reflexive stance toward actions, situations, and participants in the field setting" (Charmaz 2009, page 127-128).

Analytic ethnography and auto-ethnography are aligned to the analytic or realist tradition of the Chicago School (Anderson 2006), compared to evocative ethnography and auto-ethnography, which pursue a descriptive literary approach. Realist theories are based on the notion that *"both natural and social phenomena are assumed to have an existence that is independent of the activities of the human observer"* (Blaikie 2007, page 13).

Analytic auto-ethnography pursues a focused and strong scholarly purpose (Atkinson 2006) while obliging the researcher to be reflective (self-awareness) and but not necessarily reflexive, meaning that *"the ethnographer is thoroughly implicated in the phenomena"* (Atkinson et al. 2004, page 402).

Charmaz (2006) defines reflexivity slightly differently as:

"the researcher's scrutiny of his or her research experience, decisions, and interpretations in ways that bring the researcher into the process and allow the reader to assess how and to what extent the researcher's

interests, positions, and assumptions influenced inquiry" (Charmaz 2006, page 188).

My research journey was heavily guided by Charmaz's constructivist grounded theory approach. I used her book *Constructing Grounded Theory* (Charmaz 2006) as my main reference point and guidebook throughout the process. I subscribe to the notion that knowledge is socially constructed and that I as the researcher am part of this process. I have also consciously looked at the data and findings from different stakeholder standpoints to take the research forward and balance perspectives. Throughout the study I have reflected on my personal role in the process, applied reflexivity as defined by Charmaz (see above) and documented these thoughts in memos but also in this thesis.

Contemplating the different epistemological viewpoints and debates, I personally feel drawn to the term conventionalism – a form of pragmatism – discussed by Blaikie (2007, page 25): *"the truth status of the theories used to understand the world of objects is not important. Rather, it is what such theories allow us to do that matters"*.

2.2 Applied features of constructivist grounded theory

As discussed above, the constructivist researcher *"enters the empirical world"*, *"interprets the data through an emergent conceptual analysis"* and *"seeks to find the range of variations in the data and looks for relationships in emerging categories"* (Charmaz 2006, page 137-138).

In addition to these three listed specific constructivist components, general grounded theory concepts such as inductive logic, theoretical sampling and saturation, and constant comparison accompanied by dual-analysing the theorising as part of theoretical sensitivity, feature in the research (Bryant 2012, Charmaz 2006, 2008, 2009).

Following a constructivist grounded theory approach, I adopted an inductive logic (Charmaz 2006, 2009) with occasional abductive reasoning to compare and check emerging theories by revisiting data on an ongoing basis (Bryant 2012, Charmaz 2006). This reiterative way of working, which included constant comparison of data paired with simultaneous analysing and theorising, is the fundamental underpinning of my research activities. In the following chapters, I elaborate in detail how I applied the grounded theory methods and the ensuing findings; however, there are a number of aspects I would like to mention first.

2.2.1 Theoretical sampling

"When engaging in theoretical sampling, the researcher seeks people, events, or information to illuminate and defined the boundaries and relevance of the categories."(Charmaz 2006, page 189)

The selection of interview data was a gradual process; I started out with a small number of relationship interviews and analysed those before adding more and more sources. These first transcripts helped me identify my 'hunch', described in the first chapter, about comments not quite matching up to internal debates, and to formulate the purpose of the study.

The focal point of my research was always C-suite executives since there is so much firm internal desire to engage with this layer of senior management. However, throughout the initial phases of my analysis, I considered and evaluated a number of other interview data. For example, I looked at interviews with procurement leads, those individuals positioned one level below the C-suite, as well as win-loss interviews which could be group interviews or one-to-one sessions with someone representing the decision-makers. In the end, I removed these non C-suite interviews from my primary coding dataset for two reasons: firstly, to make sure the content was well contained and direct, based on direct personal views, and secondly to keep the sample small enough to allow for truly in-depth analysis.

Regarding the content, for example, procurement leads would discuss the general decision-making process surrounding large engagements on a relatively removed organisational level and present anecdotal comments relating to senior leaderships activities, but they provided fairly little insight into their own thought processes. Furthermore, not all organisations had a procurement or supplier management unit, so the dataset only related to a subset of the C-suite population. Win-loss interviews concentrated again only on large engagements, and the wider relationship between the organisation and the advisory firm was only occasionally discussed. Plus, there was a clear bias in these interviews: reviews were almost exclusively losses and client contacts were frequently quite apologetic for not selecting the advisory firm. Even though these comments did generate valuable insights, and I incorporated these observations into my memos; I did not include them in the primarily coded transcripts.

Initially, I also deliberated over adding interviews conducted by someone else in the client feedback team to the sample; however, I quickly dismissed this idea since I realised that I, as an individual, am very much part of the process. Due to my past experience, having worked in management consulting for many years, I approached the interviews quite differently to my colleagues, who either came from outside the industry or were part of business development functions in the past. Reading through my colleagues' transcripts, I came to recognise that I had a slightly different rapport with clients and that I picked up on comments differently, which in return was reflected in my questions and paraphrasing of answers to confirm responses. There were also moral concerns about how my colleagues might feel were I to scrutinise their interviews. Consequently, I only analysed my own interviews at an in-depth coding level and included all my other observations, which did include colleagues describing their interview experiences, in my general reflective memos.

Towards the end of the initial phases, I took stock of the number of interviews per role (e.g. number of CFOs versus number of CEOs) and also checked the number and background of each organisation. I was keen to have at least three interviews per organisation in my sample pool, in order to assess if certain messages were shared on an organisational level; I tried to include organisations with different supplier management approaches, since I picked up a shift in emphasis in the clients' comments depending on the organisational procurement set-up.

2.2.2 Theoretical saturation

Theoretical saturation is probably one of the most challenging aspects of grounded theory. Many authors recommend to *"stay in the field until no new information emerges from the collected data"* and refer to *"the thorough interrogation of the data before conclusions are arrived at"* (Goulding 2002, page 170) or simply *"categories are saturated when new data no longer spark new insights"* (Bryant 2012, slide 90).

After numerous coding reiterations, discussed in the following chapters, I ended up with eighteen in-depth coded transcripts of C-suite stakeholders. To verify saturation, I added three more interviews of an organisation with a complex supplier management approach; at this point, no new codes emerged during the analysis. Throughout the various coding reiterations, I discussed the codes I was developing and utilising with my colleagues on a code-by-code basis. I would ask peers who also interview clients if they observed similar aspects, how they interpreted the clients' comments and how they would define or describe these notions. In parallel, I was preparing a set of internal reports which were based on a much wider interview population (over 200 transcripts). These reports were based on firm-specific coding and reporting sets; I cross-referenced the outcomes of these industry reports with my academic study results and could not identify any coding gaps.

As a next step, I asked a colleague to check all my coded transcripts independently. To clarify: due to the sensitivity of the data, I was not allowed to ask for support from outside my work environment except for my PhD supervisors, which meant that I was able to discuss the general notions and ideas behind each code with other professional and academic peers, but I was not able to hand the coded transcripts to someone external. The colleague actually sat down with the Nvivo file and went through each code, comparing code definitions and checking the transcript sections that were marked with the code. I asked her to pay special attention to code definitions and possibly missing codes. We went through each code and corresponding definitions, and found that some areas were not 100% clear to her; we discussed the issues and what could be done to remedy the lack of clarity and I subsequently adjusted the wording and code definitions. Finally, I presented my codes and code categories to my professional sponsor – a senior partner in the firm who had agreed to act as a high-level sounding board and quality check during my research project. He challenged me on some of the code clustering and naming, but could not point out any aspects that were missing from the dataset. However, I felt that discussing and defending the research approach and coding results was immensely helpful and instilled a degree of confidence in me.

Based on the information I had available, I felt that a solid saturation point was reached and the focus of my study remained firmly on the senior management as specified. There is, of course, the possibility that in the future I might, as part of my role, come across an individual who communicates an aspect which differs from my existing dataset. Also, the advisory industry is constantly evolving; for example, a competitor might introduce a new way of engaging with clients, and this will, of course, be reflected in future comments. Therefore, there is no absolute guarantee of complete and long-lasting saturation. However, I do feel that at the time of writing, with the data available, I have reached an equilibrium.

2.2.3 Theoretical sensitivity

"In developing categories the sociologist should employ 'theoretical sensitivity', which means the ability to 'see relevant data' and to reflect upon empirical data material with the help of theoretical terms" (Goulding 2002, page 42 referring to Kelle 2007)

Kathy Charmaz (2006) points out that in order to gain theoretical sensitivity, the researcher needs to look at and reflect on the studied phenomena from various perspectives, make comparisons and follow up on and/or build on new ideas.

As part of my ongoing analysis and theorising, I looked at the data from numerous perspectives: on an individual level (the senior executive and the professional advisor) and on an organisational level, I analysed the data from a corporate and advisory firm perspective, as well as from the procurement or supplier management angle. Furthermore, I consulted and incorporated views of colleagues, client feedback peers working for other firms and friends who operate on the client side, as well as advisors such as my professional supervisor.

The overall analysing and theorising took time. In order to process, reflect and evolve my thinking, I requested a sabbatical to step away from my day-to-day role and concentrate on my research. Writing reiterative memos in a paper journal was critical, plus sketching out ideas in diagrams as visualisation helps me make sense of constructs and concepts.

On the other hand, I reviewed and consulted general decision-making literature to make sure that I would use appropriate terminologies and to help me place and understand the observations I was making, as well as providing an additional context and adding different viewpoints to heighten my sensitivity.

2.2.4 Timing and use of literature

"... once an area of research has been identified, the researcher should enter the field as soon as possible." And "...the literature is not exhausted prior to the research ... rather it is consulted as part of an iterative, inductive and interactional process of data collection, simultaneous analysis, and emergent interpretation." (Goulding 2002, page 296)

In principle, the grounded theory method calls for the literature review to be conducted towards the end of the research, to avoid clouding the researcher's analysis and theorising. At the same time, Glaser recommended that the researcher should not engage with the literature from the outset but should read widely (Bryant 2012). Therefore, there is a degree of flexibility as to when exactly one should dip into the literature. One key underlying requirement is that literature does not define the research (Bryant 2012). Christina Goulding pragmatically recommends that *"the researcher should read in related areas from the start and all the data to direct the literature to inform the merging theory and vice versa"* (Goulding 2002, page 165).

In this particular research project, it was clear from the beginning that due to my professional role I would enter the research field with significant background knowledge informed by past experiences, debates and general industry publications, although these experiences were of a professional nature and not academically or systematically evaluated or processed. Nonetheless, I ensured that there was a clear demarcation regarding when to initiate a comprehensive review of the literature pertaining to the research purpose and aims. During the empirical analysis involving discovery, theory building and emerging substantive models, I consciously tried to cast aside any pre-existing subject matter references and not to search for new information. However, in order to theoretically underpin and help me guide my research journey, I reviewed the peer-reviewed literature on research methodologies and also attended a grounded theory seminar (Bryant 2012).

While I was coding and analysing the data, I began to search for and read different decision-making theories, described in Chapter Four. By reading the wider decision-making literature, I was able to view my data from different theoretical perspectives, which in turn enriched the theorising process. Half-way through the empirical analysis, I experienced a phase where I was compelled to look for a comprehensive theoretical model in the literature to help me understand my findings, and which provided me with some additional indicators (elaborated in detail in Chapter Four). In summary, the wider literature on the context of my research supported the empirical stages of my study and helped me in developing my own conceptual framework and theorising.

After the empirical analysis, and while I was articulating and rationalising first substantive theories (Chapter Six), I identified areas where additional knowledge would be of help before I embarked on a review of the context literature in the field. This entry into the literature assisted me in comparing and contrasting the literature findings with the research findings in order to challenge and adjust the proposed substantive theoretical framework and include the literature findings in the study's conclusions, implications and limitations.

2.2.5 Substantive theory

Strauss and Corbin (1994) define a theory as *"a set of relationship that offer a plausible explanation of the phenomenon under study"*; within grounded theory, researchers refer to two types of theory – substantive and formal (Charmaz 2006, page 170). According to Goulding (2002), a substantive theory is *"developed from a work in a specific area"* and *"should remain parsimonious: that is, it should not try to generalise with explanations of situations for which there are no data"* (Goulding 2002, page 45-46). A formal theory, on the other hand, aims to provide an explanation across a range of situations and fields – a type of generalisation aiming at higher levels of abstraction (Goulding 2002).

Alvita Nathaniel (2007), referring to Glaser's perspective, explains formal grounded theory as

> *"not an explication of descriptive differences and similarities in a substantive area. Rather it is conceptualizations about the core category, abstracted from the particulars of time, place, and persons. Because it is empirically rooted, conceptualized, generalized, and free of particulars, it potentially applies to many substantive areas"*. (Nathaniel posted on Jun 11, 2007).

2.3 Applied features of auto-ethnography

In his article, Anderson (2006, page 378) proposes the following five features of analytic auto-ethnography:

1. *Complete member researcher status*
2. *Analytic reflexivity*
3. *Narrative visibility of the researcher's self*
4. *Dialogue with informants beyond the self*
5. *Commitment to theoretical analysis.*

Being a complete member in the *"social world under study"* (Anderson 2006, page 379) allows the researcher to gain a deeper tacit understanding of the phenomena (Charmaz 2006). In my role as a client feedback manager, I am part of the 'natural setting' and the interviews and exchanges with clients and the advisory firm processes are part of the regular processes that come with the role.

"Reflexivity expresses researchers' awareness of their necessary connection to the research situation and hence their effects upon it" (Anderson 2006, page 7 referring to Davis 1999). Reflexivity is also a key feature of constructivists' grounded theory, as discussed in previous sections. Throughout the research project, I have not only reflected on my own standpoints but also analysed the phenomena from the perspective of the different stakeholders (senior executive, client organisation, advisor and advisory firm) as stipulated by the constructivist approach (Charmaz 2009). In addition, I have documented how I struggled at times to make

sense of the data and noted down personal views and considerations in my memos. I have also addressed narrative visibility of myself in the study, as well as adopting a narrative format for this thesis document.

"The ethnographic imperative calls for dialogue with data' and others" (Anderson 2006, page 386); Anderson warns of the potential for self-absorption, a pre-occupation with or reliance on one's own views and thoughts. As a client feedback manager, acting as a communicator or mediator between client and advisory firm requires me to take note of and understand the dialogue between the two groups before I can add additional comments as well as my own perspective to the exchange. Throughout the research project, I have tried to maintain a level of objectivity, examining and understanding the phenomena from all standpoints, reverting back to the data (be it coded interviews or memos) and constantly comparing findings and concepts before drawing a number of conclusions.

By fully subscribing to a grounded theory stance, I have added rigour to the auto-ethnographic approach, exercising systematic checks into empirical data collection and analysis such as theoretical sampling, theoretical saturation and theoretical sensitivity, as elaborated in the previous section.

In retrospect, I realised that I could or perhaps should have added more personal observations and views to the debate, but I feel that this would have potentially diminished the versatility and validity of the study, especially beyond the academic remit. Overall, I feel that I have achieved a sensible balance of empirical interview data and personal field observations.

2.4 Additional research design aspects: data and tools

As previously mentioned, I was able to draw on various sources and datasets. For the in-depth empirical analysis (by which I mean re-iterative coding, analysing and theorising), I focused on 21 relationship review interviews with C-suite stakeholders (already transcribed for firm internal reporting), plus the corresponding memos, which captured my personal comments reflecting on the interview experiences and capturing observations I made while coding the transcripts. In order to develop the codes, I consulted a very wide range of sources and material:

- Relationship interviews beyond C-suite stakeholders, such as C-suite 'direct reports' and procurement leads, which I did not include in the primary coding pool (see theoretical sampling comments).

- Notes taken in preparation for the interviews: these are based on briefing meetings with the selected advisors who are involved with the stakeholders and their organisation. (Note: the lead partner normally identifies who within the firm should provide commentary for the briefing.)
- The strategic summary reports prepared for the account team and the Executive, summarising and synthesising key findings, implications and direction.
- Win-loss review interview transcripts and reports.
- The internal coding framework I developed for the firm to generate aggregated reports; the framework is based on frequently reoccurring themes as well as the strategic imperatives of the firm.
- Memos that capture my observations and thoughts that occurred to me during conversations with peers, and also general ideas I had while reflecting on experiences and data.
- Memos capturing some key thoughts and concepts I came across while investigating key decision-making theories.

I secured sign-off from my executive stakeholder and professional sponsor to officially gain access to the 21 pre-existing transcripts, which formed the basis of my analysis, as well as their general approval to carry out this academic research project.

In order to manage the vast quantities of data – some transcripts were over 15 pages long – I used the computer-assisted/aided qualitative data analysis software (CAQDAS) Nvivo from QSR International. I started out with Nvivo, as it is currently the standard software for qualitative analysis at the Business School. In previous academic assignments, I have had good experiences using CAQDAS tools for qualitative analysis. However, in this instance, I struggled with this software as there were too many unstructured codes and I could not grasp the bigger picture while coding. Therefore, for some time I went back to manual coding –hard copies, highlighters and notes on the side. Once the codes started to firm up and groupings of codes emerged, I returned to the software. A detailed account of my experiences is captured in Chapter Three.

In retrospect, I have to say that working with Nvivo was extremely helpful to pro-actively manage the codes as it enabled me to move codes around, change definitions and adjust them when needed. The query and clustering function were also beneficial during the later stages of analysing and theorising. However, I still kept paper journals so that I could write down thoughts and impressions immediately, and I also transferred data to Excel spreadsheets for further analysis and to create diagrams.

Furthermore, implementing the Nvivo software at work for aggregated reporting gave me the additional benefit of cross-fertilisation between work reporting and academic analysis. I was able to learn and 'play' with a much bigger dataset (from work) and could use these learnings for my academic analysis. In return, some of the structuring of codes in my academic set-up informed my professional reports.

Lastly, in addition to my own checking and cross-referencing of data to assure integrity and validity, I had peers spot-check my coding during the research project. As mentioned above, towards the end of the coding when I thought theoretical saturation was reached, I commissioned a colleague – the team's technical knowledge manager – to check and verify my coding and confirm saturation from her point of view.

2.5 Assessing the outcomes

There are a number of different approaches and, of course, a host of opinions on how to assess the outcomes of grounded theory research. In the initial guidelines issued by Glaser and Strauss (1967), six requirements were listed. Theory, both substantive and formal, should (Goulding 2002, page 43):

1. *Enable prediction and explanation of behaviour*
2. *Be useful in theoretical advances*
3. *Be applicable in practice*
4. *Provide a perspective on behaviour*
5. *Provide a style for research on particular areas of behaviour*
6. *Provide clear categories and hypotheses [..to be verified in present and future research].*

New assessment criteria have been proposed by different schools of thought; for example, Lincoln and Guba (1985, page 289) suggested translating existing quantitative criteria into a *'trustworthiness'* check. For example, reliability is replaced by a concept termed *'dependability'*. Opinions are split, and other authors such as Christina Goulding (2002) strongly believe that adjusted quantitative measures do not reflect the process and the outcomes of grounded theory. In this research, I adopted the assessment criteria suggested by Kathy Charmaz (2006), since I followed Charmaz's constructivist grounded theory methodology. The assessment criteria put forward by Bryant (2012) offer a slightly different take on Charmaz's perspective; both discussions provide helpful pointers.

Antony Bryant discussed four specific criteria in his grounded theory seminar (Bryant 2012, slides 104-108); they are *"fit, grab, work and modifiability"*. **Fit** refers to the need for theoretical insights to adhere to the substantive context, rather than predilections or biases of the researcher. **Grab** stands for usefulness or applicability of theory and concepts presented, both within a theoretical but also practical context. **Work** relates to the requirement to be able to use the theory as a tool or method and to be able to do something practically with the model. **Modifiability** stands for the notion to continue the grounded theory process of conceptual discovery, to try and place the theory in a different context, amend and mould it with the help of new data and insights over time.

In contrast, Kathy Charmaz (2006) has a slightly different take on how to assess or evaluate a grounded theory study. She states *"credibility, originality, resonance and usefulness"* as her four criteria (Charmaz 2006, page 182-183): **Credibility** probes if an audience is able to follow the research assessment and agree with the claims put forward. **Originality** questions to what extent the study has challenged, extended or refined existing theories and ideas. **Resonance** ponders to what degree the theories and models make sense of those individuals experiencing the phenomena, as well as offers insights into lived behaviour. **Usefulness**, which overlaps with Bryant's modifiability and work criteria, relates to not only applying and using the theory but also evolving it over time.

I will return to the four criteria and how I have applied them when I discuss theoretical saturation in detail in Chapter Four, section 4.5.3.

In conclusion, this chapter elaborates how the study's purpose and context led me to adopt a constructivist grounded theory approach combined with an auto-ethnographic stance, as well as how these methodologies informed the methods and tools utilised as part of the research process. In the next chapter, I will retrace my research journey starting with the first stage of discovery – selecting and making sense of the data and exploring the phenomena.

Chapter 3

Discovery – selecting and making sense of the data, exploring the phenomena

In this chapter, I retrace and document the first stage of my empirical research activities which I termed 'discovery'. This stage entailed, firstly, the exploration of the phenomena through a series of reiterative coding exercises, which led me to define four research questions to guide my analysis, followed by an examination of the general decision-making literature for additional perspectives in order to move the research process forward.

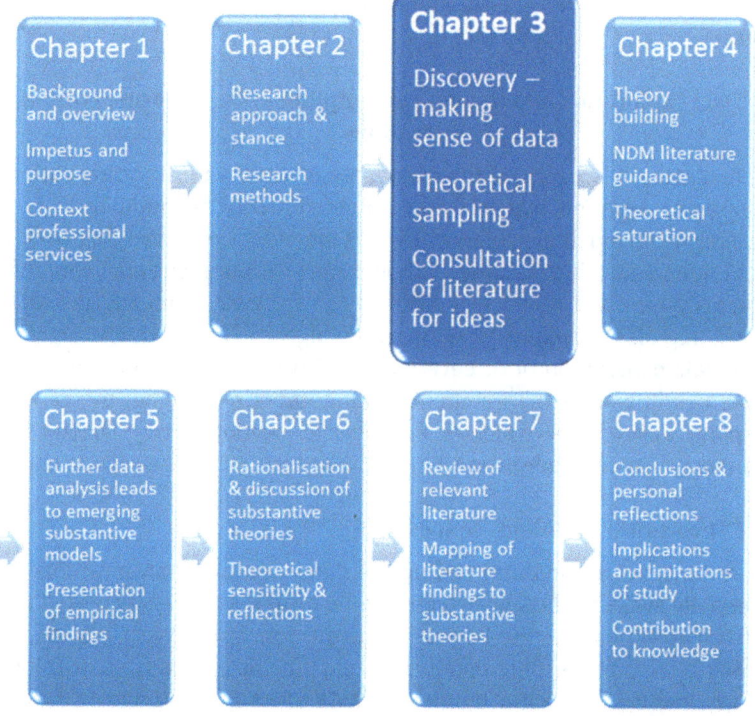

Figure 3.1 – Overview of thesis structure and content of the third chapter

Over the course of four years, the research project progressed through three distinct empirical stages: **discovery** – selecting and making sense of the data, and exploring the phenomena, in this subsequent chapter; **theory building** – development of an emerging conceptual framework and reaching theoretical saturation, to be discussed in Chapter Four; and **emerging substantive models** – analysis of findings with applied theoretical sensitivity shaped a set of substantive theories, which will be explained in Chapters Five and Six before I consult and include findings from the literature in the field in the final analysis.

On the whole, it has been a lengthy and at times rather confusing and very much personal journey, littered with numerous trials and tribulations along the way, such as balancing work commitments and academic aspirations. Since I was leading the client feedback programme effectively on a full-time basis during this first phase of the study, I was permanently exposed to new observations and emerging datasets in the field. These new findings and views, influenced by the firms and the client feedback programme's strategic initiatives, enriched the research process and provided a continuous flow of diverse new data points but also added to the complexity of the task at hand, which was to stay focused on the research purpose and select, and initially test, the most appropriate datasets.

3.1 Data exploration and theoretical sampling – first three open coding iterations

The first stage, 'discovery', of the data analysis was the most testing part of the research experience of applying grounded theory methodology. There was simply too much data, plus more and more data was emerging daily. I wasn't quite sure which datasets I should start with or focus on. I was also perpetually worried that I was drifting too far away from my research aims, going off on tangents and losing the bigger perspective. During this initial data exploration or discovery phase, I went through four iterations of open coding and experimented with a number of different theoretical sampling approaches which I describe in section 3.1.1 'Theoretical sampling – first cut' and section 3.2.1 'Theoretical sampling – second cut'.

3.1.1 Theoretical sampling - first cut

Before I started delving into coding the data, I prepared an inventory of potentially available datasets which I would be able to access as part of my work environment: At the beginning of the research project, the client feedback programme only conducted relationship reviews (no win-loss reviews). So, I identified a number of data sources associated with this review process, such as client interview transcripts (verbatim), transcript summaries prepared for the account team, partner briefing notes and summary reports to the executive. I also differentiated between audit and non-audit relationships, client account industries and internal account segmentation (into key, strategic and national accounts: this is primarily based on revenue generated and forecast over a five year period).

There was almost too much data, and I therefore decided to concentrate on the actual client comments (the verbatim client interview transcripts) and to use the firm internal data sources, such as summary reports to the executive and partner briefing notes, as supporting material to be consulted and included in research memos but not as the primary data source to be coded extensively. The main rationale was to stay as close as possible to the client perspective and to avoid a strong firm internal steer in the analysis, at least initially. Summary reports for the executive and internal partner briefing notes have a clear singular viewpoint and occasional bias towards the firm's internal agenda, which I deliberately tried to avoid.

Furthermore, I opted to exclude external audit relationship reviews, as previously mentioned in Chapter One, since the relationship dynamics are substantially different and rather more complex due to legislation and two-fold and at times adverse stakeholder interests and structure – namely the company board and senior management. To begin with, I elected to analyse only interviews I personally had conducted and therefore I was able to capture personal interview observations and other pointers gathered before and during the process in corresponding memos; consequently, I was able to prepare a memo with observations for each interview.

3.1.2 First iteration of open coding

I started off rather ambitiously and selected ten of my client interview transcripts from two relationship reviews. I included C-suite respondents, 'direct reports' and procurement leads to have a good overview of a cross-section of respondents. At this stage, I used the following process: I uploaded the transcripts in the Nvivo software, read the transcripts one by one and created corresponding observational memos for each interview (consulting other data sources such as partner internal briefing notes as well). I then coded the transcripts on an incident-by incident-level and amended the memos along the way.

Since each interview transcript was between 12 to 15 pages of fairly unstructured comments, I ended up with a very large number of diverse codes. After having coded four transcripts in completely open or unstructured (in actual fact 'in vivo'), I observed six emerging aspects of recurring comments and I decided to consider these as a type of guiding principle or questions to help me stay focused during the coding. The six facets that frequently featured in the interviews were:

1. **Expectations** – Clients listed and discussed their personal expectations of a professional advisor and advisory firm. For example, extract from CEO_1 memo: *'Later on respondent emphasises the point about how much he/she appreciated the personal coaching, preparation for the FCA interviews. Respondent does not like it when advisors are condescending ...'*

2. **Experiences** – Clients recounted their experiences, positive and negative, with advisors and advisory firms; this could be experiences linked to specific projects or general relationship or rapport experience. The comments applied to my employer but also to competitors. For example, extract from CRO_3 memo: *'Past experiences and legacy relationships feature heavily in her decision making discussions, respondent is very close to the two partners – respondent is not overly explicit around the link between these two individuals and the firm, but that's also because these partners have not changed firms.'*

3. **Perceptions** – Some clients, not all, discussed their personal and, less frequently, organisational perceptions of an advisor and advisory firm; for example, a client would say *'I perceive you to be strong in X'* or *'your 'house style' is Y'*. These comments were not necessarily based on facts or experiences per se but just general views or notions that clients held. For example, extract from CFO_5 memo: *'Respondent has a clear view as to what a professional service firm should do nor not - charge on time and material and not basis points [finance project gone wrong]. Respondent is not comfortable for the advisor to step out of these definitions.'*

4. **Actions or process steps** – A number of clients mentioned or recounted actions or steps that either they or the decision-making team made, which led to a project or considerations that informed their choice of advisor or firm. Since the interviews followed a loose feedback agenda, the comments in this regard ended up being fragmented: most of the time clients did not recount the entire process but just some selected aspects. For example, extract from CIO_1 memo: *'The bulk of the interview focuses on the supplier management programme that he/his team/the company have set up to make sense of the competitive landscape and manage the various suppliers. Companies are put in certain boxes, if they demonstrate capabilities outside the box a reconsideration or re-calibrations*

would at times ensue. There is a certain degree of rationality to the decision making - referring to selection factors - but there is also the discussion about the overall commitment between the supplier and the client company.'

5. **Individual style of respondents** – Especially in the memos, I recorded my own personal observations around the individual style of respondents. For example, when I perceived someone to be very talkative and open, I would make a note of that, whereas another client appeared more pensive or constrained, e.g. long pauses and consideration before replying to a difficult question. For example, extract from CFO_2 memo: *'Respondent is pensive, careful or guarded with his comments, occasional nervous laughter, opens up a little at the end of the interview.'*

6. **Organisational objectives, processes and culture** – Some clients emphasised organisational drivers and aspects, almost distancing themselves or providing a general context to their other comments. For example, extract from CEO_2 memo: *'Even though respondent might not be involved hands-on in the decision-making, respondent clearly keeps an eye on the advisor spend ... how much is the organisation spending with each advisory firm.'*

I coded two more transcripts in Nvivo following this method but felt slightly lost in the process and I struggled to maintain a holistic view when reviewing the coding and memos.

3.1.3 Second iteration of open coding

Even though the first iteration generated a number of different codes, I struggled to see the bigger picture and I became increasingly concerned about missing my research aims. There was simply too much data. I revised my approach and started a second iteration of open coding, again focusing on capturing a respondent's notion or train of thought and not individual words nor coding line-by-line (Bryant 2012, Charmaz 2006), plus I decided to revert to manual coding, which also allowed me to code when away from the computer.

I retained the general approach of incident-by-incident coding and memo writing, but I started to colour code different coding groups to help me visually keep oversight of the messages. I marked codes that described the clients' general expectations or experiences of working with an advisor or firm in red; comments that referred to client decision-making with regard to appointing advisors (criteria, processes and experiences) in orange; and lastly, comments that focused on organisational styles or issues in green.

Of the eight transcripts that I coded during the first iteration, I tried to pick the four, from my perspective, most diverse interviews as a starting point and applied this new colour-coded approach. This exercise went fairly well and I was able to summarise a first set of initial findings at this point, as below:

- There was a clear distinction in client comments between what they commonly referred to as 'large' or 'big' projects and 'small' projects; key differentiators between these two types of projects were total costs, budget of a project, exposure and risk on an organisational but also personal level. Furthermore, for the most part clients mentioned that organisational policies required 'large projects' to go through a formal selection process, meaning identifying and appointing a firm to deliver the project.
- Respondents also distinguished between different types of projects in terms of services expected. Clients spoke of pure delivery projects, in which the advisor or advisory firm is doing or implementing something; or pure advisory projects, in which the advisor or advisory firm provides guidance, advice or an opinion on a particular matter instead of executing something. Of course, some projects required both advice and delivery services.
- At a first glance, depending on the type of project, large/small, delivery/advice, or a combination thereof, different decision-making notions and patterns seemed to emerge.
- For advisory projects, which were often grouped as small, a solid relationship or rapport and a certain level of trust was mentioned as a prerequisite, which was not mentioned explicitly as a requirement for delivery projects.

With this in mind, I started to take note of what type of projects or services individual clients discussed throughout the interview and which other codes coincided with these.

At this stage, I felt that I had sufficiently increased my grasp of the client data, and therefore, I was comfortable to expand the research aims of my study by identifying four research questions. As already indicated in Chapter One, I set out to inquire into the social phenomenon of how senior executive clients interact with and consequently select professional advisors; now I was able to state that more specifically I aimed to explore:

- Why do senior executives engage with and employ professional service firms and their advisors?
- How do senior executives choose to interact with professional service firms and their advisors?
- How do senior executives select and appoint professional service firms and advisors?
- To what extent does the interaction (rapport between manager and advisor or firm) influence or shape the selection of an advisor to deliver a project?

With these four research questions in mind, I continued my research journey and embarked on the next round of open coding.

3.1.4 Third iteration of open coding

Since I was making good progress and I was planning on coding the remaining six transcripts following the revised approach, I decided to return to a computer-aided analysis and transferred my manual codes into an Nvivo project. While I was entering the data in the software, I started to redefine the approach a bit further and used the following statements to help guide the coding, aligning the above-mentioned colour-marked code categories to the revised ones:

- **Client decision-making** (orange) – 'this is how I decide' (taking the client's perspective), this is how I go about making decisions, this is critical to me as part of the selection process'.
- **Client expectations and experiences** (yellow) – 'these are my expectations and experiences, positive and negative, when it comes to professional advisors and firms'.
- **Organisational context** (green) – 'this is how the organisation decides or selects advisors, this is critical to the organisation'.

Of course, I applied the revised approach to the previously manually coded transcripts and then revisited the additional transcripts that I had coded during the first iteration. Although I felt I had a better grasp on the coding, a clearer definition of what I was looking for in client comments, I still felt that the larger picture or overview was missing by coding in Nvivo. I, therefore, started to create a spreadsheet summarising the key findings per transcript. I captured and organised the findings according to the following overarching attributes:

- Preferred or discussed decision-making approach or mode – for example, some senior executives preferred or felt compelled due to their role, to delegate the selection for some or all initiatives. Other respondents were keen to be involved to some degree in all selection decisions. This extract from the summary spreadsheet (memo) illustrates the attribute, CEO_3 entry: *'Based on his comments conclude that respondent primarily delegates decision-making, plus respondent very rarely appoints advisors and does not try and influence decision processes of others.'*

- Selection steps, choice patterns or sequencing of selection steps discussed – comments that alluded to certain patterns of sequencing with regard to decision-making. This extract from the summary spreadsheet (memo) illustrates the attribute, CFO_4: *'Prefers to pro-actively reach out to the advisor for assistance, if the advisor is on-site even better; respondent selects the advisor based on past experiences and perceived expertise.'*

- Individual advisor versus advisory firm preferences discussed – for example, does the respondent have a clear preference for an individual advisor or is a single person more important? This extract from the summary spreadsheet (memo) illustrates the attribute, CEO_5: *'In general strong focus on the advisory firm in respondent's narrative, respondent even talks of a house style ... when it comes to selecting firms and discussing individual pieces of work respondent does reference individual advisors; so overall focus is primarily on firm.'*

- Key criteria mentioned regarding choice or selection of advisor or firm – for example, price, experiences, access to certain staff. This extract from the summary spreadsheet (memo) illustrates the attribute, CFO_5: *'Merit is the overriding criteria - which translates into access to the A-team, responsiveness and flexibility as well as value for money. Plus balancing the spread of working between advisory firms (cooling down relationships).'*

- Organisational constraints in appointing or working with advisors discussed – for example, senior executives spoke of cost management measures to control spend on external support services, others spoke of an organisational culture that discouraged the use of external advisors. This extract from the summary spreadsheet (memo) illustrates the attribute, CFO_2: *'Clearly present but not fully discussed - appointing an advisor is equivalent to admitting to failure, not being able to handle the task. Organisation not in support of any significant advisory work (has to be under the radar).'*

- Organisational mechanisms or policies in place that might govern the selection of advisor – some respondents discussed in great detail the organisational processes and protocols that governed the appointment of advisors; however, in some interviews, this topic did not feature at all. This extract from the summary spreadsheet (memo) illustrates the attribute, COO_2: *'CFO authorisation required over a certain amount, no discussion of a formalised procurement or selection process. Agreement that for certain tasks we will always use the same provider ... An informal agreement?'*

This overview table of findings linked back to the codes helped me maintain an oversight of the codes and topics emerging and the coverage across the different data sources.

3.1.5 First emerging concepts

Over the course of the third coding iteration, a clearer picture started to emerge regarding the code categories which I colour coded, as described above, and with the aid of the overview spreadsheet (memo) various messages started to come together and coverage or gaps became more apparent.

As a first step, I attempted to summarise the general content or messaging of a relationship interview – in other words, what type of data I was able to view and make use of as part of the analysis. Almost the majority of client comments during interviews focused on the senior executive and advisor or advisory firm relationship (see 'Table 1 - Memo: Messaging inventory executive-advisor relationship' for summary). However, some senior executives tended to elaborate more on their project or delivery experiences (see 'Table 2 – Memo: Messaging inventory project or delivery experience' for summary). On average, approximately a third of the interview comments referred to project or delivery experiences (estimated based on coding categories observed in Nvivo). It was therefore clear that some respondents leaned more towards discussing relationship facets, whereas others preferred to talk about a more transactional project or delivery aspects. Interestingly enough, a fairly small number of the interview comments concentrated on overt decision-making remarks (see 'Table 3 – Memo Messaging inventory individual decision making' for summary). Tables and summary notes extracted from my research memos can be found below: 'themes' refer to primary reoccurring messaging identified in this group and 'others' captures some additional key observations I made. The estimates of data coverage are approximate averages derived from the Nvivo coding percentages for the different code groupings.

Executive - Advisor Relationships	
Data	At least 40 to 50% of interview data covers this topic
Themes	Personal relationships influencing decision making
	Networks of relationships and developments over time
	Definitions of forms of different executive – advisor relationships (confident, partner to transactional help)
	Paths and factors to a strong working relationship
	Links between advisor and advisory firm or brand, vis a vis the advisor being his/her own brand
Others	Description of relationships and how they work (positive and negative).
	Good and bad relationships – definitions and expectations.
	Relationship development over time – investment from both sides, going through peeks and trofts
	Patterns of relationships over time (continue working together after switching employers on both sides)
	Peer influence on developing relationships - networks
	Association of certain traits and attribution of personalities to different individuals
	The advisor as a brand on his/her own … what they are known for
	Organisational factors influencing relationships > ability to follow up/act upon relationship
	Big 4 a hygiene factor > important for some projects (scrutiny), safety net …

Table 3.1 – Memo: Messaging inventory executive-advisor relationship

Project or Delivery Experiences	
Data	About 30% of interview data, whereby a smaller percentage includes impact of experiences on relationships and decision making
Themes	Positive or negative project experiences influencing relationships
	Positive or negative project experiences influencing decision making
	Positive or negative project experiences shaping perception of the advisory firm
Others	Access to the A team – quality resources
	One bad experience closes the door in a particular area for good
	Can the house do it > importance of having observed a firm deliver sth, warranty

Table 3.2 – Memo: Messaging inventory project or delivery experience

Individual Decision Making	
Data	About 10-15% of overall interview data
	Occassional reference to organisational decision making processes or approaches
Themes	Decision making ownership (references as to who decided on a project etc.)
	Some discussion of decision making processes or approaches (I pick up the phone, decided in a panel)
	Comparison between different respondents when they reference organisational decision making > following the same patterns
	How do people compartimentalise their decisions
	How important is the Big 4 fact influencing decision making

Table 3.3 – Memo: Messaging inventory individual decision-making

Based on the messaging inventories presented above, I tried to chart a number of further questions or aspects that I was hoping to explore as part of the research and I concluded this exercise with a list of seven:

1. To what extent does the senior executive appoint the advisory firm rather than the individual advisor?
2. To what extent do personal relationships, between client and advisor, influence senior managers' decision-making?
3. What are the key criteria for appointing an advisor or advisory firm?
4. What is the difference between the different interactions: beyond project relationships and types of projects?
5. How important are the client-advisor relationships outside a specific project and the firm's reputation when it comes to securing large scale implementation projects or small strategic advisory projects?
6. What does a professional relationship entail? What are clients' expectations linked to these concepts?
7. Are there different types of relationships based on personal preferences and circumstances? And how do these different relationship types feature in the decision-making?

These seven questions should be seen as an evolution of the four research questions that I have already documented and discussed at the end of section 3.1.3. They are by no means a replacement for the four questions, but rather a reflexive exercise I undertook as part of the analysis to expand and investigate the four research questions in conjunction with my data exploration.

Furthermore, during the third iteration of open coding, I attempted to sketch out various emerging concepts that I was beginning to see, bearing in mind that at this point it was only a draft of various vaguely perceived concepts with no clear links or confirmed relationships. The following diagram taken from one of my memos is a graphic depiction of my thoughts (I personally prefer to capture my observations and ideas for reference in the form of sketches or diagrams, it helps me to visualise my thoughts):

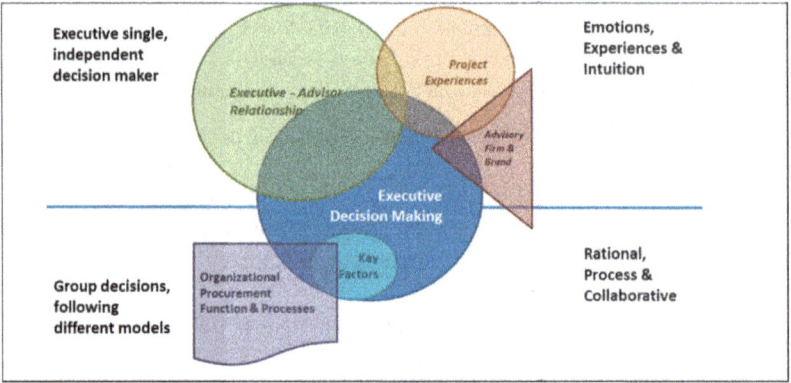

Figure 3.2 – Memo: Diagram of emerging concepts

The diagram above is thus an illustration of my thoughts as noted down in one of my memos - it is a reflection of my observations and understanding at that point in the research journey. The observations are informed by individual respondent transcript codes and memos as well as in the summary spreadsheet of observations that I discussed earlier: The colourful shapes represent client comments found in the transcripts, starting with the key aspects listed above: executive advisor relationships, project and delivery experiences and key selection factors mentioned. In addition, I identified the concept of the advisory firm and the brand, which can be, but does not necessarily have to be, wrapped into the executive-advisor relationship, plus a discrete group of comments focused on organisational procurement processes. Moreover, I started to differentiate on one level between group decision-making and executive single or independent decision-making, and on another level between two diverse approaches to decision-making. One decision-making approach is informed by processes, rationality and collaborative approaches, whereas the other is based on emotions, experiences and intuition; I observed these in the client interview data and documented them in the summary spreadsheet (memo) discussed previously. The diagram above, as well as a number of other sketches I made in my memos, helped me to capture my observations and thoughts while I was exploring and making sense of the data. At this stage, I endeavoured to pull together and mark up what I started to see in the data, taking stock of some possibly emerging concepts before I started to move on to with further coding activities.

3.2 Demarcating and firming up of research focus – fourth open coding iteration

As time moved on, a number of changes took place in my professional environment. One of the many firm-wide strategic initiatives focused on bid conversion and improving bid performance when the firm actively submits a tender or bid for a client project. As part of this initiative, the client feedback programme started to introduce 'win-loss reviews', that is, conducting a post-decision interview with client contacts to ascertain why the firm has or has not been successful in a tender situation. Furthermore, a change in leadership changed the direction of the programme, and we were asked to prepare extensive aggregated reports of client feedback data. Consequently, I started a project to install a qualitative database utilising the Nvivo software. Defining what I termed the analytical framework, entailing codes and coding structure, was a major undertaking, which took up a large amount of my time and energy. The firm's client-centric strategy and other strategic imperatives were the starting point for the analytical framework. These were supplemented with general recurring observations made during relationship reviews, and of course, the codes were then validated with a number of stakeholders of the different service lines, such as consulting, tax, corporate finance and audit, within the firm. The framework also included assigning values to codes by marking comments as positive or negative.

All these projects and activities pulled me away from my academic research for a couple of months but allowed me to step back and reflect on my progress so far. When I was able to pick up again on the study, I took some time out to review my theoretical sampling approach and coding perspectives. I was determined to tie down and articulate the study's focus more clearly.

3.2.1 Theoretical sampling – second cut

Influenced by the increasing firm internal debates around bid conversion and the role of procurement, many of the win-loss interviews were with procurement leads. I felt compelled to review the previous sampling approach and I investigated if I should include win-loss interview transcripts and relationship review interviews with procurement leads. I analysed and compared the two different sets of transcripts, win-loss and relationship reviews, and listed and contemplated the advantages and disadvantages associated with each dataset. In the end, I decided not to include win-loss review transcripts, primarily for three reasons:

1. Win-loss reviews only covered 'large' projects that had gone through a formal selection process, and therefore only matched up with a small segment of the relationship review commentary, which covered all types and aspects of projects.
2. The feedback was provided by a host of different stakeholders, most of the time procurement leads, but also business owners and other individuals. Relationship review interviews concentrated on a fairly focused population of very senior respondents compared to the mix of mid- to lower-level management contacts who provided bid feedback. Some interviews were group interviews and occasionally members of the project or the account team were present as well. Thus, the comments ranged dramatically; the group dynamics especially influenced the set-up. It became more of a discussion than feedback, which usually means client-listening and data gathering.
3. Most of the bid debriefs were loss-reviews and, from my perspective some, though not all, client contacts came across as very apologetic for not selecting the firm for a particular piece of work. There were clearly more hidden agendas and potential biases; however, I decided to exclude the investigation of these biases from the scope of this study.

As part of this theoretical sampling review, I also reassessed the general sample population of the study. In order to manage the research focus and make the study more meaningful, I decided to focus my research on C-suite respondents only, meaning very top management – individuals with roles equivalent to chief executive officer, chief financial officer, chief risk officer and so on. This would make the contribution of my study more significant, as there is only limited research in this field that is focused on very senior executives. The C-suite interviews that I used as a primary data source for the purpose of this research covered relationship, project and selection aspects, as well as formal (such as larger tenders) and informal (appointing an advisor 'on the fly') selection processes. With this theoretical sampling decision, the study had a clear demarcation regarding the scope of the research, as it would focus on the nuances of senior management decision-making processes.

3.2.2 Fourth iteration of open coding and corresponding emerging models

In retrospect, I realise that the concurrent internal win-loss debates in my professional setting did inform my outlook, and I started to look at the data in a more sequential way. One analytical and coding exercise that I experimented with was to map the interview data points and codes as a type of decision-making process diagram. For some individuals, I was able to extract and chart out a number of decision-making steps and considerations. However, for a large number of respondents I was not able to capture any definite patterns in the decision-making process.

Another perspective or coding approach that I tried out in more detail during this coding reiteration was the concept of the relationship. One of the relationship reviews I conducted involved a client-advisor relationship which was still fairly immature: the account team and the firm overall had not been working with this organisation and the client contacts for a long period of time. During the preparatory briefings with the partners but also the interviews with senior executives, it became apparent that the relationship or rapport was still in its infancy and no one from the account team had taken note of the stakeholders' expectations. Thus, I asked the senior managers outright: 'What did they expect of an advisor?', 'What would the ideal advisor relationship look like from their perspective?' and 'What is it they would like to get out of the rapport with the advisor and firm?' Of course, this approach generated some valuable insights for the account team, and I was able to discuss and present individual preferences in my summary report and presentation to the account team and senior leadership. I decided to keep this line of questioning in all my preceding client feedback interviews.

On reflection, I realised that my questioning was to a certain degree influenced by the research project. My professional and academic thinking and my work were beginning to benefit from each other. Looking at my coding results, I was detecting linkages and overlaps between expectations of an advisor and criteria for selecting an advisor, but I was struggling to dissect these further within the coding set-up that I was working with. It all blended into each other and at this stage, I took a fairly simplified approach and tried to group individuals based on dominant relationship preferences:

On one hand, I noted in my memos that there were senior managers who commented that they looked for a trusted advisor relationship. Aspects such as trust, professional and personal support, as well as emotional and softer expectations, featured heavily. On the other hand, other senior executives sought a more transactional support or rapport with an advisor and advisory firm. The comments of respondents grouped into this domain focused on expertise, access to resources and a strong emphasis on delivery. The decision-making comments were more rational, including lists of criteria with a clear indication of weighting. The diagram below, taken from one of my memos, aims to capture this emerging concept.

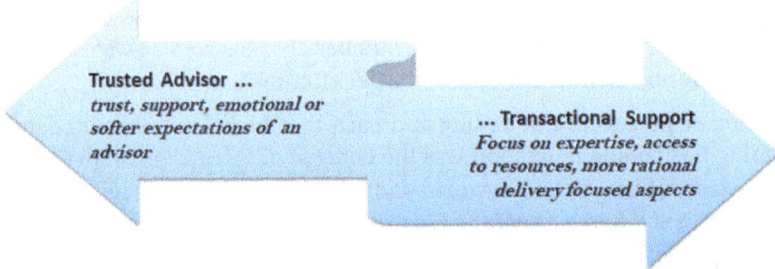

Figure 3.3 – Memo: Relationship or rapport focus diagram

The emerging concept did not quite settle or progress in this form, but I felt that what the client is looking for in terms of advisor relationship or rapport is a key element and potentially decision-making influencer of how senior executives select and appoint an advisor and a firm.

While revisiting and reflecting on the empirical coding results and the summary observations captured in the overview spreadsheet (memo), I distinguished four different ranges of senior executives' preferences, which are evolved from the six overarching attributes and the four code categories discussed in section 3.1.4:

1. Engagement or project: advising <> implementing or delivering

Some narratives discussed projects only in the context of implementing or delivering a particular service or technology, whereas at the other end of the range the focus was only on providing advice, guidance or an opinion.

2. Relationship or rapport: close partnership or trusted adviser <> supplier of services

As described in the previous concept, some respondents were keen on a very close, almost intellectually intimate relationship, sharing many, possibly all, concerns and thoughts with the advisor. This was often described by respondents as a trusted advisor relationship. Others simply saw advisors or advisory firms as suppliers of services operating at the same level as, say, IT systems and service supplier.

3. Selection or appointment focus: individual advisor focus <> firm focus

On the topics of identifying, selecting and appointing an advisor or an advisory firm, the comments ranged from concentrating only on the advisor as an individual (example: we worked with advisor X in the past, while he was actually with another firm, and since we were comfortable working with him we made the decision to reappoint X) to only discussing the firm as an entity (example: on average advisory firm X came more prepared to all the bid presentations compared to the competition).

4. Decision-making: relationship based and intuitive <> process driven and rational

Again, I observed two distinct dimensions when it came to decision-making approaches; at one end of the range were scenarios of decisions being made rather intuitively and based on relationships (see first example in selection focus section, most of the time the decision is made ad hoc or spontaneously during conversations with the advisor). Other scenarios included formal and clearly defined tender processes, with selection panels rating the advisors' proposal against a set of criteria.

Frequently, individuals would emphasise one side of a range; for example, one respondent only spoke about delivering projects and selecting partners via a structured panel-led process. Occasionally, some respondents would share views that fell into both ends of the ranges or a combination of aspects. For example, a number of respondents included both individual advisor aspects as well as firm aspects in their selection narrative. In other words, individuals had specific personal preferences, but they did not necessarily fall into a clear 'black or white' definition of these preferences or taxonomy; some individuals preferred a blend or a balance of aspects, possibly even linked to a particular situation or context.

Over the following months, I started to draft a number of different emerging models. My focus was still very much on identifying and grouping individuals, which was probably not quite right since I started to realise that preferences can blend or change depending on circumstances. However, sketching out these ideas helped me to understand and visualise my observations. I started to refer to those clients who looked for a trusted advisor relationship as betas (β) and those who sought a more transactional support or rapport as alphas (α). A few respondents could be firmly identified and placed at one end of the spectrum; a large group of interviewees had elements of both dimensions and I called them gammas (δ). Below is one of the model diagrams that I created during this phase of the analysis and documented in my memos. In retrospect, I have to admit that I did not take any of these models forward; they were simply too static in comparison to the situations described in the interviews. Nevertheless, these exercises did raise my awareness and progressed my research journey. These ideas also laid the foundation for the 'matrix' model I discuss in Chapters Five and Six, which places 'trust' at one end of the spectrum and 'control' at the other end, as in the diagram below. At this stage I linked the other axis of the decision-making matrix 'competitiveness' and 'embeddedness' to 'control' and 'trust' respectively; only later on did I recognise that these two aspects were independent of 'control' and 'trust'.

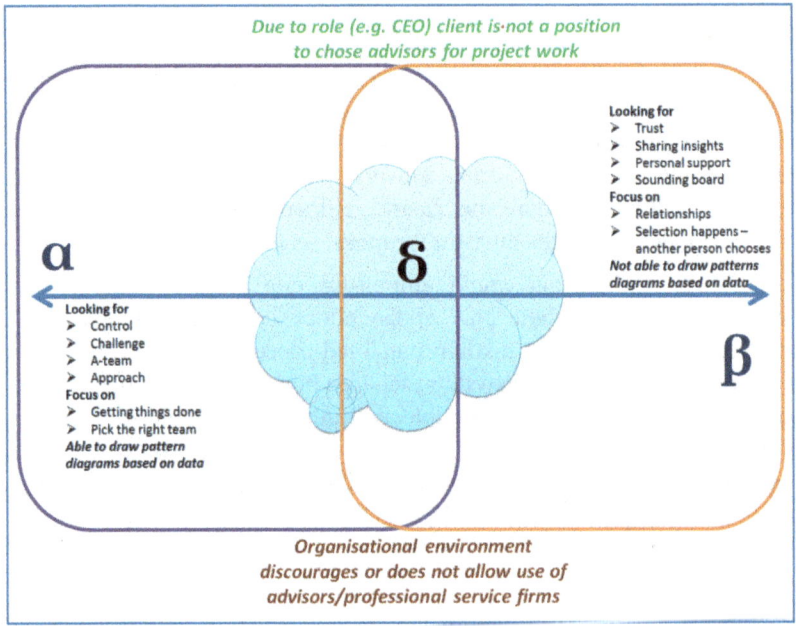

Figure 3.4 – Memo: One of the many emerging alpha-beta models

In addition to narrowing down the theoretical sample and identifying it more clearly to top management, the fourth iteration of open coding also helped me to internalise and articulate my research focus more firmly.

3.3 Summing up the discovery phase and progressing the research journey

The four iterations of open coding gave me a good grasp of the data, allowed me to narrow down and firm up my research focus and provided various first pointers and insights. A number of first concepts and models started to emerge based on the data; however, I was struggling to clearly define the concepts or assemble them into a more cohesive structure or picture. There were lots of puzzle pieces, but I could not quite make out the final picture that these pieces would create. In addition, I felt that further coding reiterations would not help me progress in my journey and therefore started to look for new impressions and inspirations in the general decision-making literature to help me understand my observations and progress the research to beyond discovery (authors and their seminal work are discussed in the ensuing section 3.4 of this chapter). However, I first took stock of my research findings and attempted to define more precisely what I was looking for in the literature:

3.3.1 Summary of discovery phase findings

Summarising the findings discussed so far in Chapter Three and drawing on my observational data documented in the summary spreadsheet (memo) and other memos, as well as the coding results, I documented the following summarising reflections:

- Three primary types of decision-making narratives appear to emerge in the client feedback transcripts and derived from material presented in section 3.1.5:
    1. A number of senior managers emphasised one or two engagements or projects and discussed these in detail, including thought processes and considerations which led to the appointment of the advisor and advisory firm – a type of reflective narrative of their decision-making.
    2. Another group of stakeholders elaborated on hypothetical decision-making processes, discussing in general terms how they preferred to engage, select and appoint advisors; occasionally respondents would use examples to illustrate their statements.
    3. Others only made intermittent comments about preferences and selection criteria.

For the first two types of narratives listed above, the commentary could often be charted as a sequence of criteria or actions leading to a choice decision.

- Interviewees also alluded to their preferred or practised decision-making modes, meaning who made decisions and how, which were at times tied to their respective role in the organisation. For example, a number of CEOs indicated that they either preferred, or felt compelled due to the oversight aspect attached to their role, to delegate appointments of professional advisors to their 'direct reports'. Others opted for a mixed decision-making mode; for example, for certain projects or initiatives they personally got involved in the selection process, but for others, they delegated the decision to their 'direct reports' or a panel of decision-makers.

- With regard to the expectations of a professional advisor, a number of senior managers personally preferred or were instructed via organisational procurement structures, to lean towards a more transactional relationship with an advisory firm. This means that someone within the organisations assesses the problem, defines a solution and then goes out to select and appoint an advisory firm to assist in the execution of a plan leading to the anticipated solution of the business problem. In this instance, the selection process is often moderated or facilitated by a third party (procurement), and appointment decisions are often made as a group or panel. Another group of respondents would draw on existing advisor relationships to jointly (with varying degrees) identify issues and devise a solution and plan to address these (often referred to as the trusted advisor model); occasionally during later execution or implementation stages, the client or the client organisation will review if the incumbent advisory firm will also deliver (execute) all aspects or phases of the plan.

- On a more personal level, some senior executives clearly communicated that they did not wish to have a close ongoing dialogue or relationship with a professional advisor; they were comfortable for interactions to be limited to project activities and to be of a more transactional nature. In contrast, another set of senior managers expressed that they did value an ongoing dialogue or exchange, and that they appreciated insights and impulses that a professional advisor could bring to the conversation, using them as a 'safe' sounding board and sparring partner for new ideas (again, part of the trusted advisor model). A small number of respondents took the relationship aspect even further and would seek personal career advice and ask the advisor to act as a coach or mentor (the focus here is often 'help me manage my reputation within and/or outside of the organisation).

- Lastly, a number of senior executives directly or indirectly referred to organisational guidelines and cultural aspects that informed the relationships and selection of professional advisors. Frequently, managers from the same organisation shared the same or similar messages or aspects.

In summary, and based on this first analysis, it became apparent that there were relationships or links between …

- o   how senior executives engage, employ or utilise a professional advisor and advisory firm, from a transactional to a trusted advisor and occasionally coaching relationship, which can vary from initiative to initiative or business to business problem;
- o   what type of benefits the executive stakeholder is seeking from that relationship and engagements;
- o   to what degree the senior manager is in a position to engage and seek the benefits within the context of the current organisational environment; and
- o   the selection and choice criteria, as well as processes, the senior executive is relying on when selecting a professional service firm.

The above-listed observations were effectively the outcome of the discovery phase. They also served as key pointers for any further investigation and the development of a suitable conceptual framework.

3.3.2 In search of new ideas and viewpoints

Even though the discovery phase of the research, as outlined in this chapter, provided a number of findings and first conclusions, I started to contemplate new sources and tools to help me understand my observations and evolve the research. Therefore, I tried to locate models and approaches in the existing decision-making literature that would help me understand the data and my findings, to explore new perspectives for investigating the data further and to adapt and customise these ideas and approaches to progress the research. The outcomes of the discovery phase and the data were still leading and directing the research; I was not looking to embrace a deductive approach by accepting an existing theory and applying it.

As part of my interpretation of the data, I turned to review general decision-making literature in search of a clearer perspective. Reflecting on the data and my first set of findings, I looked into existing discourse to understand how individuals actually operate and make decisions.

3.4 Existing decision-making theory literature – sources of new ideas and perspectives

In the following sections of this chapter and in Chapter Four, I discuss the outcomes of my literature search and how I utilised these new insights in my study. In summary, I started out by reading up on the different general decision-making theories, such as classical and normative decision-making theories, behavioural decision-making and judgement theories, and organisational and naturalistic decision-making theories. I then focused on naturalistic decision-making theories and some behavioural decision-making. I found great inspiration and new perspectives in Beach and Mitchell's *Image Theory* (1978).

3.4.1 Overview of decision-making theories

My reading of the literature indicated that decision theories have developed over time in various disciplines such as psychology, organisational behaviour and marketing, with each trying to understand decision-making of individuals or groups, albeit for different purposes and from different perspectives. Within the social science literature, I found three main schools of thought: normative, behavioural and naturalistic (Bazerman and Moore 2012, Yates 2003) as well as organisational decision-making, often discussed in conjunction with naturalistic decision-making.

3.4.2 Normative decision theories

Normative decision theory is rooted in economics and includes models such as the 'Expected Utility Theory' of Neumann and Morgenstern (1947) and the 'Subjective Expected Utility Theory' put forward by Leonard Savage (1954). Most importantly, the normative decision theory is prescriptive rather than descriptive of individuals' decision-making (Beach 1997), and it stipulates how a decision-maker should behave to obtain maximum utility (Beach 1997, Charmaz 2009, Edwards 1954). At the core of all of these models is a rational decision-maker, while two key constructs – utilities and probabilities – underpin the theories in this grouping; the models rest on the following assumptions (Shao 2006):

- Decisions are based upon unlimited information.
- Decision-makers can efficiently utilise all of the available information.
- Decision-makers know all the options available to them and the pay-offs or consequences of these options.
- Preferences between options are independent of the presence or absence of other options.
- The optimal course of action is obtained by applying the appropriate calculations of expected utilities.

When comparing the data and findings of my research project with these key principles of normative decision theories, it quickly becomes apparent that I was not in a position to characterise the senior executives as truly rational decision-makers. I could not apply or confirm any of the listed assumptions. The main aim of the study is to investigate how people make decisions, not how they ought to make decisions; therefore, as part of my search for ideas and inspiration, I quickly cast this set of theories aside.

3.4.3 Behavioural decision theories

From 1960 onwards, social scientists challenged normative theories; researchers in the field observed that decision-makers seldom make explicit trade-offs, let alone explicit use of probability (Simon 1955) and their preferences are constructed and not invariant (Beach and Mitchell 1978). Furthermore, the rational decision-maker described in normative theories was questioned by Herbert Simon (1955); he argued that decision-makers have only limited or bounded rationality and are seeking to satisfice, not maximise, as part of their decision-making. Simon observed that many individuals would choose the first feasible alternative that achieves a set of goals and not continue on in their search until all alternatives have been assessed.

Over time, various approaches and extensions of behavioural decision theories have been put forward, all of which are based on the notion that individuals are adaptive decision-makers and that their preferences are highly dependent on person, context and task-specific variables. In this body of research, it is now widely assumed that decision-makers develop a repertoire of methods for 'identifying their preferences and developing their beliefs', which in the literature are referred to as **decision strategies**. Less cognitively demanding strategies are referred to as **simple strategies or heuristics**, whereas more cognitively **demanding strategies** are noted as **analytical strategies** (Bazerman and Moore 2012, Gigerenzer and Gaissmaier 2011, Betsch and Haberstroh 2014, Dastani et al. 2005, Dillon 1998, Jennings and Wattam 1998, Mintzberg et al. 1976, Schwartz et al. 2002).

In addition, textbooks and articles describing behavioural decision theories distinguished between compensatory and non-compensatory and alternative or attribute-based decision strategies. A compensatory approach requires the decision-makers to weigh and compare different options before making a decision, whereas, in the context of a non-compensatory approach, the individual will primarily search for an option that meets a set of requirements (Beach and Mitchell 1978). In comparison, an alternative decision strategy calls for a full evaluation of one alternative at a time, while an attributed decision strategy stipulates that the decision-maker should evaluate the attributes of various or all available alternatives before making a choice (Abelson and Levi 1985, Bettman et al. 1998, Svenson 1979).

3.4.4 Organisational decision theories

Organisational decision theories evolved hand-in-hand with, and later on in parallel to, other decision-making theories (Gore et al. 2006, Rasmussen 1997, Lipshitz et al. 2001). While most general decision-making theories describe or investigate the decision-making of an individual on their own or within a group, organisational decision theories also explore group and individual decision-making but within a large context, an organisation, and at multiple levels involving individuals, groups or teams and organisational entities. Compared, for example, to naturalistic decision-making, which focuses primarily on the individual, organisational decision theories are based on a larger, system-wide model embracing different stakeholders, levels and goals (Rasmussen 1997).

There are significant synergies and overlaps between organisational decision-making (ODM) and naturalistic decision-making (NDM), and a number of articles have been written on this topic (Gore et al. 2006, Lipshitz et al. 2006). *"Both NDM and ODM focus on what decision-makers actually do and the nature of the tasks they are trying to accomplish, as defined by their organisational and real-world context"* (Lipshitz et al. 2006, page 917). Some NDM researchers leave out organisational goals and norms (Cannon-Bowers et al. 1996, Lipshitz et al. 2001), while others include these aspects as part of the decision context (Orasanu and Connolly 1993). Overall only a few NDM researchers argue explicitly that macro-cognitive functions such as decision-making, sense-making, planning and re-planning need to be performed and studied at individual, team and organisational levels (Lipshitz et al. 2006, Klein et al. 2003).

Another difference between the two groups of theories is the fact that NDM models reflect on cognitive processes whereas ODM models mainly reveal social processes, which are constrained by organisational goals and norms (Gore et al. 2006).

Returning to my own study, I realised with the help of the literature that due to the interview data and the lack of organisational level data, my research project is firmly centred on individuals and their cognitive and behavioural processes. I did code, though, during the first analytical phase, a number of incidents which can be described as organisational constraints or aspects; these relate back to senior executives' comments about their organisation and how the organisation on a general level sees and engages with external support such as advisors and advisory firms, as well as more specifically procurement or supplier management dynamics. Consequently, I would place my research project in the naturalistic decision-making group, which includes organisational aspects.

In the next chapter, I will discuss in detail naturalistic decision-making and how it applies to this research study and the emerging conceptual framework.

3.4.5 Implications for my research project

Reflecting on the literature findings and comparing these new insights to my data and findings, I was able to observe some aspects or fragments of the described behavioural decision-making theories and corresponding strategies in my dataset. Some interview comments clearly pointed towards a heuristic satisficing strategy; other interview segments involving panel decisions corresponded to, for example, compensatory attribute-based strategies. Even though the models provided further understanding, I did not feel comfortable taking on or borrowing constructs from these theories. The conceptual frameworks appeared too pre-defined and rigid, and it would have meant forcing the data into a format or structure, which is not what I was aiming for as part of my constructivist grounded theory approach. Charmaz, like many other grounded theory practitioners, explicitly stipulates that data should not be forced but should gradually evolve as part of the research process from open to closed codes, and then code groupings (Bryant 2012, Charmaz 2009, 2006)

I took away two aspects from this body of knowledge and incorporated them in my research – decision mode and decision approach. As part of the discovery analysis, I had identified these concepts and made a note of them in the form of codes and memos, but I was not quite able to place the aspects until I examined the literature. I was able to derive a clearer understanding of decision approach and mode codes, as part of my research project, from articles and books published by Frank Yates (Yates 2003, Yates and Potworowski 2012, Klein 2008). In general, Yates' theories and models aim at identifying, dissecting and understanding decision-making and by doing so to improve the decision-making process. Yates' material offers a host of well researched and thought-through deductive definitions and guidelines, which do not, however, fit an inductive constructivist grounded theory study. For example, his framework 'the cardinal decision issue perspective' addresses four aspects; *'a) what decisions are; b) what decision quality is; c) what are the modes by which people decide; and d) what are the fundamental – cardinal – issues that must be resolved in virtually all practical decision problems'* (Yates 2001, page 17). However, of the four concepts, the third – decision mode – provided some helpful guidance for my research and introduced me to a new viewpoint, which I will explain below.

Yates (Yates 2001, page 17) defines decision modes as *"qualitative distinct ways how people solve decision problems"*; the two broad mode classes are primary and secondary decision modes. *'Primary nodes'* are ones in which the decision-maker personally (possibly in a collective) derives the decision. In contrast, in secondary modes, someone else derives the decision on the decision-maker's behalf. Primary decision modes can be subdivided into analytic *("decision-maker effortfully thinks things through")*, rule-based *("decision-maker deliberately applies a rule")* and automatic *("effortless, uncontrollable and often times cognitively inaccessible"* application of rules) (Yates 2001, page 21-23). Yates proposes three major types for the secondary decision modes: agency *("decision-maker commissions someone else to make the decision")*, consultation *("decision-maker accepts or rejects recommendations developed by consultants")* and modelling *("decision-maker observes the decision of some other and simply mimics the others' behaviour")* (Yates 2001, page 21-23).

Even though I did not want to classify and differentiate between particular decision strategies or Frank Yates' (2001) decision modes as part of my coding activities, I felt compelled to view the data from these new perspectives. When I revisited the interview transcripts in the next analytical phase (described in detail in Chapter Four), I re-examined the data with this new decision mode perspective influenced by Yates' writings. I discovered a number of aspects which I had missed in previous coding iterations. Hence, while I was reviewing the client data, I identified six new codes to describe my observations pertaining to decision mode:

1. **'Follow a rational approach to selecting an advisor or firm'**, defined as 'respondent discusses that he/she/they follow a structure or more rational approach by either consulting with others, applying rules or analysing data points before making a selection decision'. For instance, a quote from CEO_2: *'I think it's a combination of making sure that you've got the right expertise; you've got the right resource both in terms of quantity and quality, the commercial terms and the strength of the relationship. I don't see any issues on any of those criteria and it's always going to be some combination of those depending on what the nature of the job is, you know.'*

2. **'Follow an ad hoc or intuitive approach to selecting an advisor or firm'**, defined as 'respondent discusses automatic decision-

making or mimicking of decision-making without greatly considering rules or conducting an analysis'. For example, a quote from CFO_2: *'And so because partner A had done work for us before, we knew him and were very happy with what he'd done. We brought him back in again to have a look at... And that project just got bigger and bigger and bigger (laughter) over the space of...'*

3.   **'Always or mostly delegate selection'**, defined as 'respondent always or most of the time delegated the selection and or appointment of an advisor or firm to one of his/her 'direct reports' or a panel of decision-makers'. To illustrate a quote from CEO_4: *'Because I mean ultimately in my role, I'm probably not the principal employer of the consulting services. It will be the people who work for me who are initiating and implementing the projects that we've agreed will form part of our strategy.'*

4.   **'Delegate for some initiatives, for other direct personal involvement'**, defined as 'respondent indicates that for certain initiatives he/she does get involved directly in the decision-making or selection process, but for others chooses to delegate the selection to someone else.' For instance, a quote from CFO_1: *'We didn't use him actually on the day because we thought it would be better to have largely our own people do it, but he was very useful in that sense. And I think we've used him a couple of other times. So I think in that kind of space I do appreciate that; on the project side, it tends to be an RFP.'*

5.   **'Selection is a group decision with some or limited senior involvement'**, defined as 'selection and appointment of an advisor or firm is a group decision and there is some senior executive involvement, either as a final sounding-board or just another vote as part of the group'. For example, this quote from CFO_1: *'It's kind of horses for courses. If we're doing a project then it's a project. We had a bidding project and I think we had an RFP, and actually it ended up being between Firm 6 and Firm 1, and the team (I wasn't really that involved) wanted to go with Firm 6 for specific expertise.'*

6.   **'Personally drive the selection of advisors'**, defined as 'respondent states that he/she personally or possibly in a collective (group) drives or shapes the selection and appointment of advisors'. To illustrate, a quote from COO_3: *'You can be very sure that I am extremely selective, and if I'm convinced that somebody delivers, I work with the person but I*

> *never work with the brand. Because for me, to be very honest,*
> *Firm 1 or Firm 4, or whatever, at that level, quality-wise, the*
> *partner should be the same. And I select by person and not by*
> *brand.'*

Beyond the theories listed above and the debate about naturalistic decision-making in the next chapter, I also engaged with other decision-making models in the literature, such as Richard Thaler's 'Choice Architecture' (Thaler et al. 2014), Daniel Kahneman's 'Thinking fast and slow' (Kahneman 2011), consumer decision-making processes (Bettman et al. 1998, Dillon 1998), as well as different decision-making routines identified in the literature (Bazerman and Moore 2012, Betsch and Haberstroh 2014, Dastani et al. 2005). All of these were interesting and intellectually engaging, but I felt that none of them settled with the grounded theory approach nor explicitly created additional inroads for my study at this stage in the research project.

In this chapter, I have retraced the discovery phase of my research journey, exploring the phenomena through a series of reiterative coding exercises, before I examined the decision-making literature for additional perspectives to move the research process forward. In the following fourth chapter, which discusses the theory building phase of the research project, I continue to elaborate on how the findings from the decision-making literature review helped me understand the phenomena and provided the impetus for an emerging conceptual framework.

Chapter 4

Theory building – emerging conceptual framework and theoretical saturation

In this chapter, I explain how, in my search for new ideas and perspectives, naturalistic decision-making theories resonated with me; in particular how the underpinning theoretical discussions associated with Beach and Mitchell's 'Image Theory' helped me to move the study forward. Furthermore, new perspectives and stimulus provided by the literature allowed me to advance – a conceptual framework started to emerge and I progressed from open coding to closed coding followed by theoretical saturation – I would describe this stage as theory building.

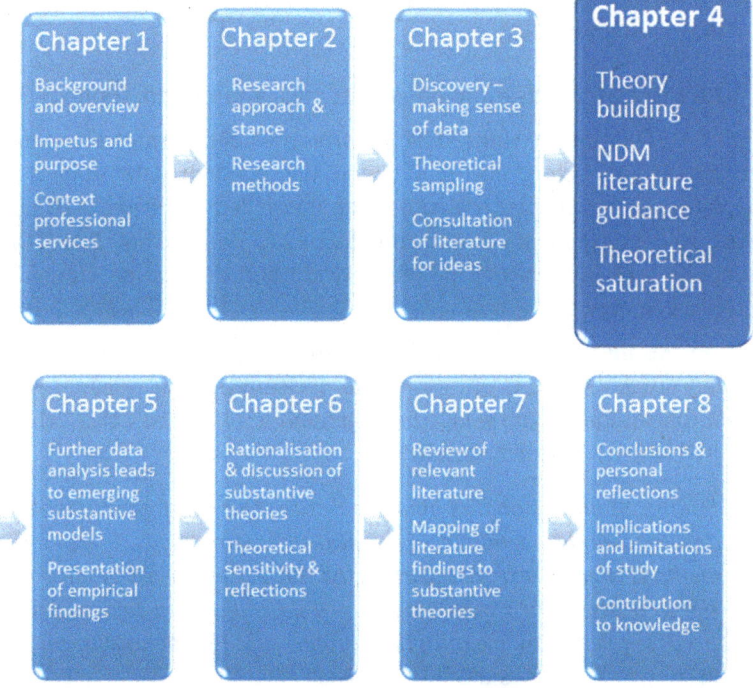

Figure 4.1 – Overview of thesis structure and content of the fourth chapter

Reflecting on the research progress reported so far, in the previous chapter I documented the initial discovery phase of the study during which I explored the phenomena through a series of open coding reiterations, supported by a theoretical sampling approach. Towards the end of this exploratory stage, I started to study the decision-making literature for additional views and insights to help me understand my observations and progress the research. In this chapter, I give an account of the next phase – theory building. During this stage, a conceptual framework, informed by my studies of the naturalistic decision-making literature, gradually emerged, and theoretical saturation was reached after a series of closed coding reiterations and validation exercises.

Towards the end of the discovery phase, described in the previous chapter, the analytical process did not progress much further. Thus, I searched for additional viewpoints in the literature to understand the data and move the empirical analysis forward. Since the underlying assumptions did not correspond so well with my dataset and research approach, I disregarded classical and normative decision-making theories as inspiration sources. However, I discovered a couple of perspectives in the behavioural decision theories, including organisational decision-making, which inspired me and enabled me to view and understand my data from a different angle.

4.1 Naturalistic decision-making – the most appropriate context?

Naturalistic decision-making (NDM) theories provided the greatest source of stimulus and helped me understand the research data from new viewpoints. In this chapter, I elaborate on naturalistic decision-making – in particular, image theory (Beach and Mitchell 1978) – and how I used the findings to take my research project forward and develop an emerging conceptual framework.

During the literature review, I discovered two statements in the peer reviewed article 'A review of naturalistic decision-making research with some implications for knowledge management' (Meso et al. 2002), which resonated with my research context:

> *"NDM aims at understanding how people use their experience to make decisions in complex, dynamic, and real time environments. It explores the methods used by experts, working as individuals or in groups, to identify and assess their situations, make decisions, and take actions whose consequences are meaningful to them ..."* (Meso et al. 2002 page 63 referring to, Gordon and Gill 1997, Beach et al. 1997)

"NDM perceives decision-making as being a process rather than a one-time, point specific event." (Meso et al. 2002, page 64)

I felt that both cited statements not only addressed the purpose of my study but also matched up with the observations I had made during my research activities so far. First of all, senior executives clearly discussed and placed their actions and decisions within the context of a larger construct, such as the organisation they were acting on behalf of, as well as their and the organisation's relationship with external advisors and advisory firms. Secondly, senior executives elaborated on decisions made by them but also in groups. Lastly, the decision to engage and work with an advisor is not necessarily a one-off decision, albeit there are unique binary decisions to appoint an advisor for a particular project; however, the ongoing rapport, mostly over years, and management of advisors is a long-term process.

Lipshitz (1993) indicates that compared to other decision theories, NDM investigates decision-making beyond the decision event and focuses on a 'sequence of activities' involved in the decision-making process where alternatives are generated. Furthermore, in contrast to behavioural and normative theories, NDM puts greater emphasis on the decision-maker's knowledge and expertise. Both aspects are of importance to my research: first of all, the study's aim was to investigate the interactions between clients and advisors, examining the client's decision-making as part of this interactive process and leading to the selection of an advisor. Within the context of the research, the client's decision-making was not a one-off decision at one particular point in time, but should be seen as part of a longer-term dialogue between client and advisor leading to appointment or no appointment decisions from time to time. Secondly, past experiences had already emerged as a key aspect in the client's decision-making comments, and, consequently, taking note of and understanding individuals' knowledge and expertise needed to be strongly acknowledged and incorporated in the research.

The need to focus on and understand the individual decision-maker and the role of his or her knowledge and expertise in the process was a key impetus for the emergence of naturalistic decision-making, which evolved within the discipline of organisational behaviour. The first NDM research programme was sponsored by the US Army Research Institute for Behavioural and Social Science in the mid-1980s (Klein 2008). These first studies were field-based and investigated the decision-making of professionals such as military commanders, jurors, medical doctors or pilots as part of their day-to-day job (Klein 2008). **Furthermore, these** early NDM studies were effectively inductive empirical research: *"Instead of beginning with formal models of decision-making, we began by conducting field research to try to discover the strategies that people used"* (Klein 2008, page 456). According to the literature, NDM as a research framework is marked by five essential characteristics or better requirements (Lipshitz et al. 2001, page 334-335):

1. Proficient or experienced decision-makers;
2. Situation-action matching decision-making rules, meaning no set sequential or decision tree type of approaches;
3. Context-bound informal modelling, denoting that decision-makers rely on a quick or better gut feeling approach instead of having time to consider or contemplate a more formal decision-making approach;
4. Process orientation, meaning that NDM does not try to predict which options will be implemented; it instead tries to capture or describe the cognitive processes of the decision-maker;
5. Empirically-based descriptions, indicating that *"NDM advocates prescriptions which are optimal in some formal sense";* however, *"if these cannot be implemented the optimal path turns worthless"*. In other words, the 'ought' cannot be divorced from the 'is'; there are no good or bad decisions as such.

An attempt to critically describe how these five characteristics of NDM apply to the datasets analysed thus far is provided below:

Proficient and experienced decision-makers – All the respondents in the current study were senior executives who had worked with and appointed professional advisors and advisory firms in the past. Furthermore, due to their level in the organisation as senior managers, they were tasked with making business-critical decisions for and on behalf of the organisation, and they had, most likely, been doing this for many years while growing through the ranks either within the organisation or in another professional environment, e.g. another company or even working for a professional advisor firm.

Situation-action matching decision-making rules – Even though for some respondents it was possible to sketch out a type of decision-making sequence or pattern, no one spoke of fixed processes or sequences when it came to working with and identifying advisors. Although some procurement leads (interviewees who spoke on behalf of the purchasing or procurement department of a client organisation) did try and advocate for a process-driven approach, the responses from senior managers clearly did not reflect a standard approach and followed more of a general situation-action making approach.

Context-bound informal modelling – Many of the senior executives spoke about making decisions quickly and at times intuitively when it came to working with and selecting advisors or advisory firms; most likely due to their years of experience, a lengthy contemplation or planning of the decision process was seldom mentioned.

Process orientation – The objective of the research project overall was to understand senior executives when it comes to working with and selecting advisors and advisory firms; my goal was not necessarily to be able to forecast how someone would decide in the future nor to prescribe a particular 'ideal' path.

Process orientation – Reviewing the transcripts and open codes, it became apparent that some individuals described either actively or hypothetically an ideal set state or series of activities; at the same time, respondents also made it clear that when circumstances change another approach needs to be taken. An example would be an emergency situation: the regulatory body threatens to shut down a part of the business and therefore a lengthy tendering process is not an option.

The underlying premises of NDM in *"trying to understand how people use their experience to make decisions in a complex, dynamic, real-time environment"* (Meso et al. 2002) resonates with the research objectives of trying to establish why and how senior managers engage, select and appoint advisors and advisory firms, and to investigate how and to what extent these interactions influence or shape the individuals' decision-making regarding appointing an advisor or firm.

4.2 Image theory – a rich source of inspiration and new perspectives

After establishing that my research project fell within the naturalistic decision-making context from a philosophical and an underlying assumptions point of view, I started to take a closer look at NDM models in order to ascertain new viewpoints and to help me understand the researched phenomena better.

In 1993, Lipshitz identified and reviewed nine relatively established naturalistic decision-making models, of which five were process and four typological models (Klein 2008). The situation assessment model (Prince and Salas 1998), model of recognition primed decisions (Klein 1993), model of explanation-based decisions (Pennington and Hastie 1988), dominance search model (Montgomery 1989, Montgomery and Svenson 1989) and image theory (Beach and Mitchell 1978, Beach 1993b, 1998, 1997) were discussed as process models. The cognitive control model (Rasmussen 1986), cognitive continuum theory (Hammond 1988), model of decision cycles (Connolly and Wagner 1988) and model of argument-driven action (Lipshitz 1988) were identified as typological models. Lipshitz's (1993) list of NDM models informed my literature explorations in the ensuing months. Over a period of time, I tried to locate and read the literature for all of the listed models. Few of the theories were discussed widely or in great detail, which meant that I was not able to extract sufficient information to compare and contrast the listed models with my empirical findings so far. However, I was able to locate sufficiently descriptive literature for Klein's model of recognition-primed decisions, Montgomery's dominance search model and Beach's image theory.

In retrospect, it was a statement and the discussion in Julie Gore's article 'Naturalistic Decision-making and Organisations: Reviewing Pragmatic Science' (Gore et al. 2006) which steered me towards image theory. Gore states*: "It appears that within the context of the organisation, and in particular the business world, decision-making inquiry requires a broad approach in order to fully understand decision complexities"* (Gore et al. 2006, page 928). In this article, Gore indicates image theory as an influential approach and discusses Beach's work extensively:

Reading through the literature (Beach and Mitchell 1978, Beach 1993a, Gore et al. 2006) explaining the three-image construct component of image theory (value, trajectory and strategic image), although not so much the screening and choice elements, I concluded that the debate surrounding this construct offered a helpful perspective for my study. The image construct debate and definitions were broad and flexible, and I felt that they would link up well with my research purpose and dataset. Thus, I started to study image theory in more detail and explored to what extent aspects of the theory could help me understand my data and take the study forward.

Regarding the other two NDM models, the model of recognition-primed decisions (Klein 1993) and the dominance search model (Montgomery and Svenson 1989) appeared to be very process-oriented and slightly inflexible compared to the at times rather fragmented and infrequently sequential data that I had available for evaluation as part of my research, and therefore, I chose not to investigate these theories in great detail.

4.2.1 Overview of image theory

In 1993, Lee Roy Beach, with the support of Terence Mitchell, formally proposed 'image theory' as an alternative process-based theory to normative decision-making in the publication *Advances in Consumer Research* (Beach 1993b). In another article, Beach credits Miller, Galanter and Pribram (1965) as the source of inspiration for the model, and in deference to the authors, Beach opted to call the model 'image theory' (Beach 1993a). Conversely, in a later publication, a group of academics claimed that Chester Barnard's model of decision-making (1938) should be seen as a historical predecessor to image theory since many of Barnard's principles and relationships are included in the conceptualisation of image theory (Novicevic et al. 2011).

Most importantly, compared to traditional decision theories, image theory offers a decision model that includes the individual's principles and values as the motivating source of decision goals and decision-related behaviour (Gore et al. 2006). Image theory encompasses two key aspects: **one is the image construct** (see Figure 4.2 below), composed of three images or schemata defined as *"schematic knowledge structures that the decision-maker applies to organise their thinking about decisions"* (Beach 1998, page 12) surrounded by a decision frame or framing, which connotes the individual's process to apply images, as well as the overall knowledge set that the decision-maker brings to bear in different situations. This is a different definition of a decision frame compared to the one found in the judgement and decision-making literature, which predominately refers to a decision frame as an individual's perspective on an anticipated set of outcomes, for example, either a gain or a loss (Tversky and Kahneman 1981).

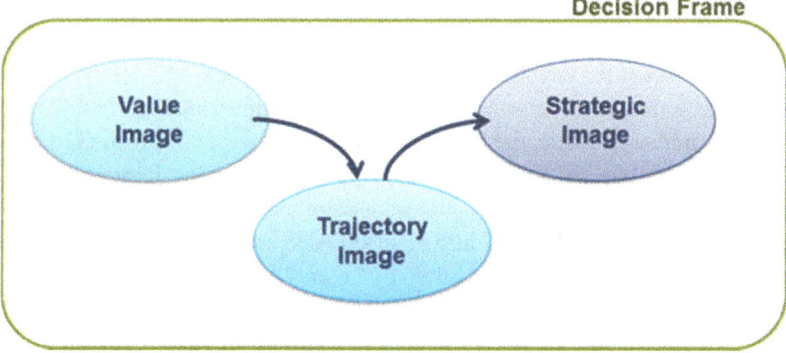

Figure 4.2 – Image Theory 'Image Construct'

The second aspect of image theory is the notion of two kinds of decisions (adoptions and progress decisions) and two types of decision tests (compatibility and profitability tests). The compatibility test examines the process of option screening, while the profitability test investigates the actual choice process, that is, the selection of one of the screened and approved options (Beach 1998).

During the course of my literature review, I found a number of image theory textbooks or chapters in textbooks, as well as publications entailing a collection of image theory studies (2014, Beach 1998, Beach and Mitchell 1978). Most of the studies that I discovered focused on the above-described second aspect of the theory, primarily employing the compatibility test and to a lesser degree the profitability test. Only a small number of empirical studies investigated the actual image construct in depth.

Nevertheless, the sources (cited above) did discuss the images and the decision framing extensively and illustratively, these explanations and discussions influenced my thoughts and understanding, and consequently led me to a number of new ideas and perspectives for the study. In the following section, I will discuss how I used the image theory discussions to help me understand the data and take the research forward.

4.3 Emerging conceptual framework

In summary, after having explored the decision-making literature in a type of 'theoretical sampling approach', I reviewed those sources, which provided the greatest inspiration and allowed me take the research forward: the image construct as I understood it from Beach and Mitchell's image theory, described above, and the decision mode definitions by Yates (2003) as discussed in section 3.4.3 in the previous chapter.

The debates and definitions linked to the image construct (schemata) of the theory provided pivotal ideas. The general underlying notion is that there are a set of images or schemata which support and influence the decision-maker in his or her decision. While comparing the results of my empirical analysis so far, I found aspects of these three images in the interview transcripts: The respondents (senior executives) made reference to expectations, requirements and ideal states to aspire to or aim for, albeit compromises featured as well – there were very few circumstances where desire and reality completely matched. Consequently, the idea of comparing or benchmarking a particular situation and features of a situation to an aspired state or image is a concept that can be found in and is supported by the research data.

In addition to the above-described image theory material, Frank Yates' discussion (2003, Yates and Potworowski 2012, Yates 2001) on the subject of decision mode, as well as the organisational dimension highlighted in the organisational decision-making literature, served as key stimuli, as described in section 3.4.3 of the previous chapter. In section 3.4.4, I described how Yates' decision mode construct (Yates 2001) provided the impetus to re-evaluate and redefine some of my codes relating to a general decision approach and decision mode.

4.3.1 Image definitions help to redefine existing code categories

The three images translate to principles, objectives or goals and plans, which many senior executives did not distinguish clearly during the interview (Beach 1998). That was one of the reasons why I struggled to see a cohesive structure between the code categories I was working with. In order to distinguish between the three images, a set of questions assisted me in classifying the data more coherently: 'Why?' – points towards the principles that motivate the behaviour; 'What?' – establishes the goals of the behaviour; and 'How?' identifies plans for how to achieve matters. The discussions that I located in the image theory literature around these three image schemata were key contributors to my empirical analysis; the debate in the reviewed literature brought new perspectives to the research endeavour. These included: revisiting the interview data and comparing it with the image theory discussions, reflecting on the meaning of each schema and underlying question allowed me to view the dataset from new angles.

The schemata-driven questions were a starting point; the detailed definitions and discussions for each image brought further clarity. Over a period of weeks, I reworked my previous unstructured code categories into a more balanced and well-defined set of constructs informed by the image theory concepts.

The first schema is the **value image,** which I started to refer to as **'imperatives'**; in the image theory literature, value image is defined as: 'strongly held broad-based principles', imperatives for personal or organisational behaviour and a gold standard criteria for adoption or rejections. After several iterations, I settled on the following definition in the context of my study:

> **The primary reasons** for engaging with an external partner. What the senior executive is looking for in an advisor or advisory firm. The gold standard that will determine if he/she will choose to engage or build a rapport with an advisor or an advisory firm.

To a large extent, this construct does overlap with the previous code category – client expectations and experiences (see list of past codes further down in this section) – nevertheless, there is a new degree of formality and clarity in the definition. Most of the codes that fell into this group were primarily based on the response to the interview question: 'How would the ideal advisor relationship look?' or 'What are your general expectations of a professional advisor such as a 'Big Four' firm?'

Trajectory image is linked to decision-maker's goal agenda, describing the ideal or desired state, a vision or just in general what the individual is trying to achieve. Within the context of my research, I started referring to this image as **'project or service trajectory or benefits sought'** and defined it as follows:

> **The reason why** the senior executive formally transacts with a professional advisor. What the senior manager is trying to achieve by engaging an advisor or advisory firm on behalf of the organisation. The objectives or goals of an engagement or interaction with an advisor or advisory firm.

Many of the codes that found their way into this construct originate with senior managers' comments and reflection on recent projects and engagements with advisors. This helped to identify the objectives and triggers for transactions or more formally engaging with a professional advisor.

In my first open coding analysis, I did not reflect strongly on this trajectory image perspective; the image theory structure and definitions helped me realise that there was indeed a trajectory image data in the transcripts, but I had overlooked these comments from this particular viewpoint. Interestingly enough, when I presented the emerging framework to my professional sponsor, this perspective also surprised him and he admitted that many advisory firms seemed to oversee or neglect this aspect outside of tender activities. During the proposal preparation, drafting of tender material, the trajectory image is, of course, the focal point, but its importance diminishes in the bigger strategic discussion involving account and relationship management.

Strategic image, the third schema, is described in the image theory literature as plans and tactics to progress towards and achieve the desired goal or goals (trajectory image). I have labelled this construct **'selection or choice actions'** and defined it in the following terms:

How the senior executive goes about identifying and selecting appropriate advisors to help execute or realise his or her goals (trajectory images). The steps that the senior manager, and with him or her the organisation, undertakes to identify and select a partner. The selection criteria and selection behaviour that are alluded to during the interview.

Many of the codes found in the previous code category – client decision-making – were organised under selection or choice actions. The codes are based on interviewees' recalling selection situations and describing key criteria for appointing advisors, either voluntarily or in response to an interview question.

For reference, during the last iteration of open coding, I was working with the following code groupings:

- Client decision-making (highlighted in orange in Nvivo) – 'this is how I decide (taking the client's perspective), this is how I go about making decisions, this is critical to me as part of the selection process'.
- Client expectations and experiences (highlighted in yellow in Nvivo)– 'these are my expectations and experiences, positive and negative, when it comes to professional advisors and firms'.
- Organisational context (highlighted in green in Nvivo) – 'this is how the organisations decides or selects advisors, this is critical to the organisation'.

The last portion of the image construct relates to the decision frame or framing. Initially, I focused on past experiences, relying on the definition of an individual's store of knowledge, learned experiences and established patterns or preferences as to how to apply the three images. Over time, I opted to include what I called organisational aspects or constraints to the decision frame. Originally, I had these codes residing in the value image group; however, I felt that there was frequently a strong distance – almost a dichotomy – between individuals' views and the organisational views mentioned by the respondent, so I decided to remove them from the value image. During the later stages of my analysis (see Chapter Five for further discussions), I also came to realise that past experiences and organisational context or constraints were two key influencing dynamics across all three structures; therefore, I was comfortable including these aspects in the decision frame.

Thus, the definition of **decision frame** in the context of this research study may be described as below and it formed the basis for another two code categories (client experience and knowledge and organisational context):

Senior executives' store of knowledge (past experiences either learned, observed or conveyed) as well as organisational context (formal or informal guidelines and/or constraints regarding working with external advisors), which the senior executive draws on when applying all three images (imperatives, project or service trajectory and selection or choice actions) as part of the decision-making activity.

4.3.2 Progression towards a closed coding framework

As part of the iterative process of developing a coding framework, I started aligning existing codes to the new code categories, which were somewhat redefined by the image theory questions that I had imposed on the data as described in the section above. Looking back, these were the key stages of the framework development:

Prior to the image theory-based re-definition, I experimented with the selection mode and approach ideas from Yates (2001). As a first step, I reviewed the transcripts to check for sufficient evidence of these six modes (primary analytic, primary rules based, primary automatic, secondary agency, secondary consultation, secondary modelling) but there was none. However, I did spot data points pertaining to decision behaviours, which I had not coded previously. As part of the reviewing activities, I developed a number of open codes found in the data while using some of Yates' (2008) terminology in the definitions. Initially, I kept the decision mode or approach codes as a separate construct; later on, I moved them into the third image – 'selection and choice actions' as one of three code categories and called them 'selection modes'. A discussion of these codes, including an example quote, can be found in section 3.4.4. of the previous chapter.

As previously mentioned, the image definitions and corresponding questions provided the impetus to redefine the macro code categories, which left me with imperatives (value image), benefits sought/future state (trajectory image), selection and choice actions (strategic image) and experiences and organisational context (decision frame). Having the definitions, and with clear demarcations, facilitated the alignment of the existing codes. Specifically, I reviewed the output of my open coding iterations and started to assign each code to one of the image components.

While I was going through this exercise, I realised that there were a number of duplicates or similar codes and I consolidated these into a set of more comprehensive codes. In addition, I made sure that the labels for each code were client-centric: I tried to articulate the code comparable to a statement or an expression that a client might share, for example, 'need to be able to trust the advisor or firm' instead of 'trust' to ensure that the code names were as precise as possible, plus I also created detailed code definitions.

Having this new overview, I created a table with code categories, listing each code underneath them. A number of codes were 'adjourned' or put to one side since they did not quite correspond with the code categories definition – they did not fit or provide an answer to the image driven questions (what, why, how and decision frame). At a later stage, and after having had a closer look at the unused or adjourned codes, I identified that these were general statements describing individuals' personal principles and preferences, and chose to include them as a separate subgroup in the imperative image. The codes would encompass messages such as 'quality has its price – you get what you pay for' or 'I like and expect to be challenged'. This was a significant step forward and gave me a more holistic view of the dataset. Over an extended period, I compared and contrasted the different codes and code categories, consolidated further and fine-tuned the definitions while constantly consulting the source data, reviewing the coded sections in the transcripts before making adjustments. Furthermore, a number of sub-groups within the code categories started to emerge and I explored and moved groups of codes around. As I mentioned in the previous section, I initially aligned the organisational context codes to imperatives and decision modes were listed as a separate group floating outside the image constructs.

The coding software Nvivo, described in Chapter Two, provided considerable assistance in the process of moving, merging and redefining codes. Nonetheless, and in parallel to developing the coding framework, I still made sure that I carefully reviewed, recoded or validated the existing coding of each of the 15 selected C-suite transcripts.

4.4 Emerging conceptual framework explained

At the end of the process, a conceptual framework of three images and a decision frame emerged. The decision mode and approach code became part of the 'selection and choice actions' construct, organisational context and constraint codes made up one angle of the decision frame, the other being past experiences. The new conceptual framework was comprised of the components depicted in the diagram below and described in detail in the subsequent sections:

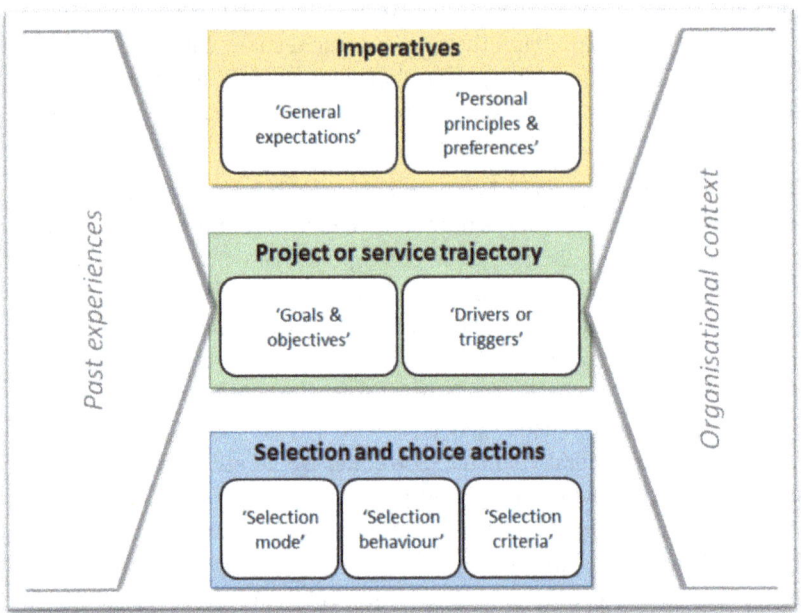

Figure 4.3 – Emerging conceptual decision-making model

Imperatives or value image: 'What is the senior executive looking for in an advisor or advisor relationship?' 'What are the criteria that will determine if he/she will chose to engage or build a rapport?'

- **Subgroup 1 – General expectations:** General expectations of an advisory or advisory firm as part of the day-to-day interactions (relationships/rapport) and engagements (projects): key qualities, attributes and characteristics or primary reasons for working with an external advisor. At the end of the analysis, I recoded eleven different codes aligned to this group; a detailed definition of each can be located in Appendix A and further discussions can be found in Chapter Five as part of the component analysis in section 5.2.

  1. Demonstrate empathy – advisor or firm should understand me and the organisation and act on that knowledge.

2. Earn my trust and bat for me – invest in the relationship and put me and the organisation first.
3. Be pro-active – advice, flag and challenge as required – don't sell.
4. Right interpersonal skills and chemistry.
5. Be embedded and hold a presence in the organisation.
6. Be able to solve problems pragmatically and collaboratively.
7. Be realistic, transparent and honest – stick to agreements.
8. Provide an external view, benchmarks and insights.
9. Help me or us understand and manage regulatory bodies.
10. Provide and assure required competence, skills and expertise.
11. Step in and help out – be responsive, accessible and available.

- **Subgroup 2 – Personal principles and preferences**: Senior executives' personal principles and preferences regarding advisors or advisory firms, as well as more generic imperative statements that go beyond general expectations. At the end of the analysis I registered twenty different codes aligned to this sub-category, below is a selection of these codes. The complete list of codes and a detailed definition of each can be found in Appendix A and further discussions can be found in Chapter Five as part of the component analysis in section 5.2.

1. Need to feel important or be a priority.
2. Need to be able to trust the advisor or firm.
3. Advisors are in the business to make money.
4. Quality has its price.
5. It is difficult to differentiate between firms.
6. Self-promotion without substance is a no go.
7. I like to stay in control – monitor advisor activities.
8. Thrive on challenge.
9. Don't like scare-mongering.
10. I do like to meet the advisor regularly.
11. I don't like to engage with the advisor socially.
12. The end result matters.
13. Integrity is important.

Project or service trajectory / benefits sought or trajectory image: 'Why do senior executives formally transact with a professional advisor? What is the senior manager trying to or tried to achieve by engaging an advisor or advisory firm on behalf of the organisation?'

- **Subgroup 1 – Goals and objectives**: Primary goals and objectives that a senior executive is looking to address by working with an advisor or advisory firm. Expected outcomes or outputs of the transaction. At the end of the analysis I recoded ten different codes aligned to this group; a detailed definition of each can be located in Appendix A and further discussions can be found in Chapter Five as part of the component analysis in section 5.2.

  1. Deliver positive results and tangible outputs.
  2. Provide guidance and advice (billable).
  3. Free-of-charge or free advice (non-billable).
  4. Be part of the organisational eco-system.
  5. Guarantee success.
  6. Fill a resource gap.
  7. Fill a knowledge gap.
  8. Teach or empower us.
  9. Help me meet a deadline.
  10. Share pain and responsibilities.

- **Subgroup 2 – Drivers and triggers**: Impetus, primary drivers or triggers for the benefits sought. Who or what called for a project or transaction with the advisor or advisory firm? At the end of the analysis I identified three codes as primary drivers or triggers:

  1. **Regulation**: Meeting or responding to demands of regulatory bodies such as section 166 reviews or implementing change requests from regulators.
  2. **Request from board or superior**. Addressing or responding to request made by the company board or a superior, or delivering an initiative that originated via someone higher up in the organisational hierarchy.
  3. **Operational response**. Keeping up with general organisational and external demands, initiative was formed or developed by respondent or with his or her input.

Selection and choice actions or strategic image: 'How does the senior executive go about identifying and selecting an appropriate advisor or firm to help execute or realise goals and objectives and respond to the triggers? Which selection criteria and selection behaviour are being alluded to by the senior manager?'

- **Subgroup 0 – Selection modes**: Different decision-making modes and approaches discussed, exploring who is making the selection decisions and how in general these decisions are made (approach). As previously discussed at the end of Chapter Three, reflecting on Yates' (2003) decision mode discussions, six codes emerged after revisiting the data with this new perspective; a more detailed definition of each can be found in section 3.4.4 and Appendix A, and further discussions can be found in Chapter Five as part of the component analysis in section 5.2.
  1. Always or mostly delegate the selection of advisors for an initiative.
  2. Delegate for some initiatives, for others direct personal involvement.
  3. Selection is a group decision with some or limited senior involvement.
  4. Personally drive the selection of advisors.
  5. Follow a structured or rational approach to selecting an advisor or firm.
  6. Follow an ad hoc or intuitive approach to selecting an advisor or firm.
- **Subgroup 1 – Selection behaviour and protocols**: What steps or actions do the senior executive and the organisation take to identify and select an advisor or advisory firm? What kind of behaviour is being discussed in the context of selection and appointment? At the end of the analysis I recorded seventeen selection behaviour codes, some of these are listed below; for a full list and definition of each code, please refer to Appendix A and further discussions can be found in Chapter Five as part of the component analysis in section 5.2.
  1. Large projects should go out for tender.
  2. Small pieces of work don't need to go to tender.
  3. Continuity creates efficiency and better results.
  4. Balance advisors – avoid over-reliance.
  5. Emergencies can bypass selection processes.
  6. Physical proximity leads to pole position for advisor or firm.
  7. Established relationships serve as a type of screening mechanism.
  8. Fire-fighting, no time to plan.
  9. Cost focus leads to DIY (meaning trying to manage projects with organisational resources).

- **Subgroup 2 – Selection criteria:** What are the criteria mentioned during interviews for selecting and ultimately appointing an advisor or advisory firm? At the end of analysis I registered 14 different codes aligned to this sub-group; a selection of these codes is listed below, for a full list of codes and detailed definitions, please view Appendix A and further discussions can be found in Chapter Five as part of the component analysis in section 5.2.

   1. Skills and experiences of individuals.
   2. Strong bid performance (presentation and question and answer sessions).
   3. Reputation and perceived house style.
   4. Brand and reputational factors are not important or less important.
   5. Relevant experiences – track record (of advisor and or team).
   6. Hunger and drive (of advisor and firm).
   7. Fair or competitive price.
   8. Previous performance and experiences.

Organisation and experiences - decision frame: Senior executives' store of knowledge as well as organisational context that the individual consults and relies on to make a decision.

- **Subgroup 1 – Organisational context:** Organisational principles, preferences and protocols for engaging and appointing advisors and advisory firms, as perceived and stated by the senior executive. At the end of the analysis I registered six different codes aligned to this sub-group; more detailed definitions can be found in Appendix A and further discussions can be found in Chapter Five as part of the component analysis in section 5.2.

   1. 'We tend to, prefer to or are not allowed to use consultants or external advisors.'
   2. 'Asking for external support is seen as a sign of failure in this organisation.'
   3. 'We know how to manage and get the most out of advisors and external support.'
   4. 'We like to monitor and balance our external support and use of advisors.'

5. 'We are not very organised in terms of managing advisors – everything is last-minute, no processes and no transparency.'

6. 'Increased focus on costs limits our use of external advisors and external support.'

- **Subgroup 2 – Past experiences**: Senior executives' personal experiences or knowledge base of working with advisors and advisory firms, including long-term (historic or legacy) experiences that the senior executives recalled during the interview or fairly recent experiences mentioned as part of the project feedback discussions. At the end of the analysis I recorded nine codes associated with historic or legacy experiences and nine more recent experiences; a selection of these codes is listed below. For a full list and detailed definitions, please refer to Appendix A and further discussions can be found in Chapter Five as part of the component analysis in section 5.2.

1. Clear association with the advisor (legacy).
2. Legacy or established relationship with the advisory firm (legacy).
3. Past experiences shape association (legacy).
4. Historic negative hands-on experiences with the advisory firm (legacy).
5. Historic positive hands-on experiences with the advisor (legacy).
6. Value for money achieved (recent).
7. Value for money questionable (recent).
8. Positive outcome or experience, achieved benefits or objectives (recent).
9. Negative outcome or experience, possibly wrong advisory firm (recent).

Just to clarify: a number of codes, values assigned to a thought or expression, were grouped together into a code category or sub-subgroup (for example, selection criteria); a number of sub-categories come together into an overarching group, which I also refer to as a component of the now emerging conceptual framework (for example, selection and choice actions). The diagram (Figure 4.3) presented at the beginning of this section maps out the emerging conceptual framework, based on the hierarchy of code categorisations discussed. A full list of all final components and codes and their definitions can be found in Appendix A and further discussions can be found in Chapter Five as part of the component analysis in section 5.2.

4.5 Closed coding, data validation and theoretical saturation

Once the emerging conceptual framework described in the previous section started to settle, I revisited the data and a range of new observations came into view as part of that process. I have noted these observations and reflections down in my memos and I will return to these in section 4.6 on the preliminary set of findings. Before I report on these thoughts, I would like to discuss my experiences regarding closed coding, data validation and theoretical saturation.

4.5.1 Closed coding

On top of reviewing and comparing the existing transcripts with the now closed codes, I also added another three senior executive transcripts of recent relationship review, increasing the number of organisations to five. In doing so, I discovered two more new codes (personal preference code 'the end result matters' and selection behaviour code 'limited exchange with my peers in terms of advisor engagement') and reviewed the wording and definition of a handful of existing codes.

Furthermore, I merged two code categories under 'benefits sought' into one comprehensive 'goals and objectives' classification (the first four codes listed in the discussion above were recorded in a separate category initially). Previously I had added types of projects – for example, pure advice versus implementation and delivery focus as a separate group – to the more general objectives, such as 'fill a resource or knowledge gap'. Please refer to section 4.4.2 above for the full list of codes in this sub-group.

I also separated 'selection behaviours and protocols' from 'selection criteria' after comparing the datasets and concluding that these aspects were sufficiently different in outlook. Selection criteria codes, for example, were more factual parameters which the decision-maker would apply, such as 'fair or competitive price' and 'hunger and drive' displayed during the bid process. Selection behaviour or protocols were more general views or ways of steering or influencing the process of selection or application of selection criteria, for example, 'small pieces of work don't need to go to tender' or 'select an advisor or advisory firm purely on merit'. These changes have been reflected in the discussion of codes in the previous section 4.4.3

4.5.2 In-depth validation of coding

Having gone through a number of coding iterations and having moved around code categories, I wanted to be absolutely sure that the coding was as rigorous and accurate as possible and nothing had been missed.

I checked the conceptual framework components and sub-groups and reviewed the definitions and codes aligned to each category. Then I assessed the coding on a code-by-code level starting with the decision frame, 'imperatives', 'benefits sought/future state' and 'selection and choice actions'. I pulled up and revisited each transcript segment for each code, comparing the different segments and making sure they were reflected in the code and the code definition. Moreover, I carried out consistency checks against the transcript and cross-referenced the codes with the memo for each respondent. This was an immensely time-consuming and tiring process, but it did provide the rigour to assure myself that the coding was of good standard.

4.5.3 Confirming theoretical saturation

Kathy Charmaz (2006) defines theoretical saturation as a moment in time during the research at which the gathering of further data does not yield any new insights, contributing or enhancing to the emerging grounded theory.

Given that adding three new transcripts during the previous iteration of closed coding only brought out two new codes, I concluded that, from a primary empirical data point of view, the research was close to being theoretically saturated, meaning the coding of the client transcripts was complete. I added three additional client transcripts, raising the overall number of coded client transcripts to twenty-one, but no new codes emerged. Once again, I examined and validated the code definitions and I was satisfied that no new codes emerged and no observations changed my perspective on code categories or the conceptual decision-making model.

For a while, I was contemplating expanding the theoretical sample to include 'direct reports' and individuals one step below the C-suite within the organisational hierarchy, but I subsequently dismissed the idea. The findings emerging at this stage were precise and firmly targeted towards senior executives' viewpoints; I was worried that by adding another layer of management the findings would become more diluted and less meaningful. Some middle managers were commenting on their bosses' behaviours, which added another level of complexity. I ultimately retained the C-suite sample population only.

In addition to the fact that the three new transcripts did not generate any new insights or data points for codes or the basic conceptual framework, I carried out two additional checks to confirm theoretical saturation.

Firstly, I had been working on a number of aggregated reports for the firm, which were primarily in-depth analyses of client comments for four industries and the audit client base. The reports were based on over 200 coded transcripts, albeit utilising the firm-wide analytical framework of codes. I cross-referenced the outcomes of these reports with my academic research project, reviewing numerous C-suite transcripts for any new codes or different takes on an existing code; no new insights emerged.

Secondly, I asked a colleague, who was very knowledgeable about coding principles and checking coding consistency in Nvivo, to review and validate my coding independently. Since she had worked with my employer in the past and had confidentiality clearance, I was able to give her access to the full interview dataset and she was able to review the entire set of codes recorded against each client transcript in the Nvivo project. Again, no new codes were identified, although I changed some of the code wordings and definitions for clarity.

Finally, I presented and discussed the emerging conceptual framework and codes and components informing client interactions and decision-making to my professional sponsor for informal sense checking and validation. No new insights regarding codes and groupings of codes emerged as part of these discussions. I adjusted some of the wording and code definitions based on his input, and I felt assured that theoretical saturation on this level was indeed achieved.

Furthermore, we also discussed in this meeting the research progress vis-à-vis the four evaluation criteria (credibility, originality, resonance and usefulness) as suggested by Charmaz (2006) and already presented in Chapter Two of this document. From a practitioner perspective, the professional sponsor was able to follow the research assessment and agreed with the claim of better summarising observations (presented in the following section 4.6) made so far, which addresses the credibility of the study. Furthermore, the findings resonated with the professional sponsor: the distinction between two decision-making processes and the fact that some senior executives might not engage in the second process due to delegating selection of advisors was particularly enlightening; on reflection, the sponsor was able to recall similar circumstances in his personal interactions with clients. On the question of originality, the research prompted the sponsor to contemplate the importance of a project or initiative trajectory in the selection and appointment process. We discussed how, as part of the firm's win-loss reviews post-tender, the focus was very much on meeting selection criteria and engaging or relating to decision makers; what the client organisation was actually trying to achieve with the project and what primary drivers had triggered the search for an advisor or firm were infrequently discussed but should really be brought more to the forefront in the future. Regarding the last evaluation criterion, usefulness, which relates to applying and using the theory and evolving it over time, we concluded that with the research project still ongoing it was premature to review this aspect, although the professional sponsor indicated that he would be keen to extract lessons learned from the study and identify opportunities for application of the model in a practical context upon completion of the research and when I returned to work.

4.6 Preliminary set of findings – first steps towards a substantive theory

Below is a consolidated summary of the reflections and first interpretations that I recorded in my memos during the final closed coding and validation activities.

4.6.1 Two distinct decision-making processes

Reviewing and reflecting on the coding results and the corresponding observations, I noted down that in my reflections it was becoming increasingly clear to me that senior executives in their interactions with professional services firms were engaged in two decision-making processes:

- **Decision process 1**: The decision to maintain or develop a relationship or rapport (depending on levels of intimacy) with a certain advisor or advisory firm.
- **Decision process 2**: The decision to appoint or transact with an advisor and advisory firm for the purpose of delivering a particular service or delivery project.

The first decision process is a personal, informal and direct decision for the senior executive regarding to what degree they would like to maintain or develop a rapport with a certain advisor or advisory firm. This decision-making relates to the intensity and proximity of the relationships. Relationships with advisors are described as very active and personal (one example I noted was of an advisor calling a senior manager in hospital offering support) or more passive, formal and even dormant (for example, a senior executive only contacting an advisor if he/she had a particular problem to discuss, with years passing in between). I came across instances in which a CEO has banned all contact with a number of advisory firms, effectively blacklisting them (Company E in the sample set). However, in general, there were few or fewer organisational constraints on this decision.

The second decision process tended to be more formal and was most likely also a contractual agreement between the organisation and the advisory firm. This decision was predominately binary: the advisory firm either was or was not appointed for a particular task. A senior executive might identify, select and appoint an advisor personally or ask another person or a group of people to be part of or take responsibility of this decision-making process.

Aspects listed under the 'imperatives' construct, general expectations of an advisor or advisory firm, clearly appeared to influence the first decision. Expectations of an advisor such as 'earn my trust and bat for me – invest in the relationship and put me and the organisation first' or personal preferences such as 'self-promotion without substance is a no go' were, from my perspective, clearly linked to the first decision-making process which informs and shapes the relationship or general interactions between client and advisor.

By contrast, elements relating to the second decision, and therefore emphasising the actual service or project, could be found in the 'benefits sought/future state' and 'selection and choice actions' constructs. The objectives and triggers of a particular initiative or project, such as 'fill a resource or knowledge gap' as discussed by a respondent, were frequently linked in the client narrative to specific selection criteria such as 'skills and experience of individuals' or selection behaviour such 'big projects should go out to tender'.

Consequently, I started to further investigate the extent to which the above-mentioned two decision-making processes were linked or informed each other. One of the selection behaviour and protocol codes was 'established relationships serve as a screening mechanism'. However, there were sufficient scenarios in interview transcripts where a CFO had decided to have a relationship with an advisor and then withdrawn from the second decision-making process by delegating selection and appointment responsibilities to a project steering group.

4.6.2 Decision-makers

In my memos I recorded that a high proportion of senior executives, particularly CEOs, referred to secondary decision modes, in which case the senior executive had little to no personal, hands-on involvement in the decision-making to select and appoint an advisor for a particular project or service (decision process 2). Many senior managers shared that they, in principle or frequently, delegated the selection and appointment decision of advisors to their 'direct reports' or a group of individuals. A couple of the interviewees explicitly stated that their aim was not to influence or get directly involved in the decisions of their 'direct reports'; one senior executive declared that this would be disempowering for his staff.

Moreover, I observed in my memos that the largest number of interviewees spoke of a hybrid approach to decision-making: for some projects or services the senior executive would directly and personally make the decision as to who should deliver the work, but for other projects he or she would either completely delegate the decision-making, ask for consultative advice from staff or participate to varying degrees in a group decision. A pattern that seemed to emerge, and which needed to be further investigated, was the following:

Small, strategic or rather personal initiatives, ranging from free-of-charge to small projects, seemed to predominately fall into the direct decision-making domain of an executive. Some respondents described decisions being made on a more intuitive or rather impulsive basis, determined by existing relationships, the perceived expertise of advisors or firms, or also availability, accessibility or continuity. Others spoke of a strong conscious effort to employ a more rational approach.

When it came to large or business-critical (visible within the organisation) projects or programmes (multiple projects) involving or affecting a number of stakeholders, a more structured selection process seemed to be the norm. This frequently involved group decision-making, whereby the senior executive was one of many decision-makers, or contributors, or acted as a referee, casting the final word if the group did not achieve consensus (this is based on observations from win-loss reviews).

An interesting observation that I made in this context is related to one specific CFO, who applied an unusual tactic. Due to his seniority and role, he was not involved directly in the selection and appointment of advisors. However, he did have some strong preferences, based on previous experiences, and he arranged for these advisors (individuals) to have increased access to the organisation by, for example, giving the advisor an office on site or introducing the advisor to key contacts within the organisation. Even when the senior executives did not feature overtly in the decision-making, they might try to influence the decision-making process by effectively putting certain advisors into more privileged positions.

4.6.3 'Project or service trajectory' determines the 'selection and choice actions'?

As mentioned above, the type of project or services sought appeared to inform how the selection and appointment decision-making evolved and the actors involved. In addition, as mentioned previously, if a project or service trajectory had a strong advisory element (to provide an opinion, to issue advice or guidance), increasing emphasis was placed on the individual advisor rather than the advisory firm or the team. Equally, if a 'project or service trajectory' had a strong delivery angle (to implement, install or change people, processes or technology), increasing emphasis was placed on the capabilities and skills of the advisory firm and the proposed team.

4.6.4 Understanding the relationships and foci

In the interview data, I found different levels of relationship proximity between senior executives, as the clients and advisor and advisory firm were a key feature in the first decision process – to maintain or develop a relationship or rapport.

Investigating and defining this relationship or rapport more closely revealed this to be an ongoing dialogue or a set of interactions between the client and the advisor. This dialogue was shaped by past experiences, positive or negative, and determined by current or future needs and circumstances on both sides, client and advisor.

The transcripts and subsequent analysis also uncovered that senior decision-makers had certain general or universal expectations of an advisor regarding the rapport or relationship with the person and the larger entity. At the same time, some respondents differentiated between various firms or firm categories (for example, *'I would expect X from a tech firm such as A but not from a 'Big Four' firm'* or *'strategy houses operate at another level compared to the 'Big Four' firms'*) and had a different set of expectations for each of them.

How did the advisory firm as an entity, versus the individual advisor, feature in senior executives' views? For many senior managers, the advisor, the individual, was the primary focal point. For others, there was a strong brand identity or 'house style' associated with an advisory firm.

Furthermore, for some senior managers, the advisory firm as an entity or presence stood in the foreground and individual advisors were in the background, present but less relevant (for example, *'I work with anyone that firm X puts forward as our lead partner'*). Whereas for others, the individual advisors were at the forefront and the advisory firm was moved into the background (for example, '*it has to be a 'Big Four', otherwise the Board would question the recommendations, but it is really the individual who presents that makes the difference'*). Further analysis will be required to work through these notions.

Lastly, I also observed a type of polarisation with regard to what was expected of an advisor, beyond delivering projects or outcomes: At one end of the spectrum, there were senior executives who valued high-level strategic discussions, presentation of industry insights and possibly a form of challenge or the advisor acting as a sounding board. For these individuals, the advisor or advisory firm was more than a pure service provider; there was an element of coaching and advising that went beyond set, contractual arrangements. For example, COO_3: '*...in such a situation you must secure a 360-degree view, and expect to be challenged [by the advisor]. And if this doesn't happen, an adviser, he's not doing his advisory work because the word itself, 'to advise', to challenge, to question and to potentially, to give a thought to potentially go a different path.*'

At the other end of the spectrum, there was a small number of senior stakeholders who were less, or not really, interested in these 'value-adding' relationship aspects. The rapport between senior executive and advisor was rather more transactional; the focus was very much on delivering projects, for the advisory firm to come in and carry out a piece of work. For example, CFO_4 expressed this view: '*There are partners now who I would phone for advice, who I may not have spoken to in four or five years, but if I've got something that's right for them, then I'll phone them.*'

The bulk of the senior executives interviewed featured somewhere in between these two extremes, valuing additional insights and occasional prompts; advice was welcome, but not a 'must have'.

What does that mean? Do individuals who do not seek this type of support or value-adding components receive input from other sources? Maybe peers, colleagues, friends, or strategy houses? Or do they simply have no need for this type of dialogue?

4.6.5 Experiences are vital

Previous experiences, either direct or indirect, featured heavily in senior executives' comments, and there was a clear link between a person's past experiences and their associations, views or opinions about different advisors or advisory firms (relating back to the code 'past experiences shape association with advisor and advisory firm'). What does that mean? Once an advisory firm starts delivering and working successfully with a client organisation in one domain (for example transfer pricing in tax), they build a reputation for expertise in this particular area. These positive project experiences serve as a reference point for future decisions. At the same time, negative experiences can have a detrimental effect on the opinions and decision references – to not make the same mistake or more precisely repeat the negative experience. Interestingly, senior executives were very open and direct with their comments pertaining to past experiences both with the firm I was interviewing for, as well as other firms.

Almost at a more elevated level were those discussions around legacy relationships with advisors, having worked with someone in the past and the outcomes having been positive. The bonding and joint experiences, including comments about growing through the ranks, seemed to be a key aspect for some senior executives and but less so for others.

It almost appears that there is a cycle of experiences, projects and relationships, which form a view of the firm and the advisor. For example, Firm X are the experts in this regulatory driven service. The more frequent and positive the experiences are with Firm X, the stronger the view in their favour – actions speak louder than words. But what happens if the advisor steps out and joins Firm Y? This was the case for Company A: previously the advisor had worked for another 'Big Four', which had built an expertise in regulatory advice with this company. When this senior advisor left the firm and joined another 'Big Four', which had a perceived expertise in finance and financial advice, the construct and association with Company A started to crumble.

4.6.6 Organisational aspects – least explored

Reflecting on the coding activities, the study found that senior executives seldom referred to organisational aspects in the interviews, and if they did it was mostly in passing; some senior managers did not mention them at all. The messages pertaining to organisational aspects can be grouped as follows:

- Organisational preferences and principles, frequently prescribed by a very senior manager such as the CEO. For example, CEO of company E banning or formally blacklisting two advisory firms.
- Organisational processes or protocols on how to engage with advisors and advisory firms, either in the form of an organisational supplier management or procurement programme or more informal guidelines.

- Existing ties and relationships with professional service providers and how these might impact screening and choice; for example, external auditor relationships, engagement with competitors or joint ventures might hinder working with a particular firm.

By taking note of and processing the above-described data points and observations, I started to formulate a first draft of substantive thoughts which were effectively a summary of the reflections recorded in my memos. However, instead of continuing down this path of simply reviewing codes and reflecting on existing memos and with that possibly jumping to conclusions, I decided to take a step back and revisit and analyse the coded material in its entirety with a heightened sense of theoretical sensitivity. The outcome of this data analysis is presented in Chapter Five, and the reflections captured in the emerging substantive theory are presented in Chapter Six.

Chapter 5

Emerging models – analysis of findings with applied theoretical sensitivity shape first theories

In this chapter, I present the results of further, rather more in-depth, analysis of the empirical client data. My objective was to take a step back and look at the client datasets in their entirety, after completion of all empirical coding activities, and to examine the coded material from various perspectives in order to expand and enrich the first preliminary findings, which I outlined in section 4.6 of the previous chapter.

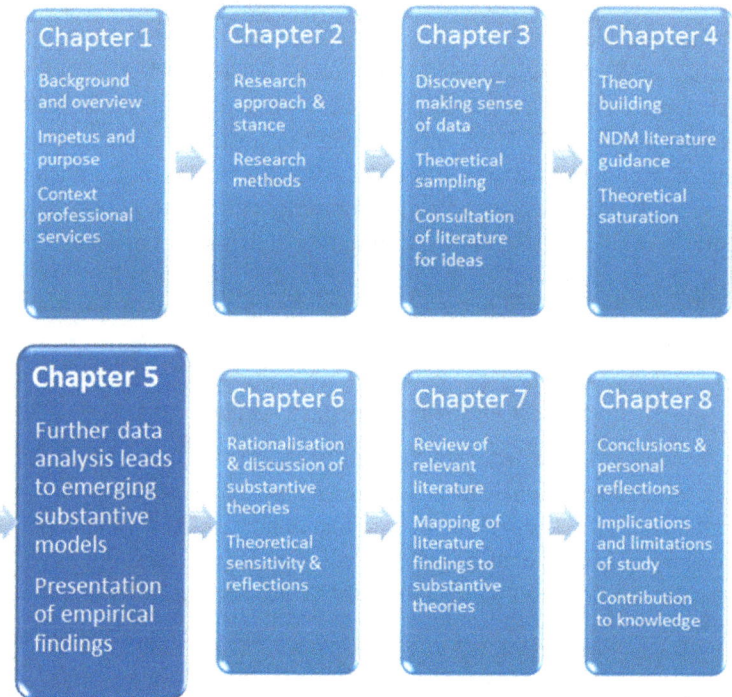

Figure 5.1 – Overview of thesis structure and content of the fifth chapter

The set of findings discussed in the preceding chapter provided the first pointers regarding the theoretical constructs that had started to emerge as a result of coding the interview transcripts and the constant comparison with the literature related to the emergent codes, concepts and categories. Instead of progressing with these first constructs, I deliberately decided to return to the data in order to systematically analyse the coding and apply the necessary level of theoretical sensitivity holistically to the entire dataset: I closely examined the data on a conceptual framework component-by-component level (a component being a grouping of code categories, for example 'imperatives – expectations of an advisor and personal preferences'). While reviewing the data, I identified patterns across components which could partly be linked to individual respondents (for example, generic role or frequently mentioned decision practices; I termed this exploration 'construct analysis') or general underlying notions such as trust, control or continuity (I termed this investigation 'leitmotif analysis'). Further description of the analytical approach taken is documented in the next section, 5.1, of this chapter.

Diligent application of theoretical sensitivity is deemed not only best practice but also one of the three fundamental requirements of grounded theory in addition to theoretical sampling and theoretical saturation (Charmaz 2006, Goulding 2002). It requires the researcher to see and reflect upon empirical data with the aid of theoretical terms (Goulding 2002, referring to Kelle 2007). Even though up to this point I had spent extensive time working with the data, I felt that I had not sufficiently stepped back and reviewed the coded transcripts and analysed the data in its entirety and systematically, illuminating the findings from different angles. In this chapter, I describe how I further analysed the data, the observations that I made and the resulting conclusions amalgamated into the first set of substantive theories.

5.1 Analytical approach taken

After having reached a degree of theoretical saturation of my primary data (client transcripts), *"when new data no longer spark any new insights"* (Bryant 2012, slide 90), and the coding had been validated independently (my colleague having extensively checked my coding), I felt confident to analyse the, for now, completed empirical dataset from a series of different perspectives.

5.1.1 Theoretical sampling – data population and limitations

As noted by Dip (2009), although theoretical sampling is widely acknowledged in the literature as a critical aspect of grounded theory, as it is vital to the emergence of theory, there is considerable ambiguity as to how the process is actually carried out. The closed coding iterations and data validation exercises, described in the previous chapters, are demonstrations of the strategy for the theoretical sampling strategy that I was engaged with. One of the contributions of this research study is an insight into the practicalities of selecting and employing a theoretical sampling strategy in the context of the research phenomenon, which is the focus of the study.

Theoretical sampling is one of the three fundamental techniques of grounded theory; it involves adding data iteratively and inductively throughout the research process (Goulding 2002, Charmaz 2006, Bryant 2012). In conjunction with theoretical saturation and theoretical sensitivity, theoretical sampling helps the researcher to achieve focus by identifying gaps and variations and allows for analytic constructs to emerge (Charmaz 2006). Throughout the research activities, I drew on a number of data sources, such as field observations, personal memos and win-loss interviews, to help me not only develop codes and a conceptual framework but also to comprehend the analytical outputs. However, I considered my client feedback interviews with senior executives and C-suite stakeholders to be my primary empirical data source, and I took careful note of their characteristics, again guided by the theoretical sampling and constant comparison techniques. Consequently, theoretical sampling of my primary data was completed with the theoretical saturation of the empirical data. The study draws on other data sources beyond my personal contribution, such as existing literature, which all formed the theoretical sampling and contributed to a state of overall theoretical saturation, to which I returned later on in my research as documented in the subsequent chapters of this thesis. The following discussion in this section aims to present the final results of my empirical theoretical sampling activities and to describe the sample population contained in this dataset. The main objective of this section is to give a general overview of the respondents who contributed to the empirical dataset and the resulting emerging substantive models.

At the beginning of the research project, I reviewed the socio-demographic and organisational backgrounds of the individuals interviewed to ensure that the sample population was varied within the given scope (C-suite executives) and to aim for a balanced view of the phenomena. As mentioned in the previous chapter, theoretical saturation was reached and confirmed with 21 senior executive interview transcripts, which were extensively coded and recoded in both open and closed formats.

Now reviewing the final population of respondents included in the study, I feel that there was a good mix of organisational roles (six CEOs, six CFOs, four CROs, two CIOs and three COOs) and companies in terms of the general corporate procurement approach taken (six companies, of which two had no or little procurement processes, two followed what is frequently termed a standard procurement process and two had implemented a fairly complex supplier management system) and backgrounds (two companies were well-established, two were the results of spins-offs from other, larger organisations and two had come about through M&A). From a theoretical sampling perspective, I felt that there were no gaps – or constellations left out – in this empirical sample.

However, on a socio-demographic level, the respondents were fairly homogenous; of the 21 respondents, as probably expected, only three were female and the vast majority were British nationals, with two Americans, two Germans and one Irish. The bulk of the individuals interviewed had held various corporate roles throughout their professional career; four had only worked for one organisation and three had previously been employed by a 'Big Four' firm. Classification details of the interview population can be found in Appendix A of this document. The theoretical sample leaned more towards an Anglo-Saxon perspective, whereas the professional background of the sample was well balanced. A similar study with, for example, French or Japanese senior executives, would likely have yielded very different results.

One unavoidable limitation or gap relating to this sample group was the fact that all of the senior executives took sufficient interest in the relationship with the advisory firm, which had certain implications. Since the client service assessment interview was positioned as an instrument to capture personal client feedback, take stock of experiences and also improve the relationship between client organisation and advisory firm, all 21 senior executives had some sort of relationship with the advisory firm and were to a certain degree keen or willing to maintain this relationship or rapport by investing an hour of their time. This, in turn, meant that clients who did not have or want a relationship or rapport with an advisory firm were not included in this sample since they most likely would have declined to be interviewed. As part of the review process, senior client contacts of company B, E and F declined interviews; according to my knowledge, in the case of companies B and F, this was due to personal differences between the respondents and the lead advisor. For one company, the CEO on principle *'did not like working with advisory firms in general'.* Consequently, the research does not include or capture the perspective of senior executives who do not want to have a relationship or closer rapport with an advisor and an advisory firm, since these individuals would not have agreed to be interviewed extensively.

5.1.2 Concentrating on the research aims

Before I embarked on more comprehensive data analysis, I recalled and reflected on my research aims and the key observations I made during the coding activities:

- Why and how do senior executives engage, select and appoint 'Big Four' professional advisors and advisory firms?
- Which aspects, and to what degree, influence or shape senior executives' views and decisions?

Keeping in mind that I had already established during the discovery and theorising stages that there are effectively two distinct decision processes:

- Decision process 1: The decision to maintain or develop a personal relationship or general rapport, depending on level of intensity, with a 'Big Four' advisor or advisory firm.
- Decision process 2: The decision to actually select and appoint a 'Big Four' advisor or advisory firm to deliver a service or project for the organisation.

However, at this point I felt that I did not have sufficient evidence regarding how these two decisions are exactly linked and to what degree. Nonetheless, I was able to pinpoint certain code categories or components of my coding framework to the two decisions:

Focal points for the Decision 1 process appeared to be what I coded as 'imperatives', meaning the general expectations of an advisor or advisory firm (for instance 'to provide an external view, benchmarks and insights'), and 'personal principles and preferences' (for example 'quality has its price or 'self-promotion without substance is a no go') when it came to working with advisors. However, contextual dynamics such as 'past experiences' and 'organisational context' also coincided with Decision 1 commentary and coding.

Decision 2 process, on the other hand, encompassed all components of the emerging conceptual framework, including the decision frame groups (past experiences and organisational context), even though the most determining components were 'selection and choice actions' (for instance, 'balance advisors – avoid over-reliance') as well as 'project or service trajectory' (for example, 'fill a resource gap' or 'teach and empower us').

5.1.3 Analytical perspectives taken

Keeping the above-mentioned considerations in mind, I progressed to investigating the client data, making use of the analytical functions of the Nvivo software as well as comparing and contrasting datasets manually. For example, I created coding profiles for each respondent in the form of a physical poster (see Appendix B for an example) which allowed me to compare and contrast individual respondents manually; for example, I organised the respondents by certain characteristics, such as role, or the satisfaction rating they provided at the end of the interview, and laid out all the profiles of a particular characteristic in front of me to scan and compare the coding information of each profile.

The overall analysis evolved gradually and encompassed investigating the interview data, primarily from different standpoints as part of four analytical stages:

- **Component analysis:** As a first step, I looked at the different conceptual framework components, such as the three image schemata and decision frame which had evolved as part of the theorising phase and discussed in Chapter 4. I examined the coding of each component and sub-component. In addition, I reviewed the coding across code categories and mapped the conceptual framework components to the two decisions. The findings are discussed in section 5.2 of this chapter.

- **Construct analysis:** While conducting the component analysis, I identified a number of cross-component patterns either linked to individual respondents' characteristics such as generic role (CEO, CFO etc.) or centred around other common denominators of individuals (for example, if a certain aspect was frequently communicated by a group of respondents, I tried to examine commonalities between these respondents). These clusters of respondents by key characteristics or observed patterns, I termed 'constructs'. In order to explore the observed patterns in more detail, I started to arrange the sample population by construct grouping. I cross-referenced and constantly compared the findings between the groups, aiming to identify constructs that generated the most indicative and polarising datasets. The most distinct construct constellations were generic role, selection approach taken and a construct I termed 'Gestalt Advisor' – I elaborate terminology and construct definition in more detail in section 5.3.2 of this chapter. The findings are presented in section 5.4 of this chapter.

- **Leitmotif analysis:** Throughout the earlier coding activities, as well as during the two preceding analyses described above, four recurring subjects or leitmotifs emerged. These four themes can be placed on two diverging continua: One continuum consists of the leitmotif 'trust and empathy' at one end with the leitmotif 'control, balance and risk management' at the other. The second continuum encompasses the leitmotif 'continuity and embeddedness' at one end and 'competitiveness and skills/merit' at the other. As a next step, I applied the most distinct construct groupings to the leitmotif structure, which provided some very insightful findings, discussed in sections 5.5 and 5.6 of this chapter.

- **Consolidation and amalgamation of findings:** As a final step, I brought the outcomes of the three analyses, described above, together, and mapped the results to the research aims and the two previously identified decisions. While synthesising the findings and working through the conclusions, a set of models emerged which underpin the resulting substantive theory, elaborated in detail in Chapter Six.

In order to confirm, challenge and further substantiate the models and theory, and to put the findings into perspective, I conducted a focused, not systematic, literature review as a next step, concentrating on the identified leitmotifs and general aspects associated with the research aims. The literature review is discussed in Chapter Seven.

A note on terminology: I am aware that personal views differ on using terms or expressions and not everyone feels comfortable with idioms such as 'component', 'gestalt' or 'leitmotif'. From my perspective, assigning and using these labels was key for me to progress with the research and conduct the analysis; they served as clear indicators and helped me to differentiate between the different perspectives taken during the research. They are very much part of my research journey, and therefore, I decided to include and use these terms in this thesis.

5.1.4 Frequency versus coverage as indicators

I was initially drawn to focus on coding frequency, especially during the first phase of the analysis investigating the components (groups of code categories) according to how many times a particular aspect was mentioned by a respondent. However, having worked with the same qualitative data for the aggregated firm reports, I quickly established that this frequency was not necessarily a reliable indicator of the importance or weighting of messages. For some individuals, frequency was key: the more often the person mentioned an idea or concept in an unstructured interview the more likely it was that he or she was trying to strongly communicate and emphasise this message. At the same time, there were other individuals in the sample population of this study who were very deliberate and focused in their communication and, therefore, even though they might mention an aspect only once but strongly in the overall messaging, that alone was, from my perspective, equivalent to many mentions from a person who was very talkative but less deliberate with their communication. Consequently, I took note of frequency, especially in the individual profiles, but I also overrode these frequency highlights manually if one message appeared particularly significant (please view example profiles in Appendix B for an illustration).

In the end, I tended to focus predominantly on coverage or presence across the respondent population as indicators: how many senior executives mentioned a particular aspect (code). If all or almost all of the respondents mentioned an aspect, I interpreted that as a type of consensus between the respondents – there was a commonality or a wider agreement amongst the respondents on an aspect or a group of aspects. If only a smaller number of respondents mentioned a specific aspect, I tried to establish the surrounding circumstances: for example, did the same group of respondents also mention other aspects differently compared to the wider population? I also had a closer look at the personal or organisational background of the senior executives in question (e.g. whether they were all working for the same organisation). This exercise of comparing and contrasting based on coding commonality or consensus across the respondent population also helped me to identify patterns which led to the identification of the previously described constructs. For example, I observed an agreement amongst CEOs that they preferred or referenced the delegation of advisor appointment decisions, which led me to group the respondents by role construct in order to compare and contrast coding.

Constant comparison and viewing the data from different standpoints is also considered good practice and a key analytical approach of the grounded theory and constructivist grounded theory (Charmaz 2006, Goulding 2002). In summary, coverage or presence proved to be a helpful indicator to identify and establish patterns, allowing me to divide and analyse the dataset beyond code categories into constructs (groupings of respondents by a particular characteristic) and 'leitmotifs' (underlying themes).

5.1.5 Application of theoretical sensitivity

Continuously throughout the research project, I aimed to apply theoretical sensitivity. Especially during both open and closed coding activities and while developing the conceptual framework, I focused on making sense of the relevant data by reflecting on my empirical data, as advocated by grounded theory (Charmaz 2006, Goulding 2002), with the support of theoretical concepts found in the general decision-making literature.

Now as part of this, from my holistic perspective, and more comprehensive four-stage analysis of the dataset, I was keen to address theoretical sensitivity by looking at and comparing the data from various standpoints, as recommended by Kathy Charmaz (2006). Furthermore, being on a work sabbatical allowed me to engage in reflexivity (Charmaz 2006) and fully concentrate on the study, view and explore the research material at my own pace, identify and develop analytical approaches that would enable a more thorough exploration of the data and document the emerging ideas and models. Having the time and not being distracted by day-to-day professional tasks was immensely helpful, and this, in turn, fostered the necessary theoretical sensitivity as part of the concentrated effort to work through the empirical data.

5.2 Results of component analysis

In this section, I present the results and key observations made as part of the component by component analysis. As part of this exercise, I went through each component, for example 'imperatives', of the conceptual framework, as the image and decision frame, and the corresponding sub-components, for instance 'expectations of an advisor'. I then reviewed the presence of aspects regarding overall coverage (how many of the respondents mentioned a particular aspect) and presence (who within the sample population mentioned certain aspects).

5.2.1 'Imperatives' or value image component

Reflecting on the 'imperative' image definition as part of the evolving conceptual framework, 'imperatives' – also referred to as the value image in the image theory (Beach 1993b, Beach 1998) terminology – can be described by answering these questions:

What is the senior executive looking for in an advisor or advisory firm? What are the primary reasons for engaging with an advisor? What are the key aspects that determine if he or she will choose to engage or build a rapport with an advisor?

I found that the imperative image was composed of two subgroups:

Subgroup 1 (VI1) - General expectations of an advisor or an advisory firm as part of the day-to-day interactions (relationship) and engagements (projects): key qualities, attributes and characteristics or primary reasons for working with an external advisor.

Subgroup 2 (VI2) - Respondents' personal principles and preferences regarding an advisor or advisory firms, as well as more general statements made, as described in section 4.3.1 of Chapter Four. These were aspects that did not readily fall into the first category, but still seemed important enough for understanding the client's expectations.

5.2.1.1 'Imperatives' - general expectations up close

As part of the coding activities, eleven aspects emerged, which were frequently mentioned by all 21 senior managers interviewed. Compared to the other conceptual framework components, the coverage for this particular sub-component group – the number of respondents out of the total sample population who mentioned individual aspects – was the highest, indicating commonality amongst the senior executives in terms of what they expected of an advisor and an advisory firm in general. Looking at the table below, it appears that there were two, possibly three, groups of aspects determined by coverage:

- The top group of expectations, up to 'VI1.10 Provide and assure required competence, skills and expertise', were widely shared amongst the respondent population (from 21 out of 21 to 17 out of 21, as indicated in the coverage column).

General expectations mentioned as part of 'Imperative' image	Coverage
VI1.1_Demonstrate empathy - advisor or firm should understand me and the organisation and act on that knowledge	21
VI1.2_Earn my trust and bat for me - invest in the relationship and put me and the organisation first	19
VI1.11_Step in and help out - be responsive, accessible and available	18
VI1.3_Be pro-active - advice, flag and challenge as required - don't sell	18
VI1.8_Provide an external view, benchmarks and insights	17
VI1.10_Provide and assure required competence, skills and expertise	15
VI1.6_Be able to solve problems pragmatically and collaboratively	13
VI1.7_Be realistic, transparent and honest - stick to agreements	12
VI1.5_Be embedded and hold a presence within the organisation	11
VI1.4_Right interpersonal skills and chemistry	10
VI1.9_Help me or us understand and manage regulatory bodies	4

Table 5.1 – List of general client expectations - 'imperatives'

- The second group of codes, from VI1.10 to VI1.4 - focusing on skills, expertise and working practices - still featured strongly amongst the respondents, with at least half of the sample population referring to these in interviews.
- The last element, 'VI1.9 Help me or us understand and manage regulatory bodies', appeared to be a unique expectation that was particular to two respondents from company A and company B. It was difficult to ascertain from the data if these were unique requirements of these two organisations, or if there was a particular need or experience which led the respondents to raise this expectation.

In summary, there seemed to be a clear indication of commonality around the majority of aspects or codes. This could possibly be a function of having worked with advisors and advisory firms for a longer period of time. There was also a common understanding as to what to expect of an advisor. This was perhaps a function of the advisor or advisory firm propagating a certain view as to what to expect – an assumption that warrants further investigation.

5.2.1.2 'Imperatives' – personal principles and preferences up close

Compared to the concentrated 11 codes constituting the subgroup expectations mentioned above, 20 rather more fragmented codes emerged regarding senior executives' personal principles and preferences. These codes had individual variation amongst respondents. The most consistently mentioned code here, 'VI2.10 I like to stay in control and monitor advisor activities', was indicated by 11 senior managers, which is a little over half of the total number of respondents.

Personal principles and preferences mentioned as part of 'Imperative' image	Coverage
VI2.10_I like to stay in control - monitor advisor activities	11
VI2.3_Need to be able to trust the advisor or firm	9
VI2.16_I DO like to meet the advisor regularly	8
VI2.9_Self promotion without substance is a no go	8
VI2.20_Integrity is important	7
VI2.4_Advisors are in business to make money	7
VI2.1_Advisor is more important than the firm	6
VI2.2_Need to feel important or be a priority	6
VI2.11_Growing through the ranks	5
VI2.14_Appreciate additional offerings	5
VI2.19_The end result matters	5
VI2.6_It is difficult to differentiate between firms	5
VI2.17_I LIKE to engage with the advisor socially	4
VI2.5_Quality has its price	4
VI2.7_Don't like getting caught up in details	4
VI2.13_Don't like scare mongering	3
VI2.12_Thrive on challenge	2
VI2.15_I DON'T need to see the advisor frequently	1
VI2.18_I DON'T like to engage with the advisor socially	1
VI2.8_Bias towards previous Big 4 employer	1

Table 5.2 – List of personal principles and preferences- 'imperatives'

- Two senior managers, CFO_2 and CFO_1, did not volunteer any personal preferences or principles. In general, fewer elements per respondent emerged; most of these were mentioned and coded as side remarks in the overall comments.

- The top three codes in the table above highlight an interesting concept, and indicated that clients like to meet their advisor regularly. The motivation for this could be to build trust and strengthen their rapport or relationship or to keep a tab or better oversight of advisors' activities. I added this thought to my 'to-be investigated further' memo log.

At this early stage of the analysis, it became apparent that compared to the previous sub-group 'expectations of advisor', there was less commonality amongst respondents. However, I began to notice that certain terms such as 'trust', 'empathy' or 'understanding', 'control' and 'a lack of trust' started to stand out. At this point, I noted my observations and picked up on these patterns again, especially in the leitmotif analysis, discussed later in this chapter.

5.2.2 'Project or service trajectory' or trajectory image component

Trajectory image dynamics (1998, Beach 1993b) map on to 'project or service trajectory' or 'future state' constructs within the conceptual framework that I utilised for the analysis of the data:

Why did the senior executives formally transact with a professional advisor? What was the senior manager trying to achieve by engaging an advisor or advisory firm on behalf of the organisation? What were the objectives or goals of an engagement/interaction with an advisor or advisory firm?

Here, I opted to differentiate between drivers or triggers for pursuing a particular future state or initiative and the actual objectives or goals that were being targeted.

Subgroup 1 (TI1) - Primary objectives and goals that the senior executive was looking to address by working with an advisor and or an advisory firm. What outcomes or outputs were being targeted as part of a transaction with the advisor?

Subgroup 2 (TI2) - Primary drivers or triggers: what was the impetus to pursue a particular future state trajectory image? Who or what had called for a project/transaction with an advisor or advisory firm?

For both subgroups, I identified codes as part of the comments on predominantly past projects: how the project came about, for example, who asked for it or what triggered it, and what the client was trying to achieve by engaging an external party.

5.2.2.1 'Triggers and objectives' as part of the trajectory image up close

Objectives and triggers as part of 'future state/benefits sought'	Coverage	Frequency
TI1.1_Deliver positive results and tangible outputs	21	85
TI1.2_Provide guidance and advice (billable)	19	66
TI1.6_Fill a resource gap	15	24
TI1.7_Fill knowledge gaps	15	34
TI1.10_A tailored approach	9	18
TI1.9_Help meet a deadline	9	14
TI1.8_Teach or empower us	8	20
TI1.11_Sharing pain and responsibilities	7	12
TI1.3_ProBono or free advice	7	13
TI1.5_Guarantee for success	6	6
TI1.4_Be part of organisational eco-system	4	10
TI2.1_Regulation	13	35
TI2.3_Operational response	11	17
TI2.2_Request from board or superior	9	20

Table 5.3 – List of triggers and objectives - 'project or service trajectory'

I have included frequency counts as an additional reference point here; the three triggers/drivers are listed at the bottom of the table. The results for the three primary triggers or drivers of advisory engagement were fairly evenly split, with regulation being a little more prominent, which might also have been due to the type of companies included and their particular circumstances.

With regard to objectives and goals (top section of the table), I differentiated between what type of project/support was required (TI1.1, TI1.2, TI1.3 and TI1.4) and what the other key objectives for engaging with an external partner were (TI1.5 onward).

- The set of codes focused on the following notion: did the project involve only advice, advice plus delivery, only delivery, free-of-charge work or actually being part of the wider ecosystem, which can be broken down as follows with regard to messaging:

- o 49 mentions discussed a combination of delivery and advice (TI1.1 and TI1.2 at the same time)
- o 36 mentions for delivery only (TI1.1)
- o 17 mentions for billable advice only (TI1.2)
- o 13 mentions for free-of-charge advice (TI1.3), with three of these being linked to billable advice (TI1.2)
- o 10 mentions of being or becoming part of the organisational eco-system TI1.4).

- For most of the senior executives interviewed, engaging with an advisor and advisory firm was about achieving or delivering something which was frequently paired up with receiving advice. Receiving free advice or free-of-charge work as part of ongoing rapport with the advisor was an objective of a third (seven) of the respondents, whereas being part of the organisational ecosystem, meaning for the professional service firm to be completely embedded in the client organisation and become part of everyday operational arrangements, was only a concern of four respondents.

- The somewhat pragmatic secondary objectives, such as filling a resource and knowledge gap, were raised by quite a few of the respondents (15 out of 21). The other key objectives were not as widely mentioned.

The extent to which the organisational culture, constraints and procurement approaches impacted these datasets needed to be validated and included in the ensuing cross-contribution analysis.

Reflecting on my own experiences, thanks to the insights I had gained, especially during win-loss review interviews, it was relatively easy to structure 'project or service trajectory' as an image, by which I mean to formulate codes and code categories. However, actually identifying the corresponding messages in the relationship review interviews was more difficult; some respondents were more outspoken in this regard than others. Reflecting on the unstructured interview agenda, I also believe that individuals spoke more about the outcomes of projects – what was actually achieved – and less about what desired state they had had in mind when they had started the project. Few executives went so far as to compare and contrast their desired outcomes with the actual results. Overall, this particular image has probably been one of the least explored components in the firm internal debate that I have been exposed to as part of my professional role, which focuses primarily on the relationship and then on the selection.

5.2.3 'Selection and choice actions' or strategic image component

The 'selection and choice action' component was the most multifaceted component, with three subgroups of code categories. Whereas the 'imperative' image could be closely linked to the first decision – to maintain or develop a relationship or rapport with an advisor or advisory firm – this component was particularly aimed at the second decision – to select, appoint and transact with an advisor or advisory firm for the purpose of delivering a particular service or delivery project (Beach 1993b, 1998). The definition questions as part of the conceptual framework were:

How did the senior executive go about identifying and selecting the appropriate advisor to help execute or realise goals and objectives and respond to the triggers? Which selection criteria and selection behaviour were alluded to by the respondent?

As previously discussed, the 'selection and choice actions' component was broken down into three distinct categories:

Subgroup 0 (SI0) – Selection modes, which included the different decision-making modes and approaches discussed, exploring who was making the selection decisions and how in general these decisions were made (decision approach).

Subgroup 1 (SI1) – Selection behaviour and protocols, indicating what steps or actions the senior executive and organisation took to identify and select an advisor or advisory firm. What type of behaviour was being discussed in the context of selection and appointment?

Subgroup 2 (SI2) – Selection criteria, meaning what criteria were being mentioned during interviews for selecting and ultimately appointing an advisor or advisory firm?

5.2.3.1 Selection mode' as part of the 'selection and choice actions' image up close

As part of the coding activities, I assigned different selection mode codes throughout the transcripts, previously discussed in Chapter Four and listed in Appendix A. While reviewing the coding results for this code category, I started to summarise the selection mode codes and identified an overarching or dominant selection mode for each respondent, which are described below. If, for example, a respondent only showed coding instances for one selection mode such as 'delegation', I would then assign the overarching or dominant selection mode code 'delegation' for this individual. Assignment was based on the selection mode codes, but also by reviewing the corresponding transcript and memos.

Delegation – These individuals predominantly delegated the selection-making decisions to, primarily, a 'direct report'; some stated this very explicitly and others made more indirect statements: four respondents fall into this group (three CEOs and one very senior CFO).

Hybrid – These individuals opted for different selection modes depending on circumstances; for example, large projects went out for tender and became a group decision; small projects could be decided directly; some smaller projects outside the area of interest could be delegated. Nine respondents fell into this group, comprising divisional CEOs, CFOs, COO and CIOs.

Primary direct – These individuals discussed their advisor choice as a direct decision-making process that they were personally responsible for; only two people referred to this model – a divisional CEO and a group CRO.

Group decision with input, at varying degrees, from themselves and others – the second largest group of six respondents predominantly referred to this selection mode. Many of the CROs and some CIO/COOs, as well as one CEO, fell into this group.

Moreover, beyond the selection mode dynamics listed above, two selection approach aspects were placed in this subgroup. 'Selection approach' identifies the senior executives' comments on how they and their organisation, in general, went about making an appointment decision:

Follow a rational approach to selecting an advisor or firm: Senior executives mentioned that he/she or they (group or organisation overall) followed a structured or more rational approach, by either consulting with others, applying rules/selection criteria or analysing data points before making a selection decision.
Follow an ad hoc or intuitive approach to selecting an advisor or firm: Senior executives referred to automatic, ad hoc or intuitive forms of decision-making, as well as mimicking the decision-making of others, more senior peers, without great contemplation, evaluation of criteria or application of rules.

A small number of senior managers alluded to using both approaches; possibly depending on the circumstances or type of support ('benefits sought') needed. The exact distribution of these aspects across the sample population is listed below:

- Eight respondents only discussed rational or structured selection approaches – interestingly, all three respondents from one company (D) responded in this manner.

- Four respondents discussed both rational and ad hoc selection processes, thus all four of them described/were better aligned to either a hybrid or group decision mode category. It might be that different approaches for different decision modes were being applied.
- Seven respondents only discussed ad hoc or more intuitive selection approaches; this does not mean that these decisions did not follow some type of direction (for example, 'for tax work I always pass on to company x'), but no conscious effort or application of selection criteria was being discussed.
- Two senior executives did not mention in detail how they approached the selection decision: CEO_3, who delegated effectively all advisor appointment decision-making, and CRO_2, who inherited a project (peers had made the decision prior to his arrival).

5.2.3.2 Cross-referencing of selection mode and approach

While analysing the selection mode coding, I started to detect a pattern for CEOs: a preference for delegating decision-making. Therefore, as a first step, I mapped the overarching dominant selection mode category (summary category of individual respondents' selection mode preferences or action, discussed in section 5.2.3.1) against the different generic roles (CEO, CFO, etc.), to ascertain if there were any clear patterns:

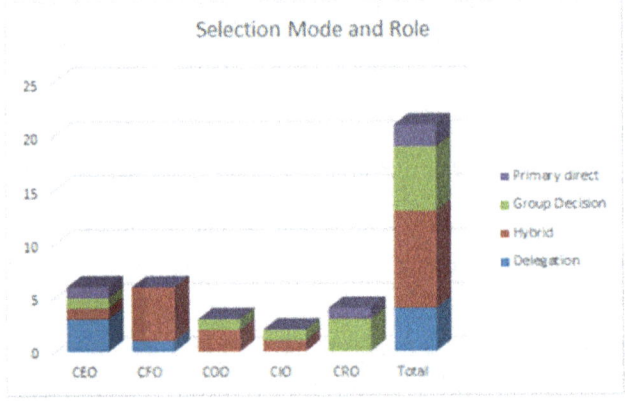

Figure 5.2 – Dominant selection mode and generic role mapped[1]

---

[1] In order to generate this figure, I mapped the dominant selection modes assigned to each senior executive (such as delegation, hybrid) to the generic role of the senior managers (CEO, CFO, etc.).

Looking at Figure 5.2 above, the 'total' column suggests that the majority of respondents were in the overarching selection mode category 'hybrid', followed by 'group decision' and 'delegation'; only a small number expressed a clear preference for 'primary direct' decision-making when it came to selecting advisors. Regarding overarching selection mode preferences per generic role, the five first columns of the figure, there appear to be no clear indicative patterns, but there are indeed a few general observations worth noting:

- CEOs appeared to favour delegation as a dominant selection mode.
- CFOs appeared to lean toward picking and choosing different selection modes (hybrid).
- CROs were more inclined to be or discuss being part of a group decision, compared to the other roles.

If I reflect on my professional experiences and internal debates, these preferences match the general expectations commonly associated with these roles. On average, CEOs tend to focus on strategic direction and oversight and leave the execution to the different domains (finance, human resources, operations etc.) and their 'direct reports', the other members of the C-suite. The domain of a CFO is frequently far-reaching, depending on the organisational structure (treasury, tax, M&A activities, internal audit as well as risk management). With this in mind, it is accepted that many CFOs delegate the appointment of advisors for certain subdomains to their 'direct reports'. However, for some projects they might insist on a panel group decision (for example large, across subdomains, or big budgeted projects as well as possibly projects perceived to be high risk) or they might make direct decisions themselves (possibly if the CFO took a personal interest in a project/service). Furthermore, many but not all CROs had a direct or dotted reporting line to another member of the C-suite (primarily a CFO but also CEO). Therefore, it is not surprising that this population of respondents spoke more frequently about group decisions.

As a next step, I cross-referenced the dominant selection mode and selection approach, and the following picture emerged:

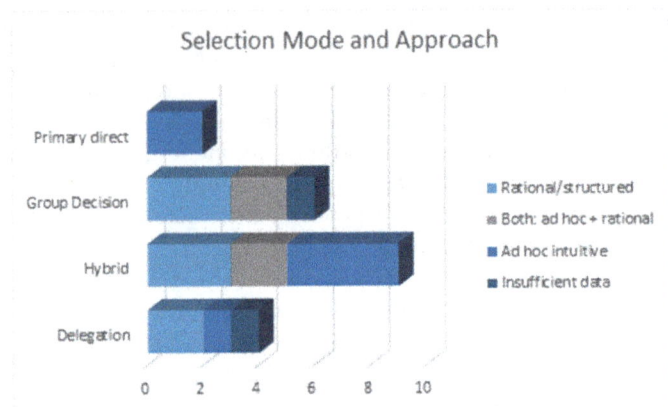

Figure 5.3 –Dominant selection mode and selection approach mapped[2]

- Senior executives aligned to a dominant selection mode hybrid (third bar chart from the top) cross-referenced with a mix of the different selection approaches (rational / structured, ad hoc / intuitive etc.). The data most likely suggests that a different selection approach is possibly being utilised depending on the circumstances and selection mode applied.
- To a certain degree, this is probably also the case for senior executives categorised under the delegation selection mode; however, the perspective is slightly skewed since senior executives in this group frequently not only elaborate on their own decision making (delegation) but also refer to decisions made by others, for example describing past projects that they are aware of but in which they were not personally involved in the decision-making process per se.
- The most indicative dataset is the top two bar charts: senior executives aligned to a primary direct selection mode only referred to ad hoc/intuitive selection approaches, whereas those aligned to group decisions primarily spoke of a rational or structured approach or a combination of rational and intuitive. Consequently, there was a clear link between these two selection modes and approaches.

---

[2] In order to generate this diagram, I cross-referenced the dominant selection mode groups of respondents (e.g. all senior executives who were aligned to delegation) with the selection modes approach codes that these individuals mentioned in the interviews.

The analysis indicated clear links between dominant selection modes and selection approaches, and to a lesser degree between senior executives' generic role and dominant selection modes. All three appeared to be strong influencers; and further data exploration, as part of the construct analysis, provided further insights.

5.2.3.3 'Selection behaviour and criteria' as part of 'selection and choice actions' image up close

Selection behaviour refers to the steps or actions that the senior executive, the organisation or a group of assigned decision-makers took that led to the appointment of an advisor or advisory firm. The data indicated that the interviewed executives described their own behaviour or that of others either as ideal, common behaviours or protocols.

Selection criteria codes capture those aspects that the senior executive, the organisation or a group of assigned decision-makers consulted and evaluated before making the appointment decision. Again, these elements could refer to past applied criteria or general criteria to be applied in future selection situations.

Selection behaviour as part of 'selection and choice actions'	Coverage	Frequency
SI1.8_Established relationships serve as a screening mechanism	15	29
SI1.3_Continuity creates efficiency and better results	12	21
SI1.16_Clear picture of each advisory firm or advisor	11	45
SI1.15_Not good to be too reliant on advisors for everything	7	20
SI1.4_Preference to pro-actively contact advisors	7	10
SI1.1_Large projects should go out to tender	6	8
SI1.13_Not in a position to spend more money on advisors	6	7
SI1.2_Small pieces of work don't need to go to tender	5	7
SI1.10_Fire fighting, no time for long-term planning	4	5
SI1.11_Cost focus leads to DIY	4	8
SI1.12_Select advisor or advisory firm purely on merit	4	4
SI1.14_Big projects are painful and be avoided	4	5
SI1.17_Limited exchange with my peers in terms of advisor engagement	4	4
SI1.5_Balance advisors - avoid overreliance	4	5
SI1.7_Physical proximity leads to a pole position	4	7
SI1.9_Projects extension and expansion	4	6
SI1.6_Emergencies can bypass selection processes	2	9

Table 5.4 – List of selection behaviours, selection and choice actions

Starting with the selection behaviour, there were a number of aspects that were more frequently mentioned during interviews as well as by a higher proportion of respondents. Here I was looking at the selection behaviour code category establishing code coverage (how many respondents mentioned a particular aspect) as well as code frequency (how many times had the particular code been mentioned by all respondents).

- Over half of the senior managers shared the view that established relationships between organisation and advisory firm serve as a type of screening mechanism, while many were of the opinion that continuity creates efficiency and better results. It, therefore, appears that firms that were already known and actively involved with the client organisation were being viewed differently during the selection considerations.
- At the same time, seven respondents shared the view that it was not good to be overly reliant on advisors.

These two opposing views informed my thinking when I developed the leitmotif analysis, described in later sections of this chapter.

Selection criteria as part of 'selection and choice actions'	Coverage	Frequency
SI2.1_Skills and experiences of individuals	14	22
SI2.2_Proposed team	14	21
SI2.12_Fair or competitive price	11	21
SI2.9_Proposition and approach	10	20
SI2.10_Legacy or established relationships	9	16
SI2.6_Clearance of conflicts of interests (e.g. audit relationships)	9	13
SI2.8_Internal insights or knowledge	9	12
SI2.13_Previous performance or experiences	8	17
SI2.7_Relevant experiences - track record	8	9
SI2.4_Reputation and house style	6	13
SI2.5_Brand and reputational factors are NOT or LESS important	4	7
SI2.11_Hunger and drive	3	5
SI2.14_Minimum threshold	3	4
SI2.3_Strong bid performance (presentation, Q&A)	3	3

Table 5.5 – List of selection criteria, selection and choice actions

The emphasis of messages was slightly different when it came to selection criteria, which are codes describing the actual criteria that respondents mentioned when it came to selecting and appointing an advisor or advisory firm for a particular project or service:

- The top four criteria, mentioned by almost half of the respondents, focused on pragmatic aspects such as skills and experiences, pricing and the proposition.
- Established relationships also featured in the selection criteria discussion, compared to the selection behaviour aspects, but were only mentioned by nine respondents. This made me reflect on whether existing relationships determined who was being considered and whether, when it came to the final choice, the relationship element was not quite so important. Would this be comparable to screening and choice? One thing to bear in mind is that many of the big advisory firms will have a type of rapport or relationship with large organisations. The relationship aspect might not have such a great advantage or exclusivity, especially in the case of larger advisory firms.
- Strong bid performance as such was only cited by three respondents; however, most respondents tended to form opinions about the skills and experiences of the team proposed via the bid performance (presentation). There, therefore, appeared to be a link between these codes, thus they should be viewed as one group.

When I looked at coding incidents for selection behaviours and criteria at an individual senior manager level, a number of interesting patterns stood out:

- A group of senior managers (CFO_5, CFO_3, CFO_4) cited a large number of different selection behaviours and criteria in their interviews.
- However, the majority of senior executives discussed elements in both categories equally, but not quite as many as the previously mentioned group, for example, CFO_1, CRO_1, CEO_2, COO_1.
- At the same time, there were some senior managers who alluded primarily to selection behaviour or practices and only to very few selection criteria, for example, CFO_2; CRO_2.

- And vice versa: senior executives referred to no or very few selection practices but a good number of selection criteria; for example, COO_3, CEO_5, CEO_4.

While reviewing the outcomes of the analysis, I was noting down the following questions in my memos: What do these findings indicate? Are senior executives in the first group the more demanding, the more involved or even possibly the more experienced clients since they are asking for many aspects? Do senior executives in the third group not really consider selection criteria at all? Is there a link between selection modes and approaches and the selection behaviour and criteria discussed?

Reflecting on the results, I was inclined to conclude that selection approaches were strong influencers, which could be associated with certain selection modes. At the same time, there were reoccurring messages regarding relationship and continuity which seemed to link up more pertinently with ad hoc selection, while a more 'rational' approach aligned more strongly with elements focusing on merit and managing advisors (avoiding overreliance). I revisit this observation below, in the construct (section 5.4) and leitmotif analysis (section 5.5) sections in this chapter.

Comparing and linking 'selection and choice actions' to objectives and goals as part of the trajectory image was not overly conclusive, which was probably due to the fact that the interview was not structured enough. Only some senior executives recounted project objectives and the selection behaviours and criteria utilised. However, based on general observations and reflections beyond the interview data, which I noted in my memos, I believe that different selection elements, both behaviour and criteria, come into play depending on the 'project or service trajectory' objectives and drivers for the planned project or service.

5.2.4 Decision framing – an integral part of the decision process

In the context of this study, the decision frame, as part of the emerging conceptual model, is made up of past experiences and organisational constraints, and defined as:

Senior executives' store of knowledge (past experiences either learned, observed or conveyed) as well as the organisational context (meaning the formal or informal guidelines and or constraints on working with external advisors) which the senior executive draws on when applying all three images as part of the decision-making.

5.2.4.1 'Organisational context' as part of the decision framing

This subgroup of the decision frame component listed the smallest number of mentioned elements. Overall, senior executive comments were rather scarce and often scattered as side remarks within the general interview commentary. However, the following observed patterns appeared to me to be of significance:

- With the exception of one interviewee – CFO_3, who frequently discussed past and recent organisational arrangements – senior executives were generally in agreement on organisational constraints and communicated identical or similar aspects as their peers in the same organisation. One organisation, company C, in particular, stood out: three senior managers who joined at the same time from another employer and who were fairly close on a personal level communicated the same messages, whereas the two other senior managers of company C were mutually contradictory.
- Two respondents – CEO_6 and COO_3 – did not refer to any organisational context or constraint regarding working with or appointing advisors. This could mean that they were unaware of these compared to their colleagues, that they chose to ignore the constraints, or that they simply did not happen to mention them during the interview.
- When clustering the organisational contextual variables, it became evident that there were two groups: organisations that did not encourage the use of advisors (notably Companies A and B) and organisations that believed they knew how to get the most out of their advisor relationships or better working arrangements (notably Companies D, E and F). For Company C, the group of respondents who recently joined the organisation together fell into the latter group, whereas the other two respondents were of the opinion that the organisation was not set up to get the most out of their advisor relationships.

In summary, there seemed to be in general agreement amongst the senior executives on the organisational context, as discussed above, in which they were operating. There were clearly also two strong organisational steers, either to avoid using advisors or only to use them as a last resort or on the other hand to manage advisors pro-actively and to a certain degree control them to make sure that the most beneficial outcome for the organisation would be achieved.

5.2.4.2 Past experiences as part of the decision framing

In contrast to organisational context, past experiences were mentioned frequently throughout the interviews. As part of the coding exercises, I differentiated between recent experiences, primarily feedback on recent projects or activities with my employer, which were marked with the prefix PER (past experiences recent), and historic experiences, when senior executives recalled impactful events and experiences of the past, which I marked with the prefix PEL (past experiences legacy). When I analysed all past experiences mentioned by coverage and frequency with the help of Nvivo, the following dataset came through:

Past experiences mentioned as part of the decision framing	Coverage	Frequency
PEL1.3_Past experiences shape association	18	62
PER1.4_Overall or on balance positive outcome or experience, some minor aspects did not go so well	17	39
PEL1.2_Clear association or legacy relationships with ADVISORY FIRM	16	51
PER1.3_Positive outcome or experience, achieved benefits or objectives	15	34
PEL1.1_Clear association or legacy relationships with ADVISOR	14	38
PEL1.5_Historic NEGATIVE hands-on experiences with the ADVISORY FIRM	10	29
PEL1.6_Historic POSITIVE hands-on experiences with the ADVISOR	9	16
PER1.1_Value for money achieved	9	12
PER1.6_Negative outcome or experience, possibly wrong firm	9	29
PER1.7_Client lesson learned, clarify objectives or services to be received up front	8	16
PER1.2_Value for money questionable	6	8
PER1.9_Client lesson learned, overreliance - we put too much into the hands of the advisor	6	19
PER1.5_Negative outcome or experiences, wrong advisor	5	7
PEL1.7_Historic POSITIVE hands-on experiences with the ADVISORY FIRM	4	7
PER1.8_Client lesson leaned, advisors overstays welcome or overcomplicates next phase	4	6
PEL1.4_Historic NEGATIVE hands-on experiences with the ADVISOR	3	4

Table 5.6 – List of past experiences, decision frame

While reviewing the results presented in Table 5.6 above, I made note of the following observations:

- There appeared to be a degree of consensus on the notion that past experiences shaped the associations that individuals had regarding advisory firms as well as individual advisors.
- Overall interview comments (codes) describing recent experiences were predominately positive. On reflection, I recognised that there could a bias since the interview was conducted on behalf of an advisory firm and therefore senior executives might have chosen to emphasise the positive. The 26 instances (frequency) linked to recent negative experiences (29 associated with the firm and only seven with the advisor) were still quite important to note.
- Remarkably, on a historical level, more positive comments were reserved for individual advisors than for advisory firms. Only three respondents referred to negative experiences with an advisor per se. It might be easier to attribute negative comments or failings to an organisation than an individual.

Summing up, past experience elements did show some interesting patterns in the in-depth analysis. The focus on advisor versus advisory firm did stand out and was a perspective of interest which was included and will be considered further in the analysis.

5.3 Component analysis conclusions inform construct analysis

5.3.1 Summary of component analysis results

The outcomes of the analysis above on a component-by-component level addressed three of the four research aims to a certain extent:

- **First research aim:** Why and how senior executives engage and interact with advisors and advisory firms on a general relationship or rapport level. The analysis found that senior executives' 'imperatives', such as general expectations and personal principles and preferences, were the crucial determining component, but that the decision framing component, encompassing past experiences and organisational context, and some aspects of the 'project or service trajectory', were also influencers.
- **Second and third research aim:** How senior managers select and appoint 'Big Four' professional service firms and advisors. In analysing for these research aims, all three image components ('imperatives', 'project or service trajectory' and 'selection and choice actions') and decision framing ('past

experiences' and 'organisational context') came into effect, with 'selection and choice actions' as well as 'project or service trajectory' components having a significant influence.

- The **fourth research aim** was to explore to what extent the interaction influenced or shaped the selection and appointment of advisors, meaning to what extent was there a link between the relationship or rapport and selection and appointment decision. The analysis of the data suggests that there were a number of relationship-type aspects, as recorded in the 'selection and choice action' component, but there was no clear indication as to how the relationship or rapport featured in the selection and choice decision.

Lastly, the results of the component analysis indicate that there were a number of constructs, such as generic role or selection approach, which appeared to be beyond, but influencing, the component structure that emerged as a result of the analysis. The clustering exercises that I engaged with indicated a number of recurring messages, such as 'controlling advisor' and 'trusting advisors' and others that spanned across components. Consequently, as a next step, I explored these influencing constructs in order to understand the phenomena.

5.3.2 Identification of constructs

As mentioned during the component analysis, a number of cross-component influencing patterns came to my attention, which I labelled constructs. These patterns were linked to generic role, selection approach and to a lesser degree selection mode, and organisational approach to managing advisors – organisational supplier management approaches.

As a next step, I conducted a series of iterations, comparing and contrasting client comments segmented by construct. For this, I grouped senior executives organised by constructs. I had three selection approach groups (structured/rational, ad hoc/intuitive and mixed) and I cross-referenced and compared the coding for these three groups across all three images and the decision-framing components. My main objective was to identify patterns or polarising comments between construct groups.

In addition to the above-listed construct definitions, I investigated a host of other potential construct groupings. For example, I looked at project and service trajectory aspects, value for money responses given, final satisfaction rating and response mode, and many more. The outcomes of these construct queries were not conclusive.

Nonetheless, working through the material I developed the idea of a gestalt construct. Already during the initial coding activities, I had observed that for some senior executives the individual advisor stood out or was placed in the foreground – they were effectively engaging and doing business primarily with this individual, whereas the firm was somewhat in the background as an assurance, a provider of resources etc. For others, it was the other way around: these senior managers spoke predominantly about doing business with the firm, regardless of who the nominated lead advisor was at the time. Lastly, there were individuals who had no clear preference or set view on this matter. I started to refer to these constructs as Gestalt Advisor, Gestalt Firm and Gestalt Balanced. I used the term 'gestalt' because it appeared to me that senior executives were trying to create a 'unified whole' construct of the entity that they were dealing with. There are a number of visual depictions used in the gestalt theory[3] (Wertheimer, Riezler 1944) and depending on the individual perception and perspective, the picture could, for example, be a vase for one person whereas for another person it is a depiction of two human profiles. Exactly this notion of perspective and creating your own perception was the basis for the gestalt construct that I introduced here.

Throughout the components of the conceptual framework, there were elements that clearly pinpointed preferences for advisor or firm; I located these in 'personal preferences and principles', 'selection behaviour and criteria' and 'past experiences' where the commentary was aimed predominantly at the advisor or the firm. Calling up these indicating elements as well as reviewing my interview memos, I was able to assign senior executives to one of the gestalt groups.

5.4 Summary of results from four key construct analysis

In addition to reviewing the empirical data from a component-by-component standpoint, I explored the coded client data from a construct perspective in order to view the phenomena from different viewpoints in line with the constructivist grounded theory approach (Charmaz 2006). In this section, I summarise the key findings of the four most insightful construct analysis: generic role, selection approach, organisation and gestalt.

---

[3] 'This "Gestalt" or "whole form" approach sought to define principles of perception — seemingly innate mental laws that determined the way objects were perceived. It is based on the here and now, and in the way things are seen. Images can be divided into figure or ground. The question is what is perceived at first glance: the figure in front, or the background.' Wikipedia Gestalt Psychology page (Wikipedia 2016)

5.4.1 Construct analysis focusing on generic roles

Generic role classification, based on organisational function and responsibilities, was the starting point for this construct. Did CFOs expect something different compared to CEOs? Did CROs favour different selection behaviours compared to CIOs? The results, especially regarding imperatives, project or service trajectory and selection and choice actions, were meaningful, but further studies would be required to explore these first points more fully.

5.4.1.1 Imperatives – expectations of an advisor or advisory firm

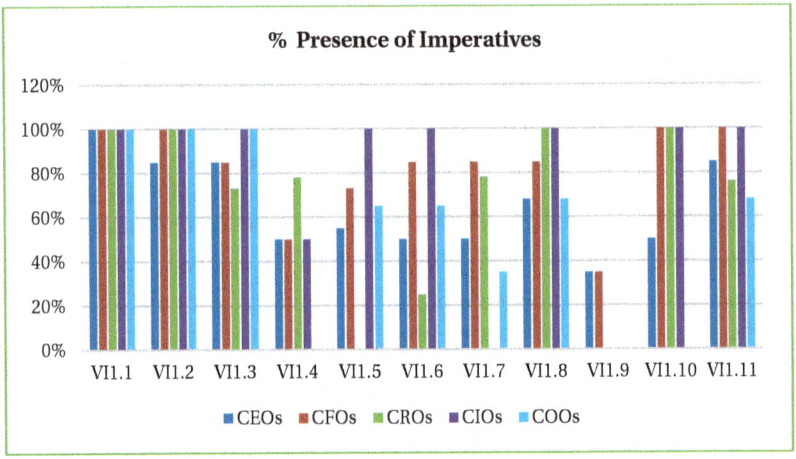

VI1.1_Demonstrate empathy - advisor or firm should understand me and the organisation and act on that knowledge

VI1.2_Earn my trust and bat for me - invest in the relationship and put me and the organisation first

VI1.3_Be pro-active - advice, flag and challenge as required - don't sell

VI1.4_Right interpersonal skills and chemistry

VI1.5_Be embedded and hold a presence within the organisation

VI1.6_Be able to solve problems pragmatically and collaboratively

VI1.7_Be realistic, transparent and honest - stick to agreements

VI1.8_Provide an external view, benchmarks and insights

VI1.9_Help me or us understand and manage regulatory bodies

VI1.10_Provide and assure required competence, skills and expertise

VI1.11_Step in and help out - be responsive, accessible and available

Figure 5.4 – Presence, in percentage, of imperatives by generic role[4]

---

[4] In order to generate this diagram, I took note of the presence of individual imperative codes mentioned by senior executives grouped by generic role; the results are shown in percentages to facilitate comparison.

There was a high level of coverage, indicating to me a type of consensus in this component group; variations were less pronounced, but there were some differences:

- Only CEOs and CFOs mentioned 'Help me or us understand and manage regulatory bodies', which could also be traced back to two specific organisations.
- Although the number of CIO respondents was small, they tended to put more emphasis on 'being embedded in the organisation' and 'being able to solve problems pragmatically and collaboratively'; at the same time, neither of them mentioned 'being realistic and transparent and stick to agreements' – perhaps this was assumed.
- Proportionally, more CROs stressed the need for the 'right interpersonal skills and chemistry' while 'being embedded and have a presence in the organisation' was not cited by any of the four respondents.
- Lastly, 'provide and assure required competence and skills' was strongly highlighted by all role groups except for CEOs. Was this possibly linked to the fact that CEOs are less involved in the day-to-day running of projects?

The results for personal preferences and principles were fairly evenly distributed; no clear patterns emerged in this dataset.

5.4.1.2 Project or service trajectory – objectives and goals

There was a consensus amongst the roles on the core objectives: to deliver positive results or outcomes and to provide guidance and advice. However,

- CIOs did not mention 'free-of-charge work' but pushed for 'being part of the organisational eco-system'; they also did not look for 'a guarantee for success' or 'call for assistance to meet a deadline' from the advisor or firm.
- Being part of the organisational eco-system was only an objective for CIOs and COOs.
- CEOs and CFOs sought a 'guarantee for success', as well as 'asking advisors to teach and empower the organisation'; CROs agreed with this view.

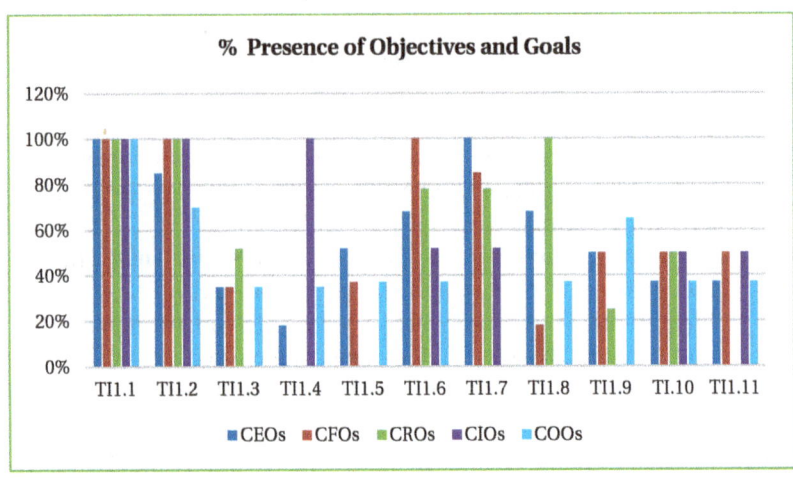

TI1.1_Deliver positive results and tangible outputs
TI1.2_Provide guidance and advice (billable)
TI1.3_ProBono or free advice
TI1.4_Be part of organisational eco-system
TI1.5_Guarantee for success
VI1.6_Be able to solve problems pragmatically and collaboratively
TI1.8_Teach or empower us
TI1.9_Help meet a deadline
TI1.10_A tailored approach
TI1.11_Sharing pain and responsibilities

Figure 5.5 – Presence, in percentage, of objectives by generic role[5]

5.4.1.3 Selection and choice actions – selection behaviour and criteria

In terms of selection and choice actions mentioned by role, indicative preferences or interests could be identified:

- CEOs made relatively few selections and choice comments, possibly because the majority of these respondents delegated the decision-making. The aspects that did stand out were: 'established relationships serve as a screening mechanism' and 'having a clear picture of each advisor and or firm within the selection practices'. When it came to selection criteria: skills and experiences were key, clearance of conflict was important and

---

[5] In order to generate this diagram, I took note of the presence of individual trajectory – goals and objectives codes mentioned by senior executives grouped by generic role; the results are shown in percentages to facilitate comparison.

reputation and house style, as well as offering a fair or competitive price.

- In contrast, CFOs cited a large range of different selection aspects. There was acknowledgement that continuity created efficiency and that established relationships served as a screening mechanism. Plus, there was a consensus that large projects should go out to tender while smaller ones did not need to, possibly linked to the group's predominately hybrid selection mode, and CFOs preferred to pro-actively contact advisors.
- CIOs, for the most part, concurred with the CEOs' and CFOs' selection practices and behaviour. Regarding selection criteria, proposition or approach, hunger and drive and a fair/competitive price came out as key aspects in this group.
- COOs mirrored many of the CFOs' selection practices and criteria, while placing a strong emphasis on previous performances and experiences with the advisor and or firm.

As mentioned previously, more substantive research is needed to confirm these patterns; there could be some symptomatic preferences associated with an individual's generic role.

5.4.2 Construct analysis focusing on selection approach

This was the most discerning construct analysis in addition to the gestalt construct, which follows later in this section. As part of the coding exercises, I identified two binary or diverse selection approach notions: individuals recounted a more ad hoc or intuitive approach to selecting an advisor or a more rational, fairly structured approach to making a choice, although some individuals made reference to both approaches. Based on senior executive comment coding, I grouped respondents as either ad hoc/intuitive, rational/structured or both.

The polarisation – by which I mean differences in emphasis between the three groups – was high in this dataset, and there were some clear preferences, especially between those individuals who communicated ad hoc/intuitive selection approaches and those who spoke of more rational or structured selection approaches.

5.4.2.1 Imperatives – expectations and personal principles and preferences

Again, there were only slight variations when it came to aspects linked to expectations, but there were a number of pronounced differences:

- All the senior executives grouped into the rational approach group called for 'earn my trust and invest in the relationship' as well as 'be pro-active – advice and challenge but don't sell'. The figures for those grouped under ad hoc were lower.
- The rational/structured selection approach group placed a stronger emphasis on 'being able to solve problems pragmatically and collaboratively' and 'to provide/assure required competence', compared to the other two groups.
- 'Help me understand and manage regulatory bodies' featured almost exclusively in the ad hoc / intuitive selection approach group.

The patterns were even more distinctive when it came to personal preferences and principles communicated.

A significant proportion of individuals who spoke of an ad hoc or intuitive selection approach stressed the following notions:

- The 'advisor is more important than the firm', and there is 'a need to feel important'; the advisor should pay personal attention to the senior executive.
- Senior managers were also more receptive to additional offerings, such as events and training sessions organised by the advisor and firm, compared to the other groups.
- Both ad hoc/intuitive and rational/structured individuals indicated an interest in meeting advisors on a regular basis. The question remains, though, what for? As discussed in the component analysis, there might be different motivations behind this request.

In comparison, very diverse dynamics showed up as critical for those senior executives grouped in the rational or structured selection approach group:

- There was a certain level of cynicism emerging, with aspects such as 'advisors are in business to make money' and 'self-promotion without substance is a no go'.
- Trust and integrity were being called on while respondents clearly had a preference for staying in control by monitoring advisor activities.

These were dissimilar preferences which signified to me that these two groups had discrete views.

5.4.2.2 Project or service trajectory – objectives and goals

Overall, regarding general objectives and goals, there was no overarching polarisation between the groups. Nonetheless, a couple of aspects stood out:

sources coded	SI0 – Ad Hoc Approach	SI0 – Adhoc and Rational	SI10 – Rational Approach Only
TRAJECTORY IMAGE 1 PRIMARY OJECTIVES & GOALS	7	4	8
TI1.1_Deliver positive and tangible outputs	7	4	8
TI1.2_Provide guidance and advice (billable)	6	3	8
TI1.3_ ProBono or free advice	4	1	0
TI1.4_ Be part of the organisational eco-system	0	1	3
TI1.5_ Guarantee for success	2	1	3
TI1.6_Fill a resource gap	6	3	5
TI1.7_Fill knowledge gaps	6	0	7
TI1.8_Teach or empower us	2	1	3
TI1.9_Help me meet a deadline	6	2	1
TI1.10_A tailored approach	4	1	3
TI1.11_Sharing pain and responsibilities	2	1	3

Table 5.7 – List of objectives and goals mapped to selection approach groups

- Senior executives aligned to the ad hoc or intuitive selection approach were keen on free-of-charge or free advice from the advisor, while the objective of meeting the deadline by engaging an advisor featured prominently as well.

- Being part of the organisation eco-system (defined in section 5.2.2 and in Appendix A) was chiefly a goal of those aligned to the rational or structured selection approach.

5.4.2.3 Selection and choice actions – selection behaviour and criteria

Regarding the selection practices and criteria mentioned, there were a number of pronounced differences between the two binary groups, namely:

Senior executives aligned to an **ad hoc or intuitive selection approach**:

- Preferred to pro-actively contact advisors while recognising that established relationships served as a screening mechanism.
- Almost half of these senior managers did not exchange details of their advisor engagement with their peers.
- Reputation and house style, experienced on a personal level, were important selection criteria for many, while the firm's brand and reputation were less critical.
- Previous performances and experiences with the advisor and firm served as a reference point for over half of this population.

Senior executives aligned to a rational or structured selection approach:

- The screening function of establishing relationship was recognised; the desire to balance advisors to avoid over-reliance was also acknowledged.
- Offering competitive or fair pricing was the most widely referenced selection criteria for this group, followed to a much lesser degree by aspects such as relevant track record and experiences (in general not with the client organisation), internal insights and knowledge and hunger and drive to secure the work.
- At the same time, this group of senior managers confirmed the importance and benefits of existing working relationships.

5.4.3 Construct analysis focusing on companies and supplier management approaches

As part of the data exploration, I ran numerous queries based on company associations and organisational supplier management directives of each company (ad hoc to no procurement, standard procurement and complex supplier management). Although the datasets were at times distinctively different, I was not able to identify any reliable patterns. For once, I observed that the organisational supplier management directive was only echoed in a small number of senior managers, meaning that an interviewee actively confirmed the existing procurement function and its possible impact on the selection process. A reasonable number of senior executives either did not acknowledge the function or ignored organisational constraints altogether. In addition, two companies (E and F) had two separate procurement directives in place: there was a complex supplier management programme for technology-related activities while the rest of the organisation operated with a standard procurement directive.

I acknowledge that the organisational supplier management or procurement directive, or a lack thereof, has the potential to influence individuals' choice of advisor. At the same time, the data indicated that not everyone within the organisation embraced these directives and some tried to circumnavigate organisational procedures, possibly in the form of selection behaviours and practices. This is clearly an area for more research in the future; however, since there were no conclusively construct-related patterns, I decided not to pursue this construct further as part of my analysis.

5.4.4 Construct analysis focusing on gestalt views

At the beginning of this section, I already alluded to the construct 'gestalt'. While coding, I observed that for some senior executives the advisor was the focal point and the firm as an entity was in the background, while another group of senior managers 'transacted' primarily with the firm regardless of who was nominated as the lead advisor. This observation led me to create the constructs 'gestalt advisor' for the first group and 'gestalt firm' for the second group. Of course, a third group that had a 'balanced' view came about as well.

In order to identify the individuals, I picked out indicating key aspects in 'imperatives - personal preferences and principles', and 'selection and choice action' comments as well as dynamics found in the past experience component. The detailed list of codes can be found in Appendix A. As a last confirmation, I cross-referenced the nodes with my memos and also reviewed the transcripts again before assigning each senior executive to one of the three groups.

5.4.4.1 Imperatives – personal principles and preferences

There were only some very minor differences between the three groups regarding 'imperatives - expectations of an advisor or advisory firm'. However, the biggest polarisation can be seen in the personal principles and preferences mentioned:

	A Gestalt_ Advisor	B Gestalt_ Balanced	C_ Gestalt_ Firm
VALUE IMAGE 2_PERSONAL PRINCIPLES	**7 (8 total)**	**4 (5 total)**	**8 (8 total)**
VI2.1_Advisor is more important than the firm	6	0	0
VI2.2_Need to feel important or be a priority	2	2	2
VI2.3_Need to be able to trust the advisor or firm	5	1	3
VI2.4_Advisors are in business to make money	2	1	4
VI2.5_Quality has its price	1	1	2
VI2.6_It is difficult to differentiate between firms	3	0	2
VI2.7_Don't like getting caught up in details	1	0	3
VI2.8_Bias towards previous Big 4 employer	0	1	0
VI2.9_Self promotion without substance is a no go	1	3	4
VI2.10_I like to stay in control/monitor advisor activities	2	2	7
VI2.11_Growing through the ranks	5	0	0
VI2.12_Thrive on challenge	1	1	0
VI2.13_Don't like scare mongering	0	0	3
VI2.14_Appreciate additional offerings	3	0	2
VI2.15_I DON'T need to see the advisor frequently	1	0	0
VI2.16_I DO like to meet the advisor regularly	3	2	3
VI2.17_I LIKE to engage with the advisor socially	1	2	1
VI2.18_I DON'T like to engage with the advisor socially	0	1	0
VI2.19_ The end result matters	1	2	2
VI2.20_Integrity is important	4	1	2

Table 5.8 – List of personal principles mapped to gestalt construct groups

The advisor as an individual was of course more important than the firm for those senior executives aligned to the '**gestalt advisor**' construct. This group also spoke exclusively about the concept of 'growing through the ranks': staying in close contact throughout their professional career regardless of employment situations. Trust and integrity were also critical aspects mentioned by a large proportion of this group.

In comparison, senior managers aligned to the '**gestalt firm** construct were keen on managing or possibly controlling the advisor and his or her activities. There was again a level of scepticism here, comparable to the rational selection approach group, via the strong presence of aspects such as 'self-promotion without substance is no go', 'advisors are in business to make money' and the 'dislike for scare-mongering'. Being able to trust the advisor was mentioned by a number of individuals in this group.

5.4.4.2 Project or service trajectory – objectives, goals and triggers

At first glance, the differences between the groups in this component were minimal, although a couple of dynamics stood out:

- A significant number of senior executives grouped under 'gestalt advisor' referred to a request from the board or a superior as a primary trigger for an initiative, whereas many senior managers aligned to 'gestalt firm' spoke about their own impetus being the driver for advisor engagements.
- In terms of goals and objectives, the comments were relatively evenly distributed between the groups. Interestingly, only senior stakeholders who fell into the 'balanced' and 'gestalt firm' groups spoke of advisors being part of the organisational eco-system, which does make sense since it is an arrangement between two organisations and not individuals. Furthermore, there was a slight increase of aspects such as 'teach or empower us' and 'sharing pain and responsibilities' for those aligned to the 'gestalt firm'.

5.4.4.3 Selection and choice actions – selection mode, behaviour and criteria

Starting with **selection mode**, there was a clear steer of senior executives in the 'gestalt firm' group towards delegation of advisor selection, whereas half of the individuals in the 'gestalt advisor' group indicated that they personally drove the selection of advisors.

Regarding the selection approaches taken, there were no strong preferences in either group. However, a larger number of senior managers in the 'gestalt advisor' group spoke of applying an ad hoc or intuitive approach (possibly mixed with a rational approach if required?).

	A Gestalt_ Advisor	B Gestalt_ 4Balanced	C_Gestalt_ Firm
SELECTION MODES	**8**	**5**	**8**
S0.1_Delegate always or most of the time selection	2	1	5
S0.2_Delegate for some initiatives, others direct personal involvement	0	2	2
S0.3_Selection is agroup decision wiht somewhat limited senior involvement	4	3	4
S0.4_Personally drive the selection of advisors	4	2	2
S0.5_Follow a rational approach to selecting advisor or firm	4	3	5
S0.6_Follow an ad hoc or intuitive approach to selecting and advisor or firm	6	3	2

Table 5.9 – List of selection modes mapped to gestalt construct groups

Regarding selection practices or behaviour, there were just a few aspects that showed up as being decisive between the groups:

- Half of those aligned to 'gestalt firm' spoke of balancing advisors to avoid over-reliance. Compared to the other two groups, more senior managers focusing on the firm indicated that big projects were painful and to be avoided while recognising that the physical proximity of an advisory firm or advisor led to a pole position.
- More individuals grouped under 'gestalt advisor' indicated a preference to pro-actively contact the advisor and admitted to having a limited exchange with peers around advisor engagements.

In terms of selection criteria mentioned during the interviews, there were a number of differences:

- Senior executives aligned to the 'gestalt advisor' construct appeared to focus on criteria based on personal experiences such as 'previous performance and experiences they had with the advisor or firm' and 'legacy or established relationships', which also explains why general brand or reputational notions mostly associated with the firm were less important.
- In contrast, senior managers in the 'gestalt firm' group more frequently mentioned knowledge-based aspects such as 'internal insights and knowledge' and 'relevant experiences and a track record', which went beyond the respondents' experience with the firm or advisor.

5.4.5 Summary of construct analysis

Analysing the sample population from diverse angles and comparing and contrasting the responses of different construct-driven groups added some valuable insights to the study. Selection approach, gestalt focus and, to a lesser degree, generic role emerged as the most determining constructs.

There was some degree of overlap between selection approach and gestalt (see table below mapping respondents to construct views), which was mirrored to an extent in the notions mentioned by each group but was not all-embracing. For example, a large proportion of respondents favouring a rational selection approach were also aligned to 'gestalt firm' instead of 'advisor'.

Respondent	Selection Approach	Procurement	Gestalt
CEO_6	Ad hoc	Standard	Balance
CFO_3	Ad hoc	Standard	Advisor
COO_1	Mixed	Standard	Balance
CEO_1	Rational	AdHoc/None	Firm
CFO_2	Ad hoc	AdHoc/None	Advisor
CRO_2	No data	AdHoc/None	Balance
CEO_3	No data	AdHoc/None	Firm
CEO_4	Rational	AdHoc/None	Advisor
CEO_5	Ad hoc	AdHoc/None	Firm
CFO_4	Ad hoc	AdHoc/None	Advisor
COO_2	Mixed	AdHoc/None	Advisor
CRO_3	Ad hoc	AdHoc/None	Advisor
CEO_2	Rational	Standard	Firm
CFO_5	Rational	Standard	Firm
CRO_4	Rational	Standard	Advisor
CFO_1	Mixed	SuppMgmt	Balance
CIO_2	Rational	SuppMgmt	Balance
CRO_1	Ad hoc	SuppMgmt	Advisor
CFO_6	Rational	SuppMgmt	Firm
CIO_1	Rational	SuppMgmt	Firm
COO_3	Ad hoc	SuppMgmt	Advisor

Table 5.10 – List of respondents mapped to key constructs

There were no clear-cut patterns between selection approach and gestalt focus or even role. Therefore, could organisational constraint or context be an influencing force that steers senior executives towards, for instance, a particular selection approach even if their general comments might point to a different gestalt construct? One hypothetical scenario might be that a senior manager leans towards the 'gestalt advisor' construct; however, some mitigating contextual influencers steer the person towards a more rational or structured selection approach. This could be a procurement directive which calls for panelled selection decision (selection mode) or even common practices of having to disclose the selection rationale to a higher entity, possibly like the company board.

5.5 Emergence of clearly identifiable leitmotifs

In the first months of my sabbatical, I spent over eight weeks examining and comparing the closed client dataset (after closed coding and data validation). During this stage, I investigated closely how the data was mapped to each component of the emerging theoretical framework, described in section 5.2; while comparing and contrasting the data per respondent I also identified a number of polarising patterns linked to individual clients' preferences or their role, which were examined as part of the construct analysis (sections 5.3 and 5.4).

At the same time, I also started to take note of a number of other cross-component patterns which appeared to me more as themes – expressions such as 'trust', 'empathy', 'control', 'balancing advisors', 'continuity', 'embeddedness', 'competitiveness' and 'merit', as well as 'skills', came up frequently in the client comments and the resulting codes. Some of these notions I had already picked up on in my earlier observations, as part of the four different senior executive preference ranges I discussed in section 3 in Chapter Three.

Reflecting on earlier and then recent observations, and after having re-examined the dataset, I started to view and articulate these patterns as four emerging themes, which I labelled 'leitmotifs' ('leading motives', translated literally from German). Over time it became clear to me that there were indeed a number of aspects with similar underlying motives, or themes, that I frequently detected and noted in the datasets. Throughout the course of the analysis, I started to refer to these four leitmotifs, as follows:

- **Control, balance and risk management** – dynamics associated with the concept of clients pro-actively managing and overseeing the advisor and firm activities, keeping a tab on their activities, sometimes but not always to manage organisational risk and avoid over-reliance. Client comments that I aligned to this leitmotif were such as the following:
  - o *'I think the bit that would be helpful for me would be the sort of overall relationship management piece. So we described all of the projects and said actually Firm has done quite a lot over the last year, but getting someone to draw them together and paint the picture of what are we doing at the moment? In the pipeline. Where do we see the opportunities? What ongoing discussions are we having? So that I get an opportunity to have some line of sight to, not just what's happening today, but how the relationship might*

develop over a three-month, six-month, 12-month time
horizon. Because it gives me an opportunity then to A)
understand in a broader context Firm's involvement and B)
maybe manage it a little bit better than I do at the moment. I
guess at the moment there's a slight feeling that if we're not
careful we get into the position where the involvement is
almost after the event you find out that there's projects going
on...' (coded as an imperative personal preference)

- o 'It's always hard to predict in advance what's happening, but
  I think we too often consult with advisers generally in
  regards to tax, that would be my observation. So I shall be
  putting the general squeeze on rather than anything
  particular.' (coded as a selection behaviour)
- **Trust and empathy** – aspects associated with the concept that a
  client needs to be able to trust and rely on the advisor or firm,
  acknowledging that the overall relationship between the two parties
  has to be on a sound footing of integrity and mutual respect. For
  instance, I noted the subsequent client quotes to this leitmotif:
  - o 'I think at this level you're looking for people you have
    complete trust in who will be very keen and support you in
    letting you know what's going on around the market more
    generally and particularly in this position, actually it's the
    trends that they're seeing from their regulatory interventions.'
    (coded as an imperative personal preference)
  - o 'I've known Name for at least ten years. I first met Name
    when she was on secondment to the Organisation as group
    compliance...head of group compliance. And, again, have
    been through, both with her and Name, some quite hairy
    times at the Organisation, you know, sort of when they were
    on secondment. And, again, it's going through things like
    that, that actually forge the relationship that carries you
    through. So I've kept in touch with Name since then. And
    they did work well ...' (coded as a selection criterion)
- **Continuity and embeddedness** – notions that refer to the concept
  of the advisor or firm being embedded and holding a presence in
  the client organisation and the benefits associated with the
  continuity of working with the same advisor and firm. The following
  client quotes I would associate with this leitmotif:
  - o 'And then, I guess ultimately getting our organisation, our
    culture, what we're about, the people, the relationships, the
    way the kind of place works. So that when there are pieces of
    work to be done, you've got that kind of connectiveness to be

> able to get quickly into step with what we're trying to achieve
> and how it fits and works and everything else...' (codes as
> imperative expectations of an advisor)

- o '...the tone that you're hearing from me is one where I have
  been quite satisfied with the work that we have done with
  Firm. And candidly developing a long-term pattern of
  interaction develops an understanding amongst
  organisations as to how best to work with each other. And to
  me that's quite important, because none of us have very
  much time and re-inventing the wheel, to me, is a
  challenge.' (coded as selection behaviour)

- **Competitiveness and merit/skills** – elements linked to the concept
  of assuring competitiveness to the client in the form of attractive or
  fair pricing, providing strong skills and knowledge and awarding
  projects based on these 'more factual' notions. For example, I would
  link client comments such as the following with this leitmotif:

  - o 'Access to good quality people and I'm talking about A teams
    and nothing less than that because we're a relatively
    straightforward business, but when we have got issues, we
    like to deal with them very quickly and very effectively. You
    just need people that can operate to a very high standard
    without too long an introduction to whatever the issue is.'
    (coded as imperative expectations of an advisor)

  - o 'So you're never going to get me to say, "Oh you guys are way
    too cheap, why don't you double your prices." You're not
    going to get me to say anything like that. But if you were so
    expensive that I didn't feel I was getting value, then we'd
    simply stop using you.' (coded as selection criterion)

5.5.1 Definition of the four leitmotifs

Once I was able to articulate and summarise the four emerging leitmotifs,
I returned to the client data and reviewed each code and the associated
client comments in order to determine if I could detect one of the four
underlying motives in the code and client remarks. Aligning codes which
encompassed previously identified keywords such as 'embeddedness' was
more straightforward; for others, I carefully examined the client
comments linked to the code before assigning them to a particular theme.

There were also a number of codes that could not be related to any
leitmotif or clearly assigned to one. For example, 'proposed team' was
frequently named as a key selection criterion. However, was the
underlying motive to assess the skills or merit of the team members, or

was there a desire for a known team, such as individuals who had worked for the client in the past? If a respondent gave further information then it would be have been coded with 'continuity creates efficiency' or 'previous performance or experience'; or if the first scenario applied, then with 'skills and experiences of individuals' or 'relevant experiences and track record'. Since the 'proposed team' code was too ambiguous and additional codes had captured the intent more clearly, I chose to not include these types of codes in the analysis.

Furthermore, similar to the scenario discussed above, codes in the trajectory image 'project or service trajectory' also did not associate clearly with one leitmotif versus another. Again, I opted to exclude these aspects from the leitmotif analysis.

After a number of assignment iterations and data checks, I ended up with the following alignment of aspects per leitmotif (Table 5.11):

Control, Balance and Risk Management	Decision Level	Sources	References
SI1.1_Large projects should go out to tender	Decision 2	6	8
SI1.11_Cost focus leads to DIY	Decision 2	4	8
SI1.13_Not in a position to spend more money on advisors	Decision 2	6	7
SI1.14_Big projects are painful and be avoided	Decision 2	4	5
SI1.15_Not good to be too reliant on advisors for everything	Decision 2	7	20
SI1.4_Preference to pro-actively contact advisors	Decision 2	7	10
SI1.5_Balance advisors - avoid overreliance	Decision 2	4	5
SI2.14_Minimum threshold	Decision 2	3	4
SI2.6_Clearance of conflicts of interests (e.g. audit relationships)	Decision 2	9	13
VI1.11_Step in and help out - be responsive, accessible and available	Decision 1	18	63
VI1.7_Be realistic, transparent and honest - stick to agreements	Decision 1	12	34
VI2.10_I like to stay in control - monitor advisor activities	Decision 1	11	23
VI2.13_Don't like scare mongering	Decision 1	3	4
VI2.20_Integrity is important	Decision 1	7	12
VI2.4_Advisors are in business to make money	Decision 1	7	13
15 variables, 6 linked to D1 and 9 linked to D2		7	229

Trust and Empathy	Decision Level	Sources	References
SI1.2_Small pieces of work don't need to go to tender	Decision 2	5	7
SI1.6_Emergencies can bypass selection processes	Decision 2	2	9
SI2.10_Legacy or established relationships	Decision 2	9	16
SI2.13_Previous performance or experiences	Decision 2	8	17
SI2.4_Reputation and house style	Decision 2	6	13
VI1.1_Demonstrate empathy - advisor or firm should understand me and the organisation and act on that knowledge	Decision 1	21	64
VI1.2_Earn my trust and bat for me - invest in the relationship and put me and the organisation first	Decision 1	19	62
VI1.4_Right interpersonal skills and chemistry	Decision 1	10	23
VI1.9_Help me or us understand and manage regulatory bodies	Decision 1	4	12
VI2.1_Advisor is more important than the firm	Decision 1	6	19
VI2.11_Growing through the ranks	Decision 1	5	10
VI2.2_Need to feel important or be a priority	Decision 1	6	13
VI2.3_Need to be able to trust the advisor or firm	Decision 1	9	25
13 variables, 8 linked to D1 and 5 to D2		*8*	*290*

Competitiveness and Skills/Merit	Decision Level	Sources	References
SI1.12_Select advisor or advisory firm purely on merit	Decision 2	4	4
SI2.1_Skills and experiences of individuals	Decision 2	14	22
SI2.11_Hunger and drive	Decision 2	3	5
SI2.12_Fair or competitive price	Decision 2	12	22
SI2.3_Strong bid performance (presentation, Q&A)	Decision 2	3	3
SI2.5_Brand and reputational factors are NOT or LESS important	Decision 2	4	7
SI2.7_Relevant experiences - track record	Decision 2	8	9
SI2.9_Proposition and approach	Decision 2	10	20
VI1.10_Provide and assure required competence, skills and expertise	Decision 1	15	40
VI1.6_Be able to solve problems pragmatically and collaboratively	Decision 1	13	24
VI1.8_Provide an external view, benchmarks and insights	Decision 1	17	49
VI2.12_Thrive on challenge	Decision 1	2	4
VI2.19_The end result matters	Decision 1	5	7
VI2.5_Quality has its price	Decision 1	4	5
VI2.9_Self promotion without substance is a no go	Decision 1	8	14
15 variables, 7 linked to D1 and 8 linked to D2		*8*	*235*

Continuity and Embeddedness	Decision Level	Sources	References
SI1.3_Continuity creates efficiency and better results	Decision 2	12	21
SI1.7_Physical proximity leads to a pole position	Decision 2	4	7
SI1.8_Established relationships serve as a screening mechanism	Decision 2	15	29
SI1.9_Projects extension and expansion	Decision 2	4	6
SI2.8_Internal insights or knowledge	Decision 2	9	12
VI1.3_Be pro-active - advice, flag and challenge as required - don't sell	Decision 1	18	63
VI1.5_Be embedded and hold a presence within the organisation	Decision 1	11	23
VI2.14_Appreciate additional offerings	Decision 1	5	8
8 variables, 3 linked to D1 and 5 to D2		*10*	*169*

Table 5.11 – Identified codes mapped to the four leitmotifs

While aligning codes to a particular leitmotif, I used a type of colour coding system which is reflected in the table above and applied in subsequent graphical presentations. The main objectives for compiling the above leitmotif table were: to have an overview of codes aligned to each motive; to document the presence of leitmotifs across components of the emerging conceptual model (image column); and to establish how many of the 21 respondents (source column) mentioned each aspect and how frequently it was mentioned in total (reference column). The table allowed me to verify that all four leitmotifs were present across the 'imperatives' and 'selection and choice' components of the model. As previously alluded to, I was not able to clearly detect one of the four underlying motives in the codes associated with the trajectory component. Looking at the total numbers of references listed at the end of each subsection of the table helped me to confirm that there was a type of balance to how often a leitmotif featured in client comments. Had there been one leitmotif with a much higher or lower frequency count, that would have been an interesting discovery to be examined further; but since there were no significant variations, I moved on to investigate and compare the four leitmotifs from various perspectives.

5.5.2 General presence of leitmotifs in the dataset

As a first step, I tried to understand the presence of each leitmotif within the conceptual framework, focusing on imperatives and selection and choice actions. Initially, I looked at how the four leitmotifs were represented within each component group (number of aspects aligned to each leitmotif by conceptual framework component):

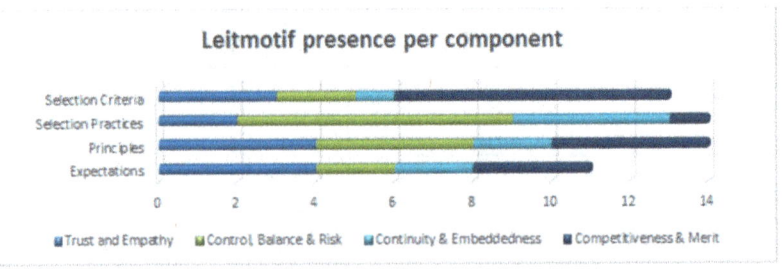

Figure 5.6 – Leitmotif presence per selected component[6]

- Expectations of an advisor and firm – 'trust and empathy' and to a slightly lesser degree 'competitiveness and skills/merit' aspects dominated this component.
- Personal principles and preferences – 'continuity and embeddedness' was the least represented leitmotif in this category; the remaining three were present at comparable levels.
- Selection behaviour – 'control, balance and risk management' clearly dominated this conceptual component, but the leitmotif 'continuity and embeddedness' also featured very strongly.
- Selection criteria – a larger number of aspects can be linked to 'competitiveness and skills/merit' motives but 'trust and empathy' featured quite strongly as well.

In summary, there were some substantial differences in leitmotifs' presence in each conceptual component:

'Trust and empathy' clearly shaped the expectations of an advisor, although the other three motifs were also important. Selection behaviour was dominated by 'control, balance and risk management' and, to a slightly lesser degree, 'continuity and embeddedness'. Reflecting on the findings, this could perhaps mean that there was an acknowledgement that continuity generates benefits but keeping the advisor in check is even more important. Selection criteria were in a way determined by the competitiveness and merit motifs; however, trust and empathy did feature as well. This is again two almost polarising views – selecting the best resource or competitive arrangement versus gravitating towards relying on trust and past experiences.

---

[6] In order to generate this diagram, I cross-referenced the number of codes by code sub-group (e.g. expectations sub-group of imperatives) aligned to the four leitmotifs.

5.5.3 Comparing leitmotif presence and frequency

Looking at the dataset from a different angle, reviewing the distribution of total count of aligned component aspects per leitmotif, the following picture presented itself:

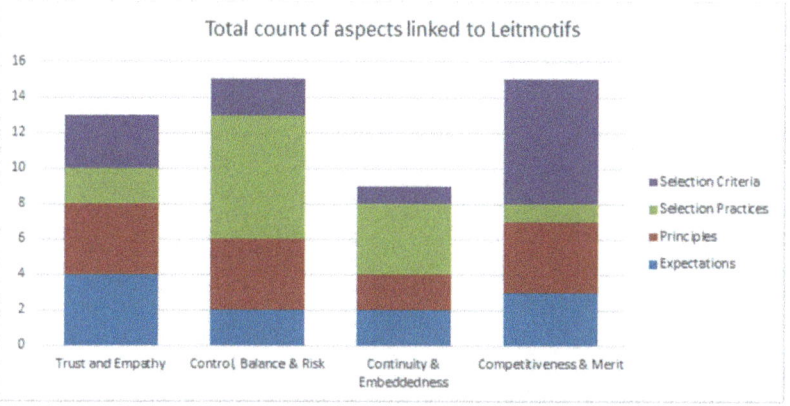

Figure 5.7 – Total count of aspects linked to leitmotifs[7]

The diagram above (Figure 5.7) depicts the total count of aspects or codes by component, imperatives – expectations and principles and selection and choice actions – selection practices and criteria, mapped to the four leitmotifs; it establishes the presence of each leitmotif across the components. For example, four imperative expectation codes are aligned to the leitmotif 'trust and empathy', in comparison two codes are aligned to the leitmotif 'continuity & embeddedness'.

When comparing the aspect count per leitmotif diagram above, with the number of references (frequency of nodes) for each leitmotif, a distinctly different view appeared.

Frequency was an interesting consideration to be added to the examination. Whereas the first diagram (Figure 5.7) focuses on presence of leitmotifs across decision-making components such as selection criteria, the second diagram (Figure 5.8), mapping frequency of client messaging of leitmotifs across components, is an illustration of client 'noise' – the more often the recipient of a message hears a certain motive, the likelihood of this message being absorbed increases. That is to say, we might communicate four different aspects, but if we state one or two of

---

[7] In order to generate this diagram, I cross-referenced the leitmotif to the number of codes by code sub-group (e.g. expectations sub-group of imperatives) – an inverse illustration of Figure 15.

these aspects more frequently, they start to stand out slightly compared to the others. Hence, when comparing both diagrams above, I made note of the following observations:

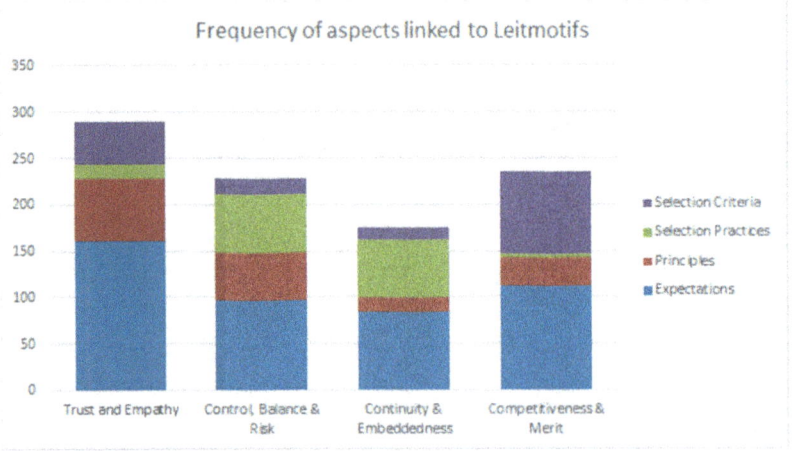

Figure 5.8 – Frequency of aspects linked to leitmotif[8]

It appears that more senior executive comments focused on expectations of an advisor (blue section of bar chart). Again, the leitmotif 'trust and empathy' featured heavily in this component.

Selection practices or behaviour and selection criteria were less frequently mentioned across all leitmotifs. This could have been influenced by individuals' rhetoric. Often respondents mentioned selection criteria only once during the interview and did not discuss these aspects again in great detail.

Therefore, an inference I would like to make based on these two datasets is: advisors or advisory firms, who are the recipients of these interviews, primarily hear or take on/absorb the messages depicted in the second diagram. The volume or frequency of client messages gathered during the client feedback conversations informs the advisors' and firm's view, meaning it is quite likely that if the client spoke primarily about the relationship, the advisor would assume that this was the most important aspect for the client:

---

[8] In order to generate this diagram, I mapped the frequency of codes by code sub-group mentioned during the interviews to the leitmotif.

- A steer towards the expectations component, which is dominated by the 'trust and empathy' leitmotif and to a lesser degree by 'competitiveness and merit/skills' comments.
- Less attention possibly being paid to selection criteria and selection behaviour or practices in particular (least frequency compared to total number of aspects aligned across motifs).

5.5.4 Further explorations of the leitmotifs

In addition to the analysis discussed above, I carried out a number of further investigations exploring the four leitmotifs in conjunction with the previously identified constructs such as gestalt. The results of these data explorations are in part documented in this thesis, and although I found these exercises were interesting and stimulating, for example trying to establish preferences of leitmotifs per respondent role, the results did not contribute substantially to the emerging substantive theory and therefore I decided not to include detailed discussion of them here.

5.6 Consolidation and amalgamation of findings

Having spent some time reviewing and reflecting on the results discussed in this chapter, the main findings and implications for theory development are outlined below, which I discuss in more detail and expand on in the next chapter on theory rationalisation.

- The conceptual model presented and discussed in section 5.3.1 had evolved, fuelled by the new findings. An additional dimension was added with the introduction of the four leitmotifs. I would describe the patterns I observed as a type of leitmotif decision-making matrix, which can be placed on the conceptual decision-making model.
- The leitmotif decision-making matrix guides the decision-maker by determining the direction and strength of foci applied as part of decision-making. Depending on the context, the senior executive is able to identify and select a leitmotif focus to guide the decision-making activities by converging on particular aspects aligned to the chosen leitmotif foci. The data has shown that when it comes to the relationship or rapport decision (context), a significantly different distribution of leitmotifs associated with 'imperatives' comes through, compared to 'selection and choice actions' in general.

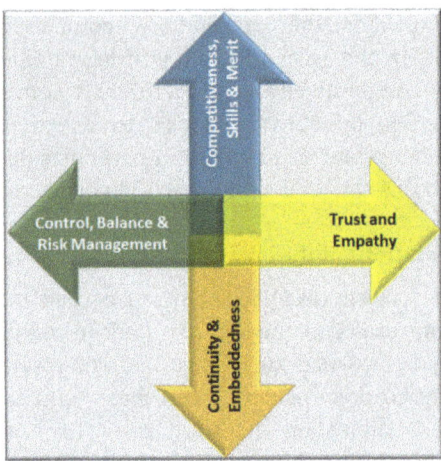

Figure 5.9 – Evolving leitmotif decision-making matrix

- This confirms to me that there are indeed two decision-making processes: to maintain a relationship and to select and appoint an advisor for a particular task. These are governed by different aspects and motives. Moreover, the relationship component does feature at varying degrees in the second selection and appointment decision in the form of particular aspects, which can be placed in the 'trust and empathy' and 'continuity and embeddedness' motives. However, these relationship dynamics are only one of many drivers that influence the selection and appointment decision.

- Furthermore, one could argue that there are four components that impact the selection and appointment decision: personal imperatives and preferences; past experiences; organisational context; and, most importantly, project-specific dynamics such as project or service trajectory and selection and choice actions. Both past experiences and organisational context have a significant bearing on the other two dimensions.

- Initially I tried to apply labels, such as alphas and betas, to senior executives, based on their decision-making behaviours; see Chapter Three, section 3.2. I have now come to realise that the decision-making process – especially surrounding selection and appointment decisions – is multidimensional and can vary greatly from project to project. The theoretical model described above illustrates the complexities and allows us to consider the different forces at play. However, as part of the analysis, I have identified three determining constructs (generic role, dominant selection approach and gestalt construct), which provide some indication as to how an individual senior executive might view and address the decision-making process.

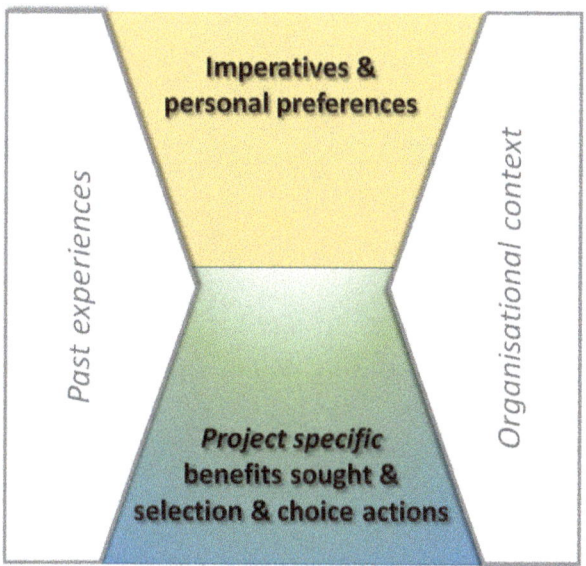

Figure 5.10 – Illustration of wider decision-making landscape

- There is clearly scope for further research, especially regarding organisational context and organisational roles. Nonetheless, I feel that these first substantive theories shed some light on a fairly unexplored black box: 'senior executives' decision-making about working with professional advisors'.

In summary, in this fifth chapter I have presented and discussed the findings of the additional, more in-depth analysis of the data from various viewpoints. The new findings and reflections have helped to shape and evolve the conceptual framework and generated some new constructs and models, such as the gestalt construct and the decision-making matrix.

Chapter Six documents how I summarised and rationalised the findings and emerging models, and captures my reflections and additional thoughts as part of this exercise.

Chapter 6

Theory rationalisation – substantive theoretical models discussed and pointers for the literature review

This chapter summarises the emerging models and substantive theory described in the previous chapter. In addition to amalgamating and discussing each emerging theory, gaps which could either be addressed with insights from peer-reviewed literature or possibly further research activities are highlighted. The chapter concludes with the objectives and plans for the literature review accompanying the study, documented in Chapter Seven.

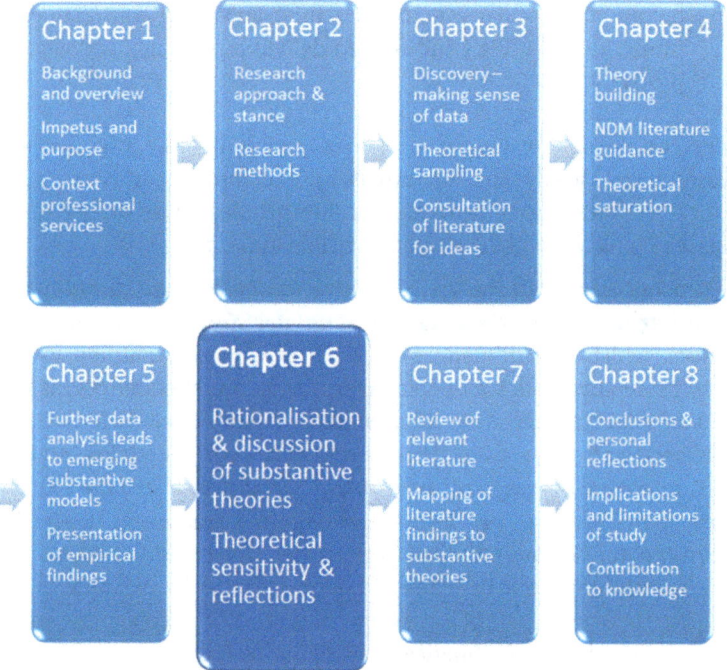

Figure 6.1 – Overview of thesis structure and content of the sixth chapter

In line with the adopted constructivist grounded theory methodology (Charmaz 2006) and the analytic auto-ethnographic (Anderson 2006) stance discussed in Chapter Two, this chapter allowed me to collect my thoughts, reflect on the research outcomes and the journey so far and plan for the next steps, particularly the literature review of similar studies.

6.1 Summary of substantive theory and models

The outcomes of the research activities so far can be summarised in the following theoretical constituents and underpinning models, which can join up or be rationalised into an overarching substantive theory (Charmaz 2006):

The study identified two decision-making processes that senior executives working for large primarily UK-based organisations utilise when interacting with 'Big Four' professional service firms and their senior advisors:

1. **Rapport Decision Process** leading to the decision to develop and maintain an ongoing personal rapport or relationship with the 'Big Four' advisory firm and their advisors.
2. **Appointment Decision Process** leading to the decision on behalf of the wider organisation to appoint and contractually transact with a 'Big Four' firm to deliver a particular service or project.

Under certain circumstances, explained later on, these two decision processes were closely aligned, otherwise the rapport or relationship element – the outcome of the first decision process – was one of many aspects which featured in the second decision-making process.

The process leading to the first decision– *to develop and maintain an ongoing rapport – was primarily a personal decision* made by the senior executives, which was influenced by a set of aspects identified in this study as 'imperatives', such as 'personal principles and preferences', as well as 'general expectations of an advisor and advisory firm'. This decision process appeared to be a *continuous and affirmative decision-making process, in which the physical proximity, intensity and intimacy of the rapport was steered or influenced by the advisor's activities*. Furthermore, the research findings suggest that this decision process was also frequently impacted by external circumstances, for example, if the senior executives were part of a steering committee of a project that might be outside their sphere of influence.

I refer to the second decision process – *to select and appoint a 'Big Four' firm and advisor for a particular service – as a binary (appoint or not appoint) decision made by the senior manager or others on behalf of the wider organisation.* The outcome of this decision process, if positive, resulted in a formal contractual transaction between the organisation, as an entity, and the advisory firm. This decision-making process, according to my findings, appeared to be informed by all three conceptual components, which I termed 'imperatives', 'project or service trajectory' and 'selection and choice actions', with aspects of the latter two featuring more frequently in the data. Moreover, the analysis revealed that the senior executive might or might not opt for a selection mode and might instead delegate the decision-making to another individual or group of individuals.

Analysis of the data found that both decision-making processes were repeatedly influenced by past experiences, either with a particular advisor, advisory firm or other situations, and also shaped by organisational context and constraints. The influence of past experiences and contextual aspects was more pronounced for the second decision, i.e. to select, appoint and formally transact with an advisory firm for a particular service. Furthermore, *past experiences and organisational context also continuously informed and shaped especially the 'imperatives' and 'selection and choice actions' aspects.* The following diagram aimed to capture the theoretical constituents discussed above.

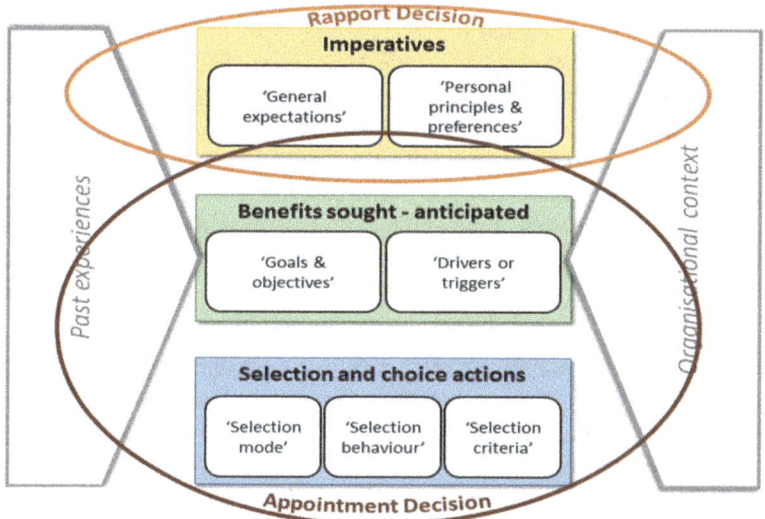

Figure 6.2 – Two decision processes mapped onto conceptual framework

As part of the research activities, I was able to construct two theoretical concepts which provide a better understanding of senior executives' decision-making:

The senior managers' decision-making took place in a *multidimensional and interactive landscape* encompassing past experiences, organisational context, personal preferences and imperatives, as well as project-specific benefits and choice actions. Although the landscape components interacted with and influenced each other, not all four components might feature equally. For example, some senior managers chose to ignore organisational constraints; plus, the 'selection and choice action' component came into consideration exclusively as part of the appointment decision process (2).

Secondly, in order to guide the decision-making approach that the senior executive appeared to be using, I refer to a type of internal *matrix configured of four leitmotifs* (i.e. overarching motives or determining notions found in the data). Depending on the type of decision to be made and the underlying landscape, the senior executive appeared to identify and weigh up decision aspects aligned to the four foci on the decision-matrix, narrowing in on a preferred position on the matrix which in turn provides guidance throughout the executive's decision-making process. The following senior executive comment illustrates such a scenario: *'Having worked with Advisor... I knew immediately I could use that approach to get things moving fast here. So we didn't do a tender and I just went straight to Advisor and said, you know, "How quickly can you help me?" Because I knew we had to move fast. The original requirement from the FSA was to produce a report I think by the end of May, which was crazy. So I managed to negotiate it back to the end of June, and the Advisor and the team came in and we quickly established terms of reference and got going.' CRO_3* In this instance, the project trajectories were linked to regulation as a driver and a key objective was to meet a deadline; in order to achieve the trajectory, the senior executive shifted the focus on the decision-matrix towards trust and empathy and continuity and embeddedness informed by past experiences, which also called for the selection practice 'emergencies can bypass selection process'.

The findings suggested that the leitmotifs on each end of the axis are not necessarily divergent motifs; however, achieving a focus on both sides could be challenging. For instance, senior executives mentioned that many professional service offerings would struggle to completely satisfy clients' demands for continuity and embeddedness while providing competitiveness, merit and skills. Consequently, *the decision maker(s)*

need(s) to be clear on the importance of each focus, potentially trading off one motive over another, to come to a final choice decision.

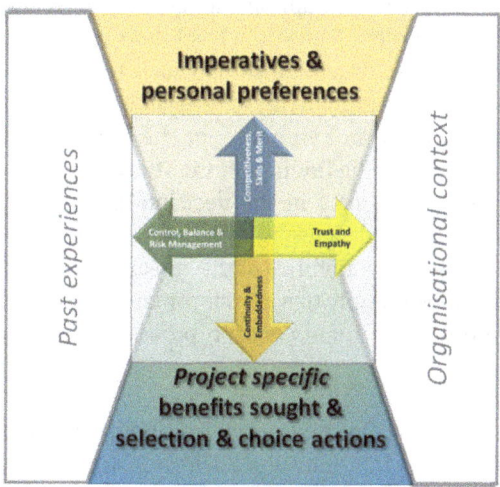

Figure 6.3 – Overview of decision landscape and leitmotif matrix

How a senior executive charts the leitmotif matrix depends on the underlying landscape, as well as the decision and task at hand. Due to this multidimensional and recurrently changing decision-making context, it is almost impossible to align individuals to a constant decision-making pattern or typology, as I tried to do initially by classifying senior managers as alphas and betas (see Chapter Three). However, the study identified ***three main constructs that provide indications*** as to how certain senior executives might choose to direct the matrix. I labelled the three constructs ***generic role, dominant selection approach and gestalt.*** In comparison, each group appeared to have differing preferences for each of the four leitmotifs. This seems to be the case for both rapport decision and also appointment decision process. Certain groups of respondents (such as CROs, those preferring an ad hoc selection approach and individuals aligned to 'gestalt advisor') favoured the 'trust and empathy' leitmotif, whereas others focused on the 'competitiveness, skills and balancing advisors' leitmotif. It is important to note that these constructs are also in part a product of the continuously evolving decision-making landscape in which the decision maker operates, meaning that senior executives might adjust their gestalt focus from 'balanced' to 'firm', for example, due to experiences or a change in the organisational context, or a CRO might move into a CFO role, which could trigger a change in decision-making patterns and priorities.

In conclusion, the outcome of the first decision, to maintain a rapport or relationship with an advisor or advisory firm, has a certain impact on the second decision, to select and appoint an advisor or advisory firm for a particular service or project. The study has found aspects pointing either directly or indirectly to the relationships which feature in the 'selection and choice actions'; interestingly these aspects were also grouped under either the leitmotif 'trust and empathy' or the leitmotif 'continuity and embeddedness'. However, the findings of the study suggest that there were many aspects that play a part in the decision-making and which were most notably influenced and shaped by past experiences and organisational context. The findings of the research project suggest that if the following conditions apply to a decision-making situation, a close link between decision process 1 and decision process 2 can be detected. If a senior executive: …

- chose to make a direct personal decision (selection mode)
- preferred an ad hoc or intuitive selection approach
- decided to tilt the leitmotif matrix towards the foci 'trust and empathy' and/or 'continuity and embeddedness'
- while the project objectives were being met, the organisational context was addressed and past experiences were positive

…then a link between the rapport and the appointment decision process could be observed. This scenario presented itself in the empirical dataset primarily in relation to free-of-charge work, advisory-only services or projects and small, low-risk projects.

The research appears to indicate that the client-advisor relationship informed by past experiences can lead to a degree of preference or even bias when it comes to exercising 'selection and choice actions', for instance, selection criteria such as 'legacy or established relationships'. Nonetheless, numerous other forces or aspects are involved, such as organisational context, service and project trajectory as well as selection modes, behaviour and criteria, which call for transparency and objectivity, and which act as a type of counterbalance to a potential relationship-driven bias. In other words, the senior executive would prefer to work with a particular advisor or advisory firm, but depending on the contextual circumstances, for example, procurement procedures for a large-scale project, the senior executive is required or feels compelled to follow a structured tender process involving a number of other decision-makers.

Taking this notion further, a 'Big Four' firm having a 'good relationship' with a senior executive does not necessarily guarantee a positive selection decision outcome. A number of other competing firms will also have 'a good relationship' with that senior manager, who might or might not be poised to directly make or actively influence the selection decision. The majority of senior executives interviewed spoke openly and positively about their relationship with other 'Big Four' and professional service firms.

Reflecting on the empirical findings and the firm internal debates, it appears to me that although the senior executive-advisor relationship or rapport can be an integral part of the selection and appointment decision, it is also a separate stand-alone paradigm and it should not be seen as simply a pathway to secure a project or sell professional services. From my perspective, the findings and observations clearly point towards a rapport that generates perpetual benefits for both the senior executive and the advisor, and their respective organisations, which extend beyond projects and services. In section 6.3.2, I document and discuss the reciprocal benefits I have observed.

Furthermore, the study uncovered that there are indeed senior executives who are less interested in a close rapport or do not value these potential relationship benefits, for various reasons. Nonetheless, the described lack of interest in a relationship does not indicate that these particular senior managers are not prepared or willing to appoint and transact with the advisory firm for services. It is, after all, a personal decision to build and maintain a rapport with an advisor, which thus needs to be respected and understood by the advisor and the advisory firm. For instance, COO_1 stated: *'... a professional services firm that's constantly calling me up and inviting me out for lunch – I never go for lunch, I just work. So I'm not looking for that type of relationship, I'm looking for a more sort of substantive relationship, whereby I can call or discuss an issue.'* CFO_4 indicated: *'There are partners who I would phone for advice, who I may not have spoken to in four or five years, but if I've got something that's right for them, then I'll phone them.'*

In the following sections, I discuss and reflect on the above-mentioned models and components (organisational context, past experiences, imperatives, service and project trajectory as well as selection and choice actions). My aim is to provide additional perspectives based on my analysis and to present reflective thoughts in addition to illuminating the substantive theory emerging from this study.

6.2 'Organisational context and past experiences' – key influencing streams

There appear to be two influencing streams which provide directive context to senior executives when it comes to interacting and appointing professional advisors: organisational context or constraints and past experiences.

6.2.1 Organisational context or constraints

The study findings indicate that senior executives either operate in an organisational context that is in general accepting and supportive of professional advisors, with certain guidelines in place to govern the interactions or are operating in an organisational context that is in general discouraging or constraining, possibly even penalising the use of professional advisors.

Those senior executives finding themselves in the latter environment were likely to have a slightly strained relationship (the result of the rapport decision process) with the advisor and advisory firm. In their interviews, they tended to shy away from discussing future advisory engagements and they were also disinclined to outline preferred selection and appointment processes and criteria. Interestingly, on a personal level, they might feel that involving an external party would be the right approach, but they were reluctant to do so. For example, CFO_2 shared the following comment: *'So generally speaking we actually don't use consultants, which probably was a mistake, right. So I think it would be (pause) I don't know... I mean we've been talking with Advisor about a couple of odd things; whether anything will happen and whether it's within his world or some other part of 'Big Four' Firm, it's difficult to say at this point.'*

In two instances, companies A and B,[1] a strong organisational steer towards refraining from engaging advisors was evident in the senior executives' interview transcripts from these two organisations. There seemed to be a clear organisational directive to try and address or manage activities and projects internally; failing to do so, and therefore having to engage external support, was seen internally as a sign of failure. These constraints not only had an impact on appointing advisors (appointment decision-making process) but also the general relationship (rapport decision-making process) between senior executive and advisor.

On a relationship level (rapport decision process), senior executives either kept advisors at arm's length, and interactions were more distant or hesitant (observed in the transcripts of COO_1, CFO_1, CRO_1), or the senior manager felt comfortable enough to be completely open with the advisor and explain his or her predicament (observed in the transcripts of

---

[1] Placeholders for senior executive and company names were installed at the beginning of the research process to assure anonymity, a complete list of senior executive codes relating them to company codes can be found in Appendix A.

CFO_2, CFO_3), for example, 'I am not in a position to spend more money on advisors'.

Regarding the process of selection and appointment decision to deliver services, the research study found that senior executives either tried to keep an engagement under the organisational radar – for example, small, contained pieces of work – or argued and convinced the organisation that certain skills were only available through a professional services firm, such as regulatory or a particular technical expertise. Time pressures were another acceptable rationale mentioned for appointing an advisory firm which came through in codes such as 'fire-fighting, no time to plan' and 'cost focus leads to DIY'.

For example, a scenario discussed in interviews pertaining to company B described how the organisation tried to manage a regulatory-driven project for several months in-house. However, only when the project was about to fail and the regulatory deadlines became unachievable did senior executives reach out, or were permitted to reach out, to an advisory firm for last-minute support in order to salvage the initiative and meet the set requirements. Naturally, a situation like this carries negative implications for the internal project team and the senior executive overseeing it. This notion was confirmed by one CFO, who openly admitted that having to resort to engaging an advisor was seen as a sign of failure within their organisation, and therefore senior executives operating in this type of context would think carefully before 'officially' selecting and appointing an advisory firm.

On the other hand, the study found that organisations which accepted or even encouraged the use of external advisors would rely on senior executives and their direct reports, as well as frequently procurement staff, to ensure that the organisation received a fair deal and the best achievable benefits. In some cases, for example, companies C and D, overt organisational strategies were in place to control and balance the use of different advisory firms, which apparently were monitored internally by senior stakeholders such as the CEO or the CFO. Both CEO_2 and CEO_3 said they compared annual billings of the 'Big Four' firms; CFO_5 even stated that if project activities with one supplier went beyond a threshold, the CFO would make a conscious effort 'to cool things down' and balance out the situation. These notions were captured in codes such as 'balance advisors – avoid over-reliance', 'it is not good to be too reliant on advisors for everything' and 'select advisor or advisory firms purely on merit'.

A key manifestation of the organisational context described in this section is the supplier management approach that an organisation has put in place. Senior executives employed by companies with little to no procurement protocols and guidelines in the study appeared to have relatively free rein in how they interacted with and appointed professional advisors. Organisations with a more traditional procurement approach (a purchasing division which oversees all procurement transactions) and even more so with a sometimes complex supplier management set-up, appeared to shape or even dictate the selection and appointment process (especially for larger or high visibility projects) as well as to a certain degree stipulate how the rapport between the two entities should be conducted. Some supplier management programmes spelled out exactly when, how and in which form the two entities – organisation and advisory firm – should interact and work together.

Both CIOs interviewed were strong proponents of well-thought-through supplier management structures; that these are not always fail-proof transpired in the interview with CIO_1. The previously identified and selected preferred supplier had provided the least competitive and developed offering for a large programme. After reviewing the different bids, the organisation decided to step away from the predefined supplier management arrangement and select another advisory firm to carry out the work.

As part of the organisational context, procurement and supplier management led by a separate leadership team exerted a significant influence by defining and managing organisational selection and appointment processes, protocols and pre-defined criteria, while installing a degree of selection transparency which challenged overtly biased or irrational decision-making.

Nonetheless, not every senior manager appeared to comply with these procurement rules. Two senior executives included in the sample chose not to discuss organisational context aspects at all, possibly ignoring constraints. Other senior executives referred to selection behaviours and practices, which allowed them to override organisational constraints, for example *'emergencies can bypass selection processes'* or by breaking down projects into smaller components that were below the procurement threshold. This suggested to me that this was a tactic adopted by a senior decision-maker who was operating under constraints. By breaking up the project, they bypassed the clearance requirements, from procurement and/or a more empowered senior executive, frequently the CFO, to appoint the advisory firm.

Concluding remarks for this section

Organisational context and constraints regarding interaction with professional advisors have a significant influence on the selection and appointment decision process as well as on the 'senior executive – advisor' relationship or rapport. In general, I observed in the interview data and via my operational memos that senior executives tend to adhere to organisational protocols for projects which are extensive from a budgetary perspective, of high visibility (e.g. outcome is presented to senior management or the board) or linked to high risk. For smaller and less critical projects, senior managers might – depending on personal preferences, circumstances and organisational consequences – push boundaries and ignore organisational guidelines.

Organisational context is a pivotal influencing stream which might or might not conflict with personal preferences and past experiences. For instance, a senior executive might prefer an ad hoc or intuitive selection approach and, based on past experiences, the senior manager might even conclude that the involvement of a particular professional advisor is the right decision. However, depending on the organisational context, a different approach might be imposed by the organisation – for example, a panelled group decision following procurement protocols or a push to manage the initiative in-house.

Overall, I believe that it is important to acknowledge the impact of organisational context on the senior executive's decision making. Organisations must carefully evaluate if the ramifications of their procurement structures lead and contribute to the desired outcomes and organisational culture. Professional advisory firms must not only tolerate, but empathetically respect and respond to, this context for the benefit of all parties involved.

All of these are considerations to be taken forward and included in the study's implications. In addition, findings from other studies found in the peer-reviewed literature might provide further insights to enrich this constituent debate.

6.2.2 Past (personal) experiences

Past experiences featured heavily in the narratives of the senior executives. Due to the nature of the interviews, to provide feedback to one of the 'Big Four' advisory firms, senior executives recounted in depth their recent experiences with advisors and the firm, but also referred to legacy experiences. This refers to experiences gathered some time ago, perhaps involving other professional service advisors and firms.

Past personal or organisational experiences, on both a relationship and a project level, informed and shaped senior managers' views of the advisor and advisory firm. Eighteen out of 21 respondents mentioned that past experiences had shaped their association with the advisor or advisory firm.

This could involve the extent to which the advisor or firm previously met agreed objectives and delivered desired outcomes; whether the respondent felt that value for money was generated; and if something went wrong, how the advisor or firm overcame these challenges. There were frequent comments about someone stepping in and fixing an issue. All these aspects appeared to have influenced rapport decisions and were reflected explicitly in the selection behaviour and criteria. Selection criteria such as 'previous performance and experiences with the advisor or firm', and 'reputation and house style which is based on past experiences' but also in the form of 'legacy or established relationships' were identified during the coding and described in Chapter Four. I interpreted selection behaviour, such as senior executives confirming that they had a 'clear picture of each advisory firm or advisor', as meaning that in their minds they had a clear view as to what an advisor or advisory firm was capable of or good at, in terms of technical delivery as well as on a relationship level.

For example, on a project level, CFO_4 confirmed that the *'firm can do finance-related projects', 'so in terms of can the house do it, yes. Good piece of work, very happy with it'* but the CFO and the organisation were holding a recent botched strategy project against the firm, indicating that credibility had been lost and the CFO and the organisation would not be looking to this particular firm for these types of services: *'That piece of work is going to be a block against winning other types of strategy assignments in here. Whether that's fair or unfair is almost irrelevant, because it's there.'* At the same time, CFO_4 confirmed that they had clear views based on past experiences when it came to individual advisors; to quote, *'partner X can do this but not that type of work'.*

Even though the vast majority of senior executives had clearly defined associations with individual advisors and advisory firms based on past experiences, only a smaller number of senior managers were prepared to generalise these views and categorically associated these to a firm's house style, or a certain expertise be it tax advisory or risk and regulation. CEO_5 indicated that *'The house style in 'Big Four'_3 tends to be more perhaps engaging, involving, a bit on the softer edges of things. I think the house style in 'Big Four'_1 is, I hesitate to use the term, but more professional, as in, it is very fact driven.'*

Another group of senior managers struggled to differentiate between the firms within a given services category, meaning that all the 'Big Four' advisory firms for them were essentially the same, with only people and past experiences setting each of them aside. A quote from a transcript illustrates this point:

> *'Because if I'm going to my board or my audit committee, whether it's got Firm_2, Firm_1, Firm_3, or Firm_4 or XX or Firm_7 or whoever, it doesn't matter. The brand becomes a hygiene factor, sorry. What matters then is the quality of what's written on the bit of paper, not the logo in the corner. You know, if I had a report from a small five partner firm of accountants from XX, it wouldn't work. So the brand becomes a hygiene factor at this level, and then it comes down to the quality of what's done, and for me that starts with the people.' CFO_4*

> *'I mean clearly I have a bias to a couple of the firms, but when I look back it's not to do with the brand, it's to do with the people that are in it. But can I see a different style in 'Big Four'_1's partners to 'Big Four'_3 partners? Not dramatically.' CRO_3*

> *'I think a lot of that is transient (distinction between the firms). Clearly you're inevitably coloured by, "Well what we're doing at the moment". I mean 'Big Four'_1 have spent a lot of time in the treasury, risk and finance space. 'Big Four'_2 have spent quite a lot of time in the finance space. 'Big Four'_4, the audit relationship dominates that; they've spent some time in looking at RDR and retail distribution.' CFO_5*

All of these views or perceptions stemmed from past direct or indirect experiences of the senior executives and they informed and shaped 'selection and choice actions' and personal 'imperatives', which influenced both types of interaction decisions between advisors and advisory firms.

Furthermore, a prominent construct which emerged out of the past experience narratives was what I termed a gestalt construct, defined in Chapter Five. The gestalt construct refers to the focal point of the decision-maker. Based on this, it appeared that when it came to engaging with an advisor or firm, for a number of senior managers the advisor as an individual entity took centre stage, whereas for another group of senior executives the advisory firm as an entity was the focal point of the interactions. A smaller group of five respondents had no clear preference. These observed phenomena have strong implications in terms of how to interpret and rationalise senior managers' comments – when a senior manager provides feedback, are these comments an attempt to describe experiences with the individual advisor or the wider advisory firm? Individuals aligned to the 'gestalt advisor' construct put strong emphasis on selection criteria linked to past experiences ('previous performance and experiences' and 'legacy or established relationships'), whereas those grouped with the 'gestalt firm' more frequently mentioned knowledge-based aspects ('internal insights and knowledge' and 'general relevant experiences and track record not necessarily linked to past experiences'). The difference in terms of impact becomes even more pertinent when an advisor changes employment and moves to another firm; in such a situation the senior executive who has taken on a 'gestalt advisor' view might readjust and align his or her outlook to the new constellation.

Concluding remarks for this section

The review of the findings of the research study suggests that past experiences not only have an immense effect on both decision-making processes, but also close the loop between the two processes. Past experiences resulting from a selection or appointment decision inform and create reference points for future selection and appointment decisions, as well as affecting the relationship or rapport between respondent and advisor and advisory firm. This means that when a senior executive selects and appoints an advisory firm to deliver a project or a set of services, on the one hand, these delivery experiences and associated interactions become past experiences and shape the senior executives' perceptions of the advisor and the advisory firm; on the other hand, the experiences are processes and mould the senior managers 'selection and choice actions' and 'personal imperatives'. Therefore, these new experiences inform the ongoing rapport with the advisor as well as future selection and appointment decisions.

Past experiences are critical reference points for senior executives which should not be underestimated. A project might not have gone well, but the actions of the advisor and firm in terms of how they address those issues determine the final outcome that is stored as a past experience. Many of the interviews alluded to challenging project situations where one of the advisors had stepped in and managed the client experience to ensure a positive outcome. It appeared to me that these situations – overcoming a challenge – were even more impactful and left a more memorable experience in the mind of the senior executives, compared to a project where everything went well without difficulties.

Reflecting on my own internal firm experiences, I believe that insufficient attention is given by the advisory firm to making sure that such project experiences are positive and memorable for the senior executives and the organisation. At least, within the context I have experienced, there is a strong firm-wide internal focus on relationship experiences in the form of marketing, corporate hospitality and other programmes such as training and events. On the other hand, project experiences are primarily subject to firm-wide risk and quality reviews with the main aim of managing or mitigating exposure for the advisory firm, and less attention is paid to the client's perspective and how this experience might shape future interactions.

One of the objectives of the post-analysis literature review is to identify previous studies that have highlighted the impact of past experiences on client-advisor relationships in a business context. The review will also seek to investigate if something comparable to the gestalt construct that I have identified in this research has been researched previously. At the end of Chapter Six, in section 6.6, 'Pointers for the ensuing literature review', I will return to these aspects, in addition to other considerations and implications for the literature review.

6.3 'Client-advisor rapport' – a multifaceted and reiterative ongoing process

The 'client-advisor rapport' is the outcome of the decision process that I have termed for the purpose of this study as 'rapport decision' by the senior executives, i.e. to develop and maintain a type of ongoing rapport. It is primarily a personal decision, which appears to be influenced by: a) the senior executive's general expectations of an advisor; and b) his or her personal principles and preferences. In addition, organisational constraints and past experiences also influence the decision and shape and mould these imperatives (see comments in previous section).

6.3.1 'Client-advisor rapport' continuously changes ...

Even though it is predominately a personal decision of the senior executive, the relationship or rapport can be constrained by the organisational context, depending on circumstances. For example, the CEO of company E had blacklisted two consultancy firms, as I was informed by the lead advisor; he and the organisation had had some very negative experiences with these two firms. A senior executive who finds him- or herself in such an organisational context might choose not to continue a dialogue with advisors from these two blacklisted entities, as a formal appointment of either firm to deliver services would create considerable tensions within the organisation.

The 'client-advisor relationship' also appeared to be an ongoing reiterative and affirmative decision-making process, in which the physical proximity, intensity and intimacy of the rapport is also steered by the advisor's activities. Very rarely did senior executives completely terminate a rapport with an advisor: many interviewees spoke of dormant relationships where they might not be in touch with an advisor for many years, but if the need arose the senior executive would pick up the telephone and contact the respective advisor.

Furthermore, the intensity and physical proximity of the rapport also appeared to vary over time. For instance, a current project might bring both advisor and senior manager together on a regular basis. In contrast, if a senior executive's role changed, and required fewer or no professional services, then the rapport might shrink to less frequent, possibly more social meetings. A small number of senior executives in the sample population spoke of having a very close relationship with an advisor, describing it at times as a personal friendship; in addition to discussing general professional concerns pertaining to their organisational role, the senior executive would also look for personal advice, for instance surrounding his or her career or how to personally manage a particular situation within the organisation.

Moreover, the data suggests that the 'client-advisor' rapport was also a reciprocal arrangement. Although the senior executive was the key driver – deciding for the most part if and how the rapport evolved – the advisor also steered and influenced the interactions with his or her actions. Most of the time it was the advisor who proposed to interact beyond current project-led schedules by offering meetings to discuss relevant topics and other networking opportunities that might be of interest to the senior executive. A small number of senior executives in the sample population mentioned that a particular advisor had not been, from their perspective, sufficiently pro-active in seeking contact and maintaining the rapport. In the transcripts, there was also evidence of senior managers' irritation about advisors who were excessively pushy and present, taking up too much of their time. Some of these senior managers went so far as to indicate that from their perspective advisor's meeting agendas, in general, appeared to be overly self-serving and opportunistic:

'Well, I compare you actually in many ways to head-hunters. Most head-hunters I don't trust as far as I can throw. They only ever ring you when they've got something and they disappear when you haven't. And you really don't want to tell them anything that you don't want passed on to other people.' COO_2.

Others pointed out that especially 'Big Four' advisors changed sides frequently, lacking a degree of loyalty towards the client, and therefore the senior executive and the organisation reciprocated this behaviour as well:

'One has a sense with the accounting firms that maybe there is less loyalty on either side so that: Would we sit here and say, we will always use 'Big Four'_1 come what may? Probably not. Would 'Big Four'_1 sit there and say, they will always supply their services to us even if there are

conflicts with other people? Probably not. So it's just a more promiscuous relationship I guess, than it is with the law firms.' CEO_4.

6.3.2 ... however, a common understanding with subtle nuances has evolved

Reviewing and contemplating the 'imperatives' – aspects which principally determine and drive the 'client-advisor rapport' – and corresponding observational memos, a number of aspects emerged.

On the subject of the general expectations of an advisor or advisory firm, there appears to be a strong consensus amongst senior executives compared to other components ('project and service trajectory' and 'selection and choice actions') in the decision-making framework. After having collaborated for a long-period of time – senior executives and senior advisors had been interacting throughout most of their professional careers in some capacity – did they have a common understanding as to what to expect of an advisor and advisory firm? Furthermore, could these notions at least in part even be shaped, almost propagated, by the advisor and advisory firms themselves? While examining the firms' marketing and project presentations, I was able to identify many of the 'imperative expectations' aspects in the material, as mentioned by senior executives as part of the study. Of course, it would be difficult to establish the source of these notions, but I would be inclined to conclude that both sides continuously repeat and therefore reinforce these notions, and consequently, a common understanding is being achieved.

Furthermore, the overall frequency of messaging of these 'imperative' aspects in the context of past and present experiences was proportionally higher compared to messages linked to 'selection and choice actions' and 'project or service trajectory'. When senior executives reflected on past experiences, the messages they shared were more frequently coded as 'imperatives – expectations of an advisor' and 'personal preferences', compared to the other two groups of codes ('selection and choice' and 'project or service trajectory'). Could this perhaps mean that senior executives were more comfortable discussing the relationship or rapport notions rather than selection and choice aspects in client feedback interviews, or could these have been easier or more pleasant sound-bites to share? Of course, one must keep in mind that the interview was set up as a client feedback discussion for one advisory firm, and therefore, the respondent was well aware of how these messages would be conveyed and to whom. Alternatively, could this emphasis (frequency) in the messaging perhaps be a reflection of the 'client-advisor rapport'? If advisors prefer to focus on these elements as well, potentially shying away from bringing up concrete selection and project objectives, then is the senior executive mirroring the advisor's behaviour by focusing on the preferred aspects of the relationship and associated past experiences?

As a result, when the advisor or advisory firm take on client feedback messages (such as the outcome of these interviews), the relationship constituent is most recurrently discussed, which in turn might lead the advisor or advisory firm to believe that this is indeed the focal point of the interactions from the senior executive's perspective, and therefore a strong rapport is the gateway to increased collaboration. Subsequently, does a strong relationship substantially influence the selection and appointment decision? I will revisit this argument in section 6.5 of this chapter.

As part of their personal guidelines and principles, a fair number of senior managers cited that they like to meet with their advisor or advisory firm regularly. Interestingly, only one senior executive explicitly stated that they did not feel that they needed to see an advisor on a regular basis. Looking at the aspects that coincide with this notion, two of the leitmotifs emerge: 'trust and empathy' – some senior managers are keen to meet the advisor regularly to strengthen the relationship and trust; others view regular meetings as an opportunity to manage and control the activities of the advisor – 'control, balance and risk management'.

6.3.3 'Client-advisor rapport': a stand-alone paradigm?

Reflecting on the data and my observations pertaining to the rapport decision process, I tried to understand and rationalise the 31 aspects (codes) associated with the imperatives component ('expectations of an advisor' and 'personal preferences') which strongly influenced this decision-making process. While examining the data, I was able to summarise the associated aspects into seven underlying motives as to why a senior executive would want to meet with an advisor on a regular basis, as well as noting what the senior manager is getting out of these interactions:

1. One motive already mentioned above is to monitor and control the advisory firm's activities, either because it is a senior manager's personal principle or an organisational policy is in place to balance advisory firms and manage risk exposure by not handing too much (be it financially or intellectually) to one person or firm. The senior executive may also be driven by a general level of scepticism about advisors' intentions, keeping a tab on the advisory firm and making sure that the advisor is not taking advantage of the organisation by selling and billing for

services that are not required from the senior managers' perspective.

2. Another motive is for the senior manager to gain rapid access to high-calibre resources and skills. For example, if a situation arises and the organisation needs external, mostly expert support quickly, having a good rapport with an advisor and their firm will be useful in getting the right resources speedily and without many complications. To fill a knowledge and resource gap are two very prominent 'project or service trajectory' aspects mentioned by senior executives.

3. A number of senior managers cited free advice and guidance as something they looked for from an advisor. This might entail simply looking through in-house prepared regulatory-driven response documents and providing feedback, or possibly a small free-of-charge project to test or validate a senior executive's idea before it is taken further internally, which might or might not turn into a fee-earning project for the advisory firm. Depending on the level of intimacy, some senior managers also look for more personal advice on their careers, possibly linked to progression within the organisation or outside.

4. This leads straight to the next motive: tapping into the advisor and advisory firm's network and asking the advisor to build bridges, either driven by a personal agenda (potential career opportunities) or for the benefit of the organisation. This could be in the form of some type of collaboration with the advisor's other clients, facilitating joint ventures, and managing dialogue with industry and regulatory bodies.

5. Closely related to the network are insights and knowledge as underlying motivations for regular dialogue. This could be technical knowledge relating to the industry or competence-specific aspects such as research and benchmarking reports. It could also be more general insights as to what is going on within an industry and other comparable organisations: what are they struggling with and how are they coping with certain issues? Of course, all of these insights are shared in confidence, which comes with a silver lining, which I will explain further on in this section.

6. Another motive is for the advisor to shoulder some of the responsibilities for the senior manager, which could be in the form of the advisor preparing and prepping the senior advisor for important meetings or the advisor presenting the material on behalf of the senior executive and potentially even

defending a particular position in a boardroom debate. In this case, the advisor is acting as an expert to give weight to an argument as an assurance (an expert has been consulted) or to even protect the senior manager from any potential critique.

7.   Lastly, a number of senior executives liked meeting with advisors or senior representatives of the advisory firm simply because *'it makes them feel important – it appeals to their ego that the advisor is spending time with them, making them a priority',* which is an interesting motive that was mentioned first and foremost by less senior respondents. It referred to the COO reporting to the CFO, who is keen to gather insights from conversations the advisor has had with more senior stakeholders in the organisation, and very senior respondents, such as a group CEO who referred to regular coffee meetings between him and another 'Big Four' firm's CEO.

Since a relationship is, most of the time, a reciprocal arrangement, and to complete my review of client-advisor interactions, I decided to add the advisor perspective in this discussion by drawing on my memos and personal observations: The lists above summarised what a senior manager might be looking for in the 'client-advisor rapport' and why. So what do the advisor and the advisory firm aim to achieve and get out of the rapport or relationship with the senior executive? Based on my experiences over the past four years, I have observed and taken note of four key benefits from an advisor or advisory firm perspective:

- On top of the list is, of course, the opportunity of steering and influencing the senior executives' and the organisations' selection and appointment decisions. By having a close rapport, the advisor and the advisory firm hope to be in a position to instigate projects by proposing ideas to senior managers to possibly secure an appointment in a 'non-compete' set up, meaning that the decision-maker will appoint the advisory firm without going through a competitive tender process. Alternatively, in the event of a competitive tender, they hope to gain valuable insights, and possibly advice, from the senior manager as to how the selection and appointment decision-making process will unfold in order to prepare the advisory firm's response accordingly. The positive appointment decision leads, needless to say, to additional revenue and profits for the advisory firm and the advisor (especially since he or she is a partner), as well as firm-wide recognition for the advisor and the account team. Securing projects in a non-compete situation is principally favoured by advisory firms and advisors. Responding to competitive tenders is a costly undertaking for the firm; producing a response document and preparing for a pitch presentation can involve numerous staff over long periods of time and production costs can be high, involving glossy documents, clever pitch videos presented on mobile devices, or even on-site visits to demonstrate certain technical solutions. For many professional services advisors, securing billable engagements in a non-competitive context is a badge of honour and a sign that they are indeed the preferred and 'trusted advisor' to the senior manager.

- In general, having a 'close' relationship with senior executives is something to aspire to, as it generates status and recognition within the advisory firm for the advisor. As part of the background description in Chapter One, I mentioned CXO-penetration as one of the recurrently applied internal measures. Being able to demonstrate a close rapport with a senior stakeholder generates significant internal benefits for the advisor.

- For an advisor to add a senior executive of a large organisation to their network also garners external benefits, elevating the advisor's standing in the business community and making him or her more attractive to other client contacts who would like to be connected to this senior manager.

- Furthermore, the senior executive might share with the advisor information and insights, in confidence, which are of immense benefit to the advisor as well as the firm. Although this is a sensitive topic, and I will pick up on this issue later on the section, these insights are being processed within the advisory firm, which is of course adhering to regulatory and ethical guidelines defined and enforced by the firm, and are being shared in appropriate formats, such as industry reports, with other clients.

Overall the 'client-advisor' rapport is multifaceted, reciprocal and rather complex. Both sides pursue personal and organisational motives and try to secure a number of benefits in exchange and as part of the interactions. Communications might not always be straightforward and honest on either side owing to fear of 'unsettling' the other party. For instance, a number of senior executives openly mentioned during the client feedback interviews that they either were 'not in a position to spend more money on advisors', mostly due to organisational constraints or that they consistently delegated all selection and appointment decisions to direct reports. Consequently, they were not really in a position to actively and positively influence a selection and appointment decision for the advisor.

Instead of communicating these facts overtly, they chose to emphasise in the client feedback interviews that they especially appreciated the relationship constituent and frequently requested additional knowledge and insights from the advisor and advisory firm. Stepping away from the coded scenarios and reflecting on these observations, to some extent it appears as if senior executives might not want to communicate their limited decision-making reach, in fear of unbalancing the rapport – the senior manager is keen to retain and keep the 'client-advisor relationship' progressing. On reflection, I was pondering if the increased demand for insights and thought leadership noted by the firm in the past five years might possibly be a function of this situation: clients want to maintain a dialogue and make use of the relationship benefits, but are effectively not in a position to commission professional services, and therefore utilise the thought leadership debate as a way to stay engaged with a number of advisors.

Senior executives' narratives showed that gaining access to industry and competitive insights was probably one of the biggest incentives for some of the senior managers, albeit not all. Obtaining insights into what other organisations, possibly competitors, are currently doing: which challenges they discuss, how they are overcoming these challenges, how successful they are and how they achieve these successes, as well as how the senior executive's organisation compares to the other companies in the market, is an interesting proposition to a number of senior executives. Firm internal observations captured in my memos suggest that these insights are amassed by, most likely, other advisors of the advisory firm, or a research department, and then processed by a knowledge management unit within the organisation or even shared informally between individuals, depending on circumstances and within set regulatory and ethical guidelines. Senior executives were, of course, aware of and made reference to these arrangements, and thus there is a silver lining attached to these insights, which in effect turns into a type of game from a senior manager's perspective: to reveal little or just enough to the advisor, but to gather as much insight and competitor information as possible in return. Based on my past experience, I am aware that some organisations categorically step out of this cycle. For instance, one of the life sciences companies I worked for was neither keen on personnel who had worked on competitors' projects, nor interested in material which summarised competitor activities. Even within the sample population, a number of senior executives were very sceptical of the notion of such insights and challenged their value.

Concluding remarks for this section

The 'client-advisor rapport' is reciprocal and complex and constitutes and informs the senior executive's interactions with the advisor and advisory firm. Even though the senior executive-advisor relationship or rapport can be an integral part of the selection and appointment decision, it could be seen as a separate stand-alone paradigm and should not be seen as simply a pathway to secure a project or sell professional services, even though this is frequently the primary reason or benefit cited by the advisor. There are a number of different motives and benefits that each side might aim for as part of this exchange paradigm. From a senior executive's point of view, the 'client-advisor rapport' is mainly determined by personal imperatives, although at times organisational context and constraints can significantly alter this arrangement.

An evolution of the 'client-advisor rapport' is the notion of a 'trusted advisor', which is commonly referred to, discussed and aspired to within the 'Big Four' firm where I am employed and in the professional services industry more widely. The concept of a preferred or 'trusted advisor' has only been mentioned explicitly by one senior executive describing his rapport with a lawyer and a law firm. Elements of a trusted advisor notion are somewhat present in the imperative – general expectation code 'earn my trust and bat for me …' – and in the benefits sought – 'sharing the pain and responsibilities of a project'. This led me to contemplate and question to what degree this construct is really requested and determined by the client.

Could it be that over the years the professional service industry has created the construct of a 'trusted advisor' and by communicating the idea repeatedly and widely, installed the notion in receptive clients? The 'trusted advisor concept' is frequently linked with the proposition or promise of delivering value add or providing value beyond project context. Interestingly, I only found these aspects in the 'imperatives' constituent general expectations of an advisor and not overtly in project-specific 'benefits sought'. It would be of interest to explore the underlying drivers of these notions, although I am inclined to speculate that the main impetus for these constructs is of a self-serving nature for the advisor and advisory firm, driven by a quest to distinguish the firm's presence and offering in the marketplace. Perhaps as part of the literature review, these questions can be addressed and clarified.

6.4 Project or service-specific 'selection and appointment decisions'

The second decision-making process, i.e. to select and appoint a professional advisor for a particular service, is a binary choice (appoint or not appoint) with a concrete outcome at a certain point in time. The outcome is an agreement to deliver a specific service or project. It is a formal understanding between the organisation and the advisory firm, compared to the primarily personal decision of the senior executive to develop and maintain a rapport with an advisor or advisory firm. This level of formality and the elevation to an organisational choice permeates into the decision making.

Project-specific 'trajectory or benefits sought' and 'selection and choice actions' actively drive the selection and appointment decision. Past experiences and organisational context are pivotal influences and to a certain degree imperatives and the 'client-advisor rapport' feature in this second decision-making process. In the next section of this chapter, I discuss in more detail the links between the two identified decision-making processes. At this point, I would like to mention that for some, not all, senior executives, having an ongoing rapport with their advisory firm is a prerequisite and assumed, which is captured in the selection behaviour code 'existing relationships act as a screening mechanism'. However, it is important to note that senior executives and their organisations frequently maintain a rapport with many professional service firms; this is often also determined by procurement and supplier management agendas. Imperatives and the associated 'client-advisor rapport' are an integral part of the selection and appointment decision and are reflected in a number of the 'selection and choice actions', but in the decision-making landscape it is probably a less prominent constituent.

6.4.1 'Project or service trajectory' and key influencers

'Project or service trajectory' is the driving conceptual framework component for the selection and appointment decision. Project triggers, goals and objectives are key influencers of how the selection and appointment decision will unfold. Each project is different, some more so than others, and circumstances might change and will, therefore, call for unique decision-making processes. Even while a tender or selection process is underway, goals and objectives may change, and these adjustments will most likely pervade into the 'selection and choice actions' employed.

During the data analysis, I uncovered three somewhat equally present triggers – an impetus for a project or a demand for professional services;

regulation, requests from the board or superiors; and operational response, which was primarily driven by the senior executive or his or her team. Objectives and goals can be broken down into two subcategories: the type of project or services sought, and which supporting goals are being targeted. A project or a service agreement to deliver an output, for example, to deploy a technology, or to install revised operational processes, and to provide advice and guidance at the same time, was the project type most commonly mentioned during the interviews. Advice-only projects were less frequently cited, while free-of-charge work and being, or better becoming, part of the organisational eco-system were only sporadically mentioned. Other supporting goals were aspects such as 'filling resource or knowledge gaps', 'teach and empower us', 'tailored approach', 'guarantee for success' and so on, where filling a resource and a knowledge gap were the most repeatedly mentioned project and service trajectories. It is important to keep in mind that these 'project or service trajectories' were mentioned by senior executives in the context of engaging with a 'Big Four' advisory firm; I would anticipate a different distribution of benefits to feature in the context of, for example, law firms or tech companies. Tech companies such as IBM or SAP tend to offer services aligned to technical products which require some advice (which one to select and how to deploy them). The primary focus of the services is to assist clients with installing and operationalising these new products, thus the emphasis is more on delivering services than providing advice.

In summary, with the help of the Nvivo clustering tool, I was able to identify five project or service trajectory patterns, asking the advisory firm to:

1. 'Fill our internal gaps and deliver as agreed' (most common request)
2. 'Pragmatic and collaborative working, paired up with free advice'
3. 'Use the right interpersonal skills to teach an empower us'
4. 'Be embedded in the organisation and share the pain and responsibilities'
5. 'Help manage regulatory bodies and deadlines, make sure it is a success'

On reflection, I was surprised by the lack of tangible or measurable target definitions. For regulatory-driven assignments, the primary aim was of course to satisfy the regulator, and by addressing regulatory demands the project achieved its ultimate goal. However, senior executives felt that there was little value to the organisation, except of course the fact that the organisation would not get fined by the regulator and business operations would not be disrupted. Beyond the regulatory debate, only two senior executives spoke of achieving tangible goals in the form of organisational KPIs (key performance indicators). While many senior managers were happy to make general statements to the effect that the professional services delivered the results they were looking for, most likely based on some general evaluation or gut feeling, numerous other senior executives circumnavigated the value for money discussion by either engaging in a general debate about the value for money concept or by focusing the commentary on pricing, lamenting that the advisory firm or all advisory firms were too expensive. These data points led me to believe that a concrete and measurable definition of goals and benefits and how to assess these after a project are maybe not as commonly discussed between senior executives and advisors as one would assume. It is certainly a difficult task and the senior executive and the project team might feel overwhelmed or struggle to define these goals independently, or possibly the time pressures are so immense that this aspect is recurrently pushed to the side. Nevertheless, why does the advisor not make a stronger effort to force this debate? Again, maybe there are time constraints, or they may be too eager to get a project started, but assessing or measuring the outcomes and outputs of a project might create some uncomfortable and unfavourable situations for the advisor and the advisory firm. Perhaps certain findings in the literature review will shed some light on these considerations.

Concluding remarks for this section

Some of the 'project and service trajectories' translate into selection criteria such as the skills and expertise of individuals, relevant experiences and track record, proposition and approach as part of the 'selection and choice actions'. In retrospect, and informed by a firm internal analysis of win-loss reviews I conducted in parallel, I anticipated more apparent links between 'project and service trajectory' and 'selection and choice actions'. The lack of clear connecting indicators is probably due to the type and format of the interviews. Senior executives only occasionally recounted a particular project and the selection and appointment process. Also, in the case of a group decision, senior managers might not have been so closely involved in the actual process, which was often handled by procurement. There is definitely scope for more research in the future, mapping from project goals and objectives to selection and choice actions, possibly based on win-loss reviews. However, such an exercise would probably capture more formal or rational selection processes or group or panel decisions managed by a decision-making facilitator such as procurement.

6.4.2 'Selection and choice actions' aim to deliver the 'project or service trajectory'

In addition to 'project or service trajectory' as part of the planned project, the actual choice process is largely determined by the component 'selection and choice actions', which encompasses selection mode and approach, selection behaviours or protocols and selection criteria. As indicated above, I have detected some links to triggers, objectives and goals as part of the 'project or service trajectory'; however, no clear patterns emerged from the dataset. The two influencing constituents – past experiences and organisational constraints – also come to bear, as well as the general ongoing relationship that the client has with the advisor.

The starting point of the 'selection and choice actions' is the selection mode (determining who makes the decision) and the general selection approach (how in principle the selection is going to be made); here, I found a number of interdependencies:

- The senior executives' generic role appeared to inform the selection mode chosen. For instance, CEOs were more inclined to delegate selection responsibilities to direct reports or teams. Senior executives with very far-reaching organisational domains, such as CFOs, tended to use different selection modes depending on the project or services in question. For example, the CFO would always delegate appointment decisions for a subdomain such as tax to the head of tax; large projects would call for a group decision involving a number of key individuals, whereas if a small project or initiative was of personal importance to the CFO, he or she might make a decision personally and directly.
- Organisational context in the form of procurement protocols or a lack thereof. Senior executives spoke of some basic rules, which were reflected in the selection practices. This involved large projects going out to tender and following structured and often panelled decision-making process; small projects had no fixed guidelines. The two respondents who actively supported (and also created) their supplier management programme referred to a take-on process whereby the professional services

firm was included in the strategic supplier programme, and with that, the firm would subsequently be added to the choice set. If no procurement guidelines were in place or were not sufficiently enforced, senior executives were free to choose how and who would select an external partner for a project.

- The personal principles and preferences of the senior executive championing the project also came into effect; these were often further manifested in the general selection approach commentary. Some senior managers leaned towards a more rational or structured decision-making approach, also present in the selection behaviour 'select advisor or advisory firm purely on merit'. Other senior executives tended towards a more ad hoc or intuitive selection approach. Interestingly, this intuitive selection approach coincided quite frequently with the selection mode to 'personally drive the selection of advisors or firms' in organisational contexts where there were no or weak procurement protocols.

Selection behaviour or practices refer to how the process unfolds and how the selection criteria are applied, whereas the selection criteria are used to evaluate an offering of an advisory firm and are often found as part of a scoring mechanism, either documented or kept in mental storage.

Recalling experiences of the win-loss reviews I have conducted in the past, it seems to me that advisors and advisory firms, as well as procurement staff, tend to focus on selection criteria. Selection behaviour and practices have only been intermittently discussed, but I would argue based on the empirical findings that they are equally important. The widely cited selection behaviours listed below were key incentives to the development of the leitmotif matrix:

- 'established relationships serve as a screening mechanism',
- 'continuity creates efficiency and better results'
- 'it is not good to be too reliant on advisors for everything'
- 'balance advisors – avoid overreliance'.

As I mentioned previously, having an established relationship acts as a screening mechanism, although a number of professional service firms will have a rapport with the organisation. Beyond the screening aspect, the selection behaviours and criteria clearly point towards a four-pronged underlying pattern – the leitmotif decision-making matrix:

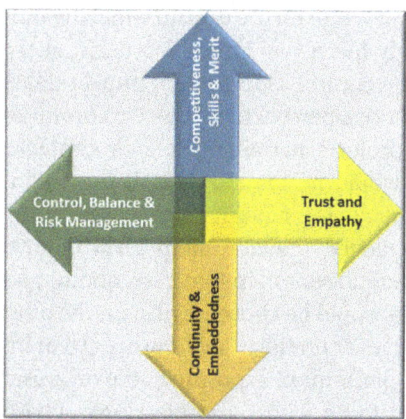

Figure 6.4 – Leitmotif decision-making matrix

Initially, I interpreted the observed patterns as a type of selection dichotomy, whereby the decision-maker would have to weigh up certain dimensions – trust, competitiveness, continuity and control – which evolved over time into the leitmotif decision-making matrix presented in Figure 7.4 above. The following scenarios aim to explain the model:

A large number of senior executives confirmed in their interview narratives that 'continuity' created strong benefits, meaning working with an advisor or advisory firm that they had worked with in the past, had good experiences with or maybe who had completed a first phase of a project or a related project. According to the senior executives, this particular advisory firm had the advantage of: a) possibly knowing the challenges and subject matter expertise relevant to the project; and also, b) knowing their way around the organisation – stakeholders, internal processes etc. Selecting and appointing this advisory firm would be fairly straightforward in terms of getting them up to speed and making contractual and other arrangements; furthermore, there would be fewer risks of delays, confusion and impact on business continuity. At the same time, the decision-maker would be keen to get the best professional service firm for the job from a general skills and knowledge point of view, but also in terms of general competitiveness and price. If a different professional services firm offered a better team and better skills and knowledge, having done the same project for another organisation, or was offering a more attractive pricing arrangement, what would happen then? The decision-maker(s) would have to rethink and balance priorities: 'continuity and embeddedness' versus 'competitiveness, merit and skills'.

Two other dimensions might come into effect as well in this scenario. Control in the form of monitoring and balancing advisors is another dimension which will weigh on the decision-making thought process. If an advisory firm already has a very strong footprint, in terms of projects, in the organisation, the control aspect might impact the selection outcome. For example, from a risk perspective, the decision-maker might conclude that awarding all projects pertaining to one strategic initiative to one external company would be too risky. Or, if the organisation follows an internal policy of balancing advisors, this could mean that an advisory firm might have reached the maximum level of involvement deemed appropriate by the organisation. In that case, another advisory firm with a comparable offering would be chosen. Trust, on the other hand, could also be a dominant influencer on the thought process. For instance, if a project is deemed high-risk in terms of exposure to the organisation, the decision-maker(s) might opt to go with the professional advisory firm that they place the most trust in to deliver or manage the project sensitively, even though this firm might not have put forward the most competitive offering or is not yet embedded within the organisation.

Concluding remarks for this section

It is important to keep in mind that individuals who make selection decisions need to be prepared to substantiate their choice rationale to others. Of course, if a senior manager makes a direct decision and it is a small project, the decision rationale will not be documented as such. However, group or panel decisions will most likely follow a structured process, which includes evaluating competing offerings with a set selection criteria and possibly having an open debate to facilitate consensus. Individuals involved in the decision-making process might steer or have a bias towards one firm versus another (possibly from more positive past experiences or a stronger rapport), but they still need to justify their views to the other decision-makers in the group. The same holds true in the case of an individual making a direct decision – he or she needs to be able to articulate a cohesive choice rationale when questioned, for example, by the board or another senior figure.

6.5 Linking rapport and appointment decisions

The overall aim of this study is to investigate inductively and systematically the interactions between professional advisors and senior executive clients, with an emphasis on the decision-making process of these senior executives regarding relating to, selecting and appointing advisors.

As a result of this research, two overarching models, Figure 6.4 (the leitmotif decision-making matrix) and Figure 6.2 (the two decision processes mapped to the conceptual framework) have emerged, which summarise the proposed substantive theory. Senior executives' decision-making takes place in a multidimensional and interactive landscape consisting of past experiences, organisational context, 'imperatives' and project-specific 'project and service trajectory' and 'selection and choice actions'. This decision-making process is guided by a type of internal decision-making matrix, which the senior manager operates based on circumstances, in order to align his or her decision-making with the help of four indicative leitmotifs; the senior executive focus and navigates the matrix depending on the type of decision either concentrating on a specific project or the ongoing rapport.

The matrix configurations for 'rapport or relationship decisions' and project-specific 'selection and appointment decisions' were found to be distinctively different for each respondent. On average, the matrix appears to be more level or balanced in regards to 'rapport or relationship decisions', although certain senior executives tended to lean towards 'trust and empathy' or 'control and managed'. The consolidated matrix configuration for 'selection and appointment decisions' was more pronounced in particular directions depending on the senior executives' commentary. Please refer to Chapter Five for a detailed discussion.

These two distinct matrix configurations confirm the already observed phenomena of two decision-making processes: the primarily personal decision of the senior executive to develop and maintain an ongoing rapport with an advisor and advisory firm; and the decision by the senior manager or someone else on behalf of the organisation to select and appoint or not appoint (binary) an advisor or advisory firm for a particular service.

6.5.1 Interdependencies between rapport and appointment decision processes

The study has observed some links between the two separate decision processes, described above. First of all, relationship or rapport-related aspects can be found in 'selection and choice actions'. The following two notions stand out in particular:

- 'Established relationships serve as a screening mechanism' was mentioned by 15 of the 21 senior executives as a selection behaviour.
- 'Legacy or established relationships' was cited by nine of the 21 senior managers as a selection criteria.

Secondly, the interview comments clearly indicated that the overall rapport or relationship with the advisor provides a backdrop to the selection and appointment decision process, most notably in the form of past experiences which shape the associations or views the senior executive might hold in regards to the advisor and the firm. To that effect, the resulting 'client-advisor rapport' informs the selection and appointment decision, just as organisational context and past experiences do as part of the underlying decision-making landscape.

Furthermore, the 'selection and appointment decision' can in turn also influence the 'client-advisor rapport' both positively and negatively. For instance, during one of the win-loss reviews I encountered the following situation: a large multi-million pound technology implementation programme was at the end of a lengthy tender that was awarded to another advisory firm. The two partners who lost out on the deal were, of course, disappointed and requested a meeting with the CIO, with whom they did not necessarily have a very close relationship, to discuss the outcome of the tender. This was despite that fact that the CIO had delegated the decision-making to a group of middle managers. It was clear from the partners' comments that they aimed to challenge the appointment decision in the planned conversation. The CIO repeatedly cancelled the requested meeting before calling it off completely. Needless to say, the rapport did not improve.

Overall the impact of the 'client-advisor rapport' will vary from appointment decision to appointment decision. In summary, I took note of the following key observations while reflecting on the research findings pertaining to the 'client-advisor rapport':

- Not every senior executive who has a relationship or rapport with the advisor is actively involved in the selection and appointment decision-making process, as in the scenario discussed above.
- Moreover, CEOs in particular expressed interest in maintaining a rapport with the advisor, but then also clarified that they would not get directly involved in the selection process (delegating this task to someone else), and would remain impartial, either out of respect for their direct reports who effectively owned the selection and appointment process (disempowering) or by seeing themselves as a guardian who oversees the use of advisors (primarily in those organisations which aim to balance advisors). Therefore, these client executives on a personal level only actively engaged in the first

decision-making process (rapport with an advisor) and took on a more removed or monitoring role in the second decision-making process (selection and appointment of advisors).

- Only one respondent tried to indirectly influence the selection process by giving the advisor physical access to the organisation (office) or by providing insights or tips as to what would be important to achieve a positive outcome.

- Otherwise there was consensus amongst senior managers that significant engagements either from a scope, budget or visibility point of view should ideally go through a competitive tender, accompanied by a structured and transparent decision-making process facilitated by an internal resource; this indicates a more formal decision-making process, as indicated in the selection and appointment decision-making process described (2nd decision process).

- An active, positive 'client-advisor rapport' appeared to frequently secure a spot in the choice set regarding who the tender request would be issued to. In other words, the first decision-making process relating to establishing rapport could have a positive impact, in that the advisor would be asked to submit a tender for a particular project or programme, but was not viewed as a key criterion informing the second decision-making process – the actual selection and appointment of an advisor or advisory firm to deliver the project.

- For an advisory firm to be physically present and embedded in an organisation, either via project work or a general close rapport, speed was a key concern in terms of getting projects started quickly. Being present, and having an active or live rapport, was shown to be beneficial in terms of being considered and asked to submit a tender for a project. However, being present does not always lead to a positive outcome in the second decision-making process, unless of course continuity and embeddedness is a key influencing motive in the decision-making.

- Small projects and free-of-charge work are on average less exposed to organisational scrutiny and, therefore, the decision-maker has scope for a more informal decision-making approach. Depending on the senior managers' preferences, a positive rapport might then become the driving force for selection, and might even act as a trigger for project needs in the first place. In this instance, the rapport and the selection decision-making process is closely aligned.

In summary, the 'client-advisor rapport' will feature from time to time in some shape or form in the selection and appointment decision process. However, I would argue that past experiences, which also inform the rapport decision-making, are important and prevailing influencers. Managing project and rapport experiences proactively should be of the utmost importance to a successful advisory firm and advisor. This is not always the case. Frequently, I have observed a strong firm-wide focus on managing and supporting the client relationship, often administered by marketing-type functions. Project experiences, particularly towards the end of an engagement, do not appear to receive the same level of attention and support, which often leads to rather negative comments in client feedback interviews. Ironically, these project experiences can become a key determinant for the advisory firm's future success or failure in selection and appointment decisions in future, and perhaps more mundane, projects.

6.5.2 Scope to widen the decision-making agenda

I believe that the 'client-rapport' should not be seen as a means to an end – helping the advisor to place and sell new services in exchange for personal favours and insights – but a value-generating paradigm for all four parties involved: the senior executive, the client organisation, the advisor and the advisory firm. Casting aside the selection and appointment decision, it becomes apparent that the most important output of the 'client-advisor rapport' is essentially knowledge exchange and opportunities for networking, ideally not just for the senior executive and the advisor but also for the two organisations behind the two individuals. Distancing the 'client-advisor relationship', or at least parts of it, from a pure marketing and sales agenda, and viewing and supporting it from a knowledge management and market presence perspective might help to generate new benefits and bring about tremendous change. Concurrently, it is important to acknowledge that the present study has uncovered that there are senior executives and organisations who do not want to participate in and contribute to this paradigm for various reasons, but who are still interested in transacting and receiving project-specific services from the advisor and advisory firm. It is pivotal that the advisor and advisory firm understands this position and respect it.

While writing down these thoughts, a particular discussion in Julie Gore's article (2006) comes to mind. Julie Gore (2006, page 927) describes two distinct paths which developed within NDM inquiry: the first path is focused on exploring *"what people do wrong and offering suggestions for improving decision making"*. Daniel Kahneman and colleagues (2011) are mentioned as the proponents of this view. The second path looks at *"what people do right"* and uses *"close examination of heuristics and expertise in order to learn more powerful heuristics"*. Pliske and Klein (2003) are cited as the originator of this thought path.

Reflecting on the outcomes of my study so far, I am not quite sure where to place my research project and its contributions. Overall, as part of this study, I have tried to understand what people do, regardless of right or wrong. By simply understanding decision-making processes and different perspectives taken, I was hoping to be able to create a mutually more beneficial and respectful decision-making environment. Instead of different stakeholders trying to use the knowledge gained to manipulate or shape decision outcomes to their advantage, I would hope to promote a more understanding and supportive environment from which everyone involved is able to benefit.

6.6 Pointers for the literature review

Since the research is based on a constructivist grounded theory approach (Charmaz 2006), I decided to follow grounded theory recommendations (Bryant 2012, Charmaz 2006, Goulding 2002) and deferred the review of other literature in the field until the emerging substantive theory of my study was on a somewhat sound footing. The main point for this deferral was to ensure that the literature would not influence or even force the emerging theory.

Kathy Charmaz (2006) recommends to focus on the most significant literature in relation to aspects addressed in the emerging and now developed grounded theory and to analyse and critique the literature from this particular angle.

Consequently, the objective of this study's literature review is to enrich, supplement, expand or challenge the research findings and the proposed substantive theory. I was aiming for a focused review of the literature, concentrating exclusively on material that responds to my research aim and falls within the remit of professional services. I am conscious that with this approach I might miss some interesting concepts which could have taken the debate further. At the same time, the professional advisor context is rather complex and unique, and it would be difficult to extrapolate which aspects of, for example, a consumer business study could be realistically transferred to this context.

Throughout this chapter I have made reference to how additional findings, either in existing literature or via future research activities, could enhance and support the debate of this research project. As part of the literature review, I aimed to investigate specifically studies or peer reviewed opinions concentrating on the following:

- Senior manager and advisor relationships, in particular, the 'trusted advisor' concept
- Reputations and branding of professional services firms and their impact on buying behaviours
- Organisational buying of professional services
- Impact of past experiences on professional services' relationships and buying behaviours.

With these four focus areas, I intended to stay as close as possible to the original research aims – focusing on the interactions between professional advisors and senior executive clients, with an emphasis on the decision-making process of these senior executives when it comes to relating, selecting and appointing advisors – and the emerging substantive theory and models discussed in this chapter. In Chapter Seven, which is dedicated to the literature in the field, I describe how I approached the literature review, and summarise and discuss the findings.

Chapter 7

Comparison of emerging theory with literature findings; discussion and reflection

In this chapter, I discuss the approach I have taken and the findings of my review of the literature in the field, mainly relevant peer-reviewed articles investigating the same or similar phenomena. Furthermore, I map and elaborate on the literature findings vis-à-vis the empirically informed substantive theories which have so far emerged as part of this research.

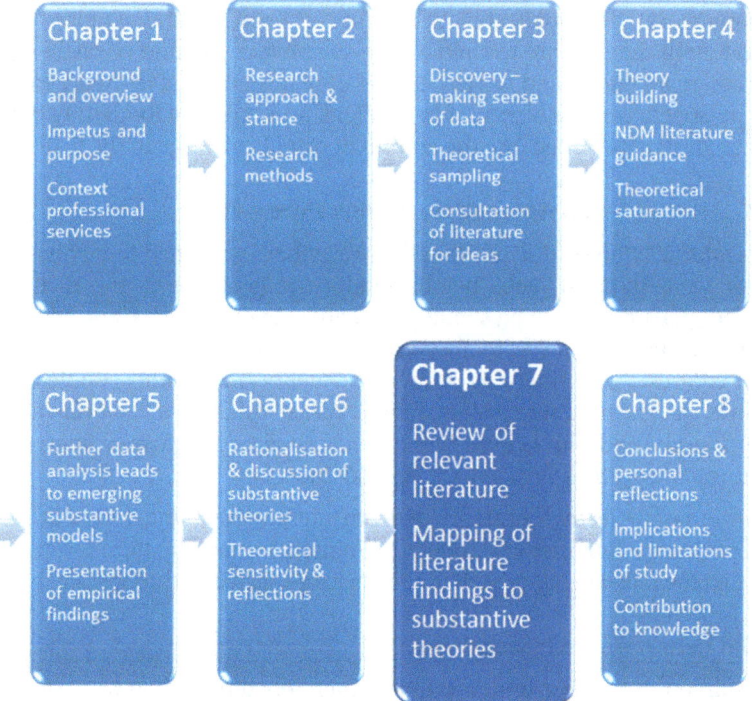

Figure 7.1 – Overview of thesis structure and content of the seventh chapter

The literature review was an ongoing phase of reflexivity as part of the research, although it is listed here as a separate chapter. In constructivist grounded theory research, existing literature is not primarily used as a theoretical background, but should rather be viewed as an additional data source to be included predominantly during later stages of the reiterative, reflective analysis (Charmaz 2006, 2008, Bryant and Charmaz 2007). Grounded theorists should validate and complete emerging concepts by collating further data (Goulding 2002), which should also include data extracted from existing literature (Charmaz 2006). Charmaz (2006, page 165) states that *"the intended purpose of delaying the literature review is to avoid importing preconceived ideas and imposing them on your work"*. By delaying the literature review, the researcher creates an intellectual space to develop and articulate their own unique ideas.

As part of this research project, I started to draw on the general decision-making literature after the initial discovery stage, to help me understand the observed phenomena in the empirical data (Chapter Three). It also provided new perspectives and ideas to devise and develop a conceptual framework (the theory-building stage described in Chapter Four).

At this stage, having rationalised and reflected on the emerging theory (Chapter Six), the main objectives for reviewing and including the literature in the field are twofold: firstly, to enhance, support or challenge the emerging theory and to view and analyse the substantive theory from the perspective of the literature in the field, and secondly to identify how this study can be placed into the current body of knowledge in the field.

7.1 Approach to the literature review

Charmaz (2006) recommends that the researcher's grounded theory has to be there in the first place before adding the literature in the field as another perspective, which should help conclude the analysis. She advises using the literature review to investigate relevant publications, to compare and contrast the emerging grounded theory to existing bodies of knowledge. The literature review should *"position your study and clarify its contribution"* and *"reveal gaps in the extant knowledge and state how your grounded theory answers them"*. (Charmaz 2006, page 168).

With these objectives in mind, and considering the points raised at the end of the previous chapter under 6.6 'Pointers for the literature review', I applied the following approach to the literature search and analysis.

7.1.1 Literature search boundaries

In addition to the four topical pointers mentioned in section 6.6 – senior executive-advisor relationships, reputations and branding of professional services firms and their impact on buying behaviours, organisational buying of professional services and impact of past experiences on professional services' relationships and buying behaviours – the scope of this literature review included primarily peer-reviewed articles pertaining to professional services.

I decided not to include empirical research that focuses on the public sector since relationships with public sector senior managers were beyond the scope of the study and I did not conduct or include relationship interviews with public sector clients.

Furthermore, I also chose not to include discussions of general leadership and team dynamics or management, unless the research explicitly included external professional advisors.

7.1.2 Literature search

Following the theory rationalisation described in Chapter Six, I reflected on the emerging concepts and categories from the transcripts of the interviews, my memos, observations and ethnographic experiences. In doing so, I put together the subsequent list of search terms:

Professional services		Relationship
Professional service firm		Decision-making
Professional advisor		Choice
Consultancy		Selection
Consultant		Appointment
Professional partnership	+	Interactions
		Buying or purchasing
		Experiences
		Project outcomes
		Brand
		Reputation

Table 7.1 – Literature search terms

The data sources for the literature review were Web of Science, Google Scholar, ProQuest, EBSCO and Emerald. Employing the above-listed search terms and combinations of terms, I found that there were three primary debates in the literature: concentrating on relationship management and marketing; marketing measures or constructs such as loyalty and satisfaction; and purchasing or procurement of services.

After organising and assigning the first wave of papers to the three debates, I investigated each area in more detail. From then on, I followed a type of 'snowball' search approach, looking up relevant studies cited in the peer-reviewed articles or tracing citations of especially pertinent research. There were numerous articles which were interesting, but did not quite apply to my research focus and objectives for the literature review as described above. Over time, a state of saturation set in. I did find new studies and articles, but they did not provide any new ideas or findings, and at that stage I decided to conclude the active literature search. I believe that the 25 studies I examined in detail provide a comprehensive and thorough view of the literature, albeit I am conscious that this is by no means a systematic and exhaustive review of all of the literature available.

7.1.3 Grounded theory and naturalistic decision-making literature

In addition to the literature search outlined above, I conducted further literature searches to confirm that no studies had been missed that were comparable from a methodological point of view. Queries of the databases Web of Science, EBSCO, Emerald and ProQuest for the keywords 'professional services' combined with 'grounded theory' retrieved a handful of articles pertaining to the field of business; there were also numerous medical or health care-related studies. The results are listed in the bibliography; I took note of three studies concentrating on human resources and gender (Kokot 2015, van Rooij and Merkebu 2015, Fischer et al. 2014), one research project exploring change readiness and knowledge sharing (Rusly et al. 2014), one study concerned with professional accountants acting for small and medium enterprises in Iran (Kamyabi and Devi 2012) and a further study investigating the advisor relationships with non-paying clients (McColl-Kennedy et al. 2015). When I combined 'professional services' and 'naturalistic decision-making or image theory', I located only one research project, which examined branding and brand recognition for audit firms and screening of clients (Asare 1996). Moreover, in Lee Roy Beach's book *Decision-making in the Workplace* (Beach 2014), I found two studies making use of Image Theory in regard to auditing decisions made by audit firms within the context of the audit and the screening or take-on process of new clients by audit firms. Although these two topics are somewhat related and part of the 'Big Four' domain, external audit, as I mentioned earlier, is very distinct compared to the advisory business and was not within the scope of this research.

In summary, although I found some literature discussing the use of grounded theory or naturalistic decision-making in the context of professional services, there were not many.

7.2 Overview of literature findings

In line with grounded theory recommendations (Charmaz 2006, Bryant and Charmaz 2007, Goulding 2002), my overall aim was to absorb the key concepts and debates in the literature regarding my research topic and, therefore, I was keen to take stock of the wider breadth or reach of the literature. By closely analysing the literature review sections of the selected articles, I was able to take in the depth of the discussions and the different viewpoints within those.

7.2.1 Key debates in the literature

While reviewing the different articles, I identified two principal concurrent debates within the management literature: one discussion located within the marketing discipline and the other in the business operations and purchasing domain. The marketing debate focused primarily on the individual client-advisor interactions or relationships and corresponding measures and concepts associated with these constructs; these were labelled as relationship management or relationship marketing regarding professional services. This debate overlaps significantly with the first decision-making process identified in my research, which leads to a rapport or relationship between client and advisor. Whereas the operational dialogue emphasised the role of the organisation and organisational functions relating to procurement set-ups or purchasing criteria of professional services, new organisational models such as preferred or strategic supplier programmes were also examined. The discussion pertaining to this body of literature has significant overlaps with the second decision-making process which emerged from my analysis, resulting in the selection and appointment of an advisor or advisory firm.

I also read a number of practitioner books, articles and studies; I included three of these in the detailed analysis: an insightful study commissioned by the Financial Times (Financial Times, Managing Partners Forum and Meridian West 2012), David Maisters' *Managing the Professional Service Firm* (Maister 2007), which is written from an external or client perspective, and a type of how-to guide for consultants titled *Guerrilla Marketing for Consultants* by Levinson and McLaughlin (2011). Other works consulted are prescriptive or directive, even including checklists either for the client buyer or the consultant or advisor seller; others are personal accounts of experiences.

Besides the two debates mentioned above, relationship management and organisational purchasing, I found references to the role of advisors as part of an organisation's strategic decision-making, as well as how top management teams and in particular CEOs interact and make decisions. Advisors in this case could be a number of different individuals and also professional advisors such as a partner from a 'Big Four' firm – the actors in my research.

7.2.2 Summary of literature findings

Table 7.2 presents the literature overview and findings and sums up the attributes and key concepts that I was able to understand from my engagement with the literature. The literature findings presented in the table can be mapped to the two identified decision-making processes as indicated above: 'relationship' marked literature is primarily aligned to the first decision-making process (to develop and or maintain a rapport with the advisor) and the 'purchasing and process criteria' marked literature is predominately aligned to the second decision-making process (to select and appoint an advisor for specific services).

Author(s) & Year	Topic	Key Findings	Type of study	Perspective taken	Respondents/ seniority
J. Chelliah, D. Davis 2010	Relationship *structure and aspects*	Charts relationship as a reciprocal exchange of benefits; confirms a parallel informal contract to assure psychodynamics delivering personal benefits for client; no differentiation between project and ongoing rapport.	Psycho-dynamics-led study, use of semi-structured interviews	Advisor perspective	21 mid-level primarily management consultants
J. Chelliah 2010	Relationship *Structure and aspects*	Proposes a conceptual framework encompassing a formal and informal contract running in parallel; contracts are based on three layers of expectations: technical competence, professional contribution & personal style; in addition to future sales opportunities; self-satisfaction is one reason for the consultant to go the extra mile.	Literature review to develop a conceptual framework for future research	Advisor perspective	N/A
J. Mattila et al. 2013	Relationship *development as part of project*	Outlines and confirms the reciprocal client-advisor relationship via documenting consulting project interactions from both perspectives; definition of five distinct interaction phases.	Longitudinal observational case study over three 3 years.	Client and advisor perspective	Mix of individuals involved in the project
K. Karantinou M. Hogg 2009	Relationship *development and types*	Alerts to high credence and experiential nature which leads to clients being more interested in the process than outcome; confidentiality issues add to complexity; study differentiates between within and in-between project relationships and clients who are relationship seekers or switchers.	Qualitative interviews of advisors (15) and clients (6)	Primarily advisor, some client	Multiple levels within advisors firms, no specifics on clients
Nikolova et al. 2015	Relationship *aspect trust*	Successful client-advisor relationships are based on trust; study explores and adapts the ABI model and generic modes of trusts and	Qualitative open-ended interviews of advisors (16) and clients (15)	Client and advisor perspective	Independent advisors – contractors and clients involved in

		establishes that trusting is a process with involves three social practices: signalling ability & integrity, demonstrating benevolence and establishing an emotional connection; past experiences and also reputational aspect determine trust.			selection
J. Seth 2009	Relationship *'Trusted Advisor'*	Presentation slides summarising the concept of trusted advisor (values and characteristics) and general expectations associated with the concepts; interesting comment – the expectation of a loyal client is for the advisor not to work with competitors.	No information available	Client and advisor perspective	No information available
M. Mohe, D. Seidl 2009	Relationship *Social systems theory*	A-theoretical research dominates literature in the field, a small number of theories have been applied: role and agency theory, social network and learning theory, theory of rites, psychodynamics and concept of otherness or parasites; main objective is to test social-systems theory in the management consultancy context; changes for the client can only take place from within the system, some advisory firms are now testing and applying the concept.	Theoretical application supported by findings of other studies	Client and advisor perspective	N/A
J. Sieg et al. 2012	Relationship *aspect dialogue*	Relationship marketing requires ongoing pro-active dialogue from advisor; dialogue leads to competitive advantage, generates free insights and can be used as a catalyst to move forward; in addition to solving problems dialogue can create trust, control, competence and continuity.	Constant comparison method, field work with a branch of one of the 'Big Four' firms	Client and advisor perspective	Multiple levels, 33 advisors & 16 clients
S. Avakian et al. 2010	Relationship *aspects trust & culture*	Examination of trust and culture in interpersonal and inter-organisational relationships; proposes the notion that both client and advisor at times attempt to create a hybrid culture as part of their relationship.	Literature review and discussion, not empirical	Client and advisor perspective	N/A
L. Bagdoniene, R. Jakstaite 2009	Relationship *aspect trust*	In-depth investigation of multidimensional trust concept as part of the client-advisor relationship as it evolves, relationship is a process of mutual understanding and value	Literature review and discussion, not empirical	Client and advisor perspective	N/A

		creation in cooperation.			
D. Maister, G. Wilson 1993 & 2003	Relationship *experiences observations*	Frank personal experiences and views of professional service industry from a client perspective; identifies types of work procedural, brain and grey hair; walks through selection process – qualifications & selection; closes with an in-depth client account and very outspoken.	Case study based on personal experiences and observations	Client perspective	N/A
J. Levinson, M. McLaughlin 2005	Relationship *experiences advice*	Pendant to R11b, the relationship and interactions described from the advisor perspective as part of a how-to guide for consultants. 'No matter how good you are, you can't count on client loyalty.' In a recent survey over 50% of clients confirmed that they felt indifferent to their existing consultants.	Case study based on personal experiences and observations	Advisor perspective	N/A
R. Trasorras et al. 2009	Relationship *satisfaction, loyalty & retention*	Definition of satisfaction, loyalty and retention in the context of professional services based on empirical research. Satisfaction – to what extent do experiences meet expectations; loyalty cannot be achieved without utility; satisfaction is the first step; other aspects that define loyalty are personal determinism and social bonding; satisfaction and loyalty drive retention.	Deductive approach, utilising quantitative survey	Client and advisor perspective	Independent advisors and their clients
M. Haverila et al. 2011	Relationship *selection satisfaction*	Comparative study of key client satisfaction drivers in consultancy engagement (US compared to rest of the world); prior experience and reputation decisive selection factors, identified four macro groups of drivers: consultant/team characteristics, project management, customer focus, value and enterprise consideration; there are some differences between the two geographies.	Quantitative and open-ended survey informed by literature review	Client perspective	Senior executives, 35 US and 22 non-US
FT Research conducted by Meridian West 2012	Relationship *overview*	Key client messages: what matters the most is consistent service delivery, desire for more strategic, big picture dialogue and value add. Significant gaps between client and advisors' views.	Interviews and quantitative survey	Advisor and client perspective	Senior partners and executives, focus on partners
Tale Skjølsvik 2012	Relationship & Selection; *impact of relationships on selection*	Study uncovers three main relationship benefits: contextual knowledge, chemistry and past experiences, but also	Use of an adapted RBV framework, structured interviews and	Advisor and client perspective	Senior partners and client managers at various levels

		acknowledges sacrifices – mainly lack of work effort and knowledge loss. Research suggests that buyers have indeed become more professionalised and moved beyond relying on the trusted advisor concept.	field observations		
E. Day, H. Barksdale 1994	Purchasing process and criteria	Explores purchasing activity as decision-making process and advocates to include post-project evaluation; calls for clear differentiation between selection and evaluation criteria; discussed complexities and challenges of decision-making.	Literature review and discussion, not empirical	Organisatio-nal view	N/A
E. Day, H. Barksdale 2003	Purchasing process and criteria	Continuation from earlier works, key conclusions: relevant experience of firm, project manager and team are vital; competence and capacity evaluated via hard criteria, beyond that client relies on softer criteria informed by perceptions and judged during interview/presentation; all things being equal chemistry with the project team can be deciding factor.	Explorative qualitative interview results informed open ended survey, use of thematic analysis	Client view – purchasing professionals	Not disclosed, focus on architecture, construction and engineering services
M. Sonmez, A. Moorhouse 2010	Purchasing process and criteria	Identified six high-level criteria in order of importance: competence, knowledge & understanding, product & services, reputation, organisational capability and cost (last); most important criteria were to meet client needs; clients struggle to evaluate possible outcome and effectiveness; a good rapport with delivery team is a deciding factor; most decisions subjective based on judgements; authors call for more formal and subjective processes and criteria	Review of RFPs, small face to face interviews followed by an online quantitative survey	Client view – purchasing and learning & development professionals	Mid to senior level
F. Pemer et al. 2014	Purchasing policies and systems	Investigates increasing formalisation of service procurement utilising transaction cost economics model, which is linked to the maturity and life cycle of the organisation; formalisation takes place either via policies or guidelines or installing a preferred supplier programme whereby the latter has a limited positive impact on purchasing effectiveness.	Quantitative survey informed by transaction cost economics model	Client view – purchasing professionals	Mid-level
M. Mohe	Purchasing	Claims increasingly	Based on field	Organisatio-	N/A

2005	strategies and policies	uncontrolled consulting spent has triggered organisations to review procurement of professional services; presents rationale for increased professionalization and three generic strategies employed by client organisations: increase expertise and deploy one of our purchasing strategies, build in-house consulting expertise or build governance expertise.	observations and literature	nal view	
M. Mohe 2008	Purchasing and cultural aspects	Presents a framework to investigate purchasing at various levels in the context of cultures – micro, meso, macro and inter-culture; demonstrates complexities of relationships and interactions; in the absence of objective measures, clients assign great importance to cultural fit with consultants.	Literature review and discussion	Organisatio-nal view	N/A
D. Höner, M. Mohe 2009	Purchasing and goal divergence	With the help of agency theory investigates the goal divergence between managers and organisations; organisations have the option of a number of control or incentive-based measures to manage the issue; identifies how organisation and individual manager influence and intervene in the purchasing process.	Case study with one major client organisation, mixed method qualitative & quantitative surveys	Organisatio-nal view	Mid-level managers
J. Sieweke, S. Birkner, M. Mohe 2012	Preferred supplier programme (PSP)	Exploration of why organisations install preferred supplier programmes; establishing corporate not individual relationships and decreasing transaction costs are one of the rationales for an installation; almost equal split between both views – companies who had little professional service spend felt expense of setting up and operating preferred supplier programme would not justify savings; points out significant strategic and cost implications for advisory firm.	Web-based quantitative survey	Client view – purchasing professionals	Presume mixed levels

Table 7.2 – Summary of literature findings

7.3 Comparison of the two literature debates

Scanning through the introductory comments and results of studies, authors refer to an increased academic interest in the professional services and consultancy in the past fifteen years (Höner and Mohe 2009, Karantinou and Hogg 2009, Sieweke et al. 2012). Many studies follow an explorative approach and, as Michael Mohe and David Seidl (2009) point out, are 'a-theoretical' (not applying a particular theoretical approach), albeit a number of authors put forward new conceptual frameworks and models for future use (Mohe, Seidl 2009, Skjølsvik 2012, Day and Barksdale 1994, Höner andMohe 2009, Werr and Pemer 2007).

In addition, professional services is a field marked by complexity and multi-dimensionality, and due to the *"closed and secretive nature of consulting organisations"* (Karantinou and Hogg 2009, page 251), access to the appropriate and necessary data can be a challenge. With reference to the client-advisor relationship in particular, the studies attempt to capture clients' views and expectations (Karantinou and Hogg 2009, Nikolova et al. 2015, Sieg et al. 2012, Trasorras et al. 2009, Mattila et al. 2013, Haverila et al. 2011, Skjølsvik 2012, Financial Times, Managing Partners Forum and Meridian West 2012, Wilson 2003). However, clients consistently make up a smaller proportion of those interviewed and the client's view is regularly communicated by the advisor and not directly the client (Chelliah and Davis 2010, Karantinou and Hogg 2009, Financial Times, Managing Partners Forum and Meridian West 2012). Only infrequently is the client's position or functional focus in the organisation explicitly mentioned in the documents or considered in the analysis (Financial Times, Managing Partners Forum and Meridian West 2012, Haverila and Bateman et al. 2011).

"To theorize the client-consultant relationship, researchers have variously drawn on role theory, agency theory, social network theory, rites theory, situated learning theory and the theories of otherness and parasites, all of which treat the 'difference' between clients and consultants in different ways" (Mohe and Seidl 2009, page 2).

In their article, Mohe and Seidl (2009) hypothetically apply Niklas Luhmann's (2005, 1986) social systems theory and conclude that change for a client organisation can only take place from within the client system; however, consultants' activities might trigger actions which lead to the desired changes. In other words, it is the advisor's influence or interferences – Mohe and Seidl (2009) call them *"perturbations"* – with the client system that could or would bring about change within the client organisation. It is an interesting conclusion, especially in light of the fact that a number of consultancies are, according to the authors, now experimenting with this approach.

Regarding the operational purchasing debate, I took note of the following theories, in addition to non-theoretically-based explorations of primarily selection criteria or rationales for adopting one strategy or approach, such as preferred supplier programmes, over another: standard buying decision-making process (Day and Barksdale 1994 referring to, Bateson and Hoffman 1991, Stock and Zinszer 1987), transaction cost economics model (Werr and Pemer 2007 referring to, Rindfleisch and Heide 1997), agency theory (Höner and Mohe 2009 referring to, Jensen and Meckling 1979) and the resource-based view (Skjølsvik 2012 referring to, Lowendahl 1992, Lowendahl and Revang 1998). Comparing the two debates in the literature, there were a number of observations that stood out for me.

7.3.1 Client-advisor relationship debate

Four reoccurring aspects emerge in the wider relationship literature.

1 - The majority of studies imply that client-advisor relationships are effectively continuous processes that take place at multiple levels and are informed by cultural spheres and aspects such as the professional service firm and client organisation's culture (Avakian et al. 2010, Mohe 2008).

2 - Client-advisor relationships are found to be of a reciprocal nature with each party pursuing specific objectives and motivations, and aspiring to achieve a number of benefits from the interactions (Chelliah and Davis 2010, Chelliah 2010, Mattila et al. 2013, Karantinou and Hogg 2009, Nikolova et al. 2015, Sieg et al. 2012, Avakian et al. 2010, Bagdoniene and Jakstaite 2015, Maister 2007, Levinson and McLaughlin 2011, Trasorras et al. 2009, Haverila et al. 2011, Financial Times, Managing Partners Forum and Meridian West 2012, Skjølsvik 2012). Chelliah (Chelliah and Davis 2010, Chelliah 2010) refers to formal, primarily organisational, contracts (e.g. to provide project deliverables such as response to regulatory demands) and informal, hidden and personal, contracts (e.g. to coach and help the client manager to progress his or her career) between client manager and advisor.

3 - An ongoing dialogue between projects and good communications during projects, according to the existing literature, not only assures a positive experience but also strengthens the relationship (Chelliah and Davis 2010, Karantinou and Hogg 2009, Nikolova et al. 2015, Sieg et al. 2012, Bagdoniene and Jakstaite 2015, Wilson 2003, Levinson and

McLaughlin 2011, Maister 2007, Trasorras et al. 2009, Haverila et al. 2011, Financial Times, Managing Partners Forum and Meridian West 2012, Skjølsvik 2012).

4 - The outcomes of the interactions appear to be client satisfaction, trust, loyalty and retention, where satisfaction, meaning the client perceives they will receive utility or value from the interaction, is the pre-requisite for all other mentioned constructs (Karantinou and Hogg 2009, Nikolova et al. 2015, Avakian et al. 2010, Bagdoniene and Jakstaite 2015, Maister 2007, Trasorras et al. 2009, Haverila et al. 2011, Financial Times, Managing Partners Forum and Meridian West 2012)

The literature that has investigated the 'client-advisor relationship' is mostly at an individual level of analysis, the individual client being the manager receiving the services with the advisor or consultant proposing or offering the services. Many studies (Chelliah and Davis 2010, Nikolova et al. 2015, Trasorras et al. 2009) focus on sole operator or independent consultants and have not studied consultants operating within a larger firm or network. Interestingly, the research, which includes large professional services firms such as the 'Big Four', does not in particular elaborate on how the client perceives the individual advisor (Mattila et al. 2013, Karantinou and Hogg 2009, Sieg et al. 2012, Haverila et al. 2011) except for the general multi-level cultural debate, for example, presented in detail by Avakian et al. (2010). Therefore, the decision to interact with, select and appoint an advisor appears to be linked to that individual client manager; the involvement of others, such as selection panels or procurement staff, does not feature in the existing research. These findings corroborate the notion I put forth in the proposed substantive theory, that the client-advisor relationship decision is indeed a personal decision. I am surprised that no significant references are made in the literature to organisational constraints which might impact the individual's decision. I also did not find any reference comparable to the gestalt concept (i.e. clients focusing on either advisor or firm as a primary reference point) that I put forward in my analysis.

7.3.2 Operational dialogue

In contrast to the client-advisor debate, the operational purchasing literature focuses chiefly on organisational strategies, programmes and processes to improve and professionalise the selection and procurement of professional services (Werr and Pemer 2007, Mohe 2005, Höner and Mohe 2009, Sieweke et al. 2012). They dissect the general selection process and applied criteria, distinguishing between hard (meaning tangible and measurable) and soft (relying on personal judgement and perceptions) criteria (Day and Barksdale 1994, 2003, Sonmez and Moorhouse 2010, Mohe 2008, Höner and Mohe 2009). Past experiences are widely viewed as the most pertinent reference point; however, post-project evaluation and therefore an ex-ante (prior to project) definition of objectives is due to the high level of credence and makes the experiential nature of the services a challenge (Day and Barksdale 1994, 2003, Sonmez and Moorhouse 2010, Mohe 2008, Höner and Mohe 2009). A fair number of papers (Höner and Mohe 2009, Mohe 2005, Werr and Pemer 2007, Skjølsvik 2012) highlight the fact that close collaboration between an advisor or advisory firm over a longer period of time provides significant benefits but also point out the downsides, such as lack of effort and loss of new competitive knowledge and insights.

The operational purchasing debate primarily takes on an overarching organisational perspective and occasionally investigates the views of purchasing professionals within larger companies. Selection and appointment of professional service providers is discussed as an organisational decision, encompassing a number of different individuals linked to the service recipient business units and procurement (Day and Barksdale 2003, Sonmez and Moorhouse 2010, Werr and Pemer 2007, Mohe 2005, Sieweke et al. 2012). What strikes me is that there is little to no explicit discussion regarding different types of professional projects or services and how these could be subject to distinct decision-making processes and criteria. David Maister (2007) refers to three categories of work (*"procedural, brain and grey hair"*) requiring distinct levels of expertise but which, from my point of view, also deliver very different outcomes and benefits to client organisations, and which I tried to capture as 'project and service trajectory' in my research. Interestingly, Maister (2007) does not explicitly differentiate between or elaborate the three categories of work when it comes to selecting an advisor or advisory firm, therefore implying that the same selection process or approach is used for all three.

7.3.3 First conclusions

To a certain degree, one could argue that the marketing-driven 'client-advisor relationship' dialogue predominantly takes into consideration the interests of the advisor and advisory firms, whereas the operationally-driven purchasing debates in the literature look at wider client organisational interests. The general premise of the relationship literature is that a strong relationship leads to a strong position for the advisor, or even a competitive advantage, and therefore should transfer and impact favourably on the selection decision (Chelliah and Davis 2010, Chelliah 2010, Karantinou and Hogg 2009, Nikolova et al. 2015, Sheth and Sobel 2000, Sieg et al. 2012, Levinson and McLaughlin 2011, Trasorras et al. 2009).

Interestingly, only one study I located – 'Beyond the trusted advisor' by Tale Skjølsvik (2012) – unequivocally links both concepts (client-advisor relationship and the selection of a professional advisor) and identifies the impact of relationships on the selection decision. Obviously a number of studies (Chelliah 2010, Karantinou and Hogg 2009, Sheth and Sobel 2000, Sieg et al. 2012, Day and Barksdale 2003, Höner and Mohe 2009) refer to or mention both aspects – rapport and selection – but there appears to be a gap in the literature regarding seeking to understand the impact of the relationship on the purchasing process.

Moreover, the discussions and findings of this body of literature addressed some of the aspects that I have raised pertaining to the proposed substantive theory in Chapter Six. In the next section, I compare the literature findings with the outcomes of my data analysis so far and identify any remaining gaps that could be addressed in future research.

7.4 Mapping literature findings to the research project

The previous section has provided a general overview of the different debates and points of view that I found in the literature. In this section, I compare the literature findings to what I have understood from my research project. I consider aspects such as past experiences and their impact on the client-advisor relationship and selection of advisors; the selection process, criteria and organisational point of view; and lastly the client-advisor relationship set-up. As indicated earlier, there is significant overlap between the relationship management or marketing debate that I found in the literature and the first decision-making process leading to the rapport or relationship. There is a similar overlap between the more operational procurement discussion located in the literature and the second decision-making process, identified as part of my empirical analysis, which informs the actual selection and appointment of an advisor for a particular project.

In the following section, I critically evaluate how the client-advisor relationship could impact the advisor selection process and reflect on the findings. Mapping the data from the review of current literature and emerging concepts and then relating them to my ethnographic experiences in the process of developing theoretical sensitivity has been a challenging but rewarding process. The process of constant comparison (Charmaz 2006, Bryant and Charmaz 2007, Goulding 2002) has enabled me to put the pieces together and create a more coherent picture of the phenomena.

7.4.1 Impact of previous performances and past experiences

Since professional services are intangible (their outputs or outcomes might be tangible), experiential and based on credence, selecting the best offering, advisor and firm is perceived to be a difficult or even risky task for the client and client organisation.

"However imperfect, past performance usually is used as the predictor of future performance" (Day and Barksdale 1994, page 47) and can function as a key influencer in the client's selection and decision-making process.

At the same time, assessing past experiences and performances is challenging; individuals tend to focus on 'psychosocial' outcomes linked to service delivery or interactions with the advisor, instead of performance or success measures (Day and Barksdale 2003, Sonmez and Moorhouse 2010)

Researchers (Haverila et al. 2011, Mattila et al. 2013, Day and Barksdale 2003, Sonmez and Moorhouse 2010, Trasorras et al. 2009, Mohe 2005) contributing to both debates, relationship marketing and organisational purchasing, suggest that a more structured evaluation, a priori and ex post, of the service delivery experience and outcome would have a positive impact on the selection process. This could also provide a more grounded approach, mitigating high levels of credence and the reliance on clients' perceptions or gut feelings.

The evaluation of services, and with that client satisfaction, is not an easy undertaking. Mohe (2005) reports in his study that two out of every three German firms do not evaluate post-project, which corroborates the lack of measures or KPIs as part of the value for money conversations I uncovered as part of my research project. I took note of a number of facets in the existing literature which should inform a service or project evaluation:

- In order to assess service performance and outcomes, the client needs to define – ideally with the advisor – the project objectives and expectations, keeping in mind that these can or will change during the course of the project or service, either due to contextual changes or personal changes (Day and Barksdale 1994, Werr and Pemer 2007, Mohe 2005, Höner and Mohe 2009, Maister 2007, Trasorras et al. 2009).

- Objectives and expectations need to be realistic and should, if possible, be set within a wider context in order to address the wider client organisational issues. Bundling of projects and the cohesive setting and tracking of objectives against organisational problems would generate the most impactful result (Mohe 2005). Moreover, Mohe (2005) warns in his article of *'problem re-interpretations'* by consultants to match the advisory firm's skills and offerings, which might miss the actual cause of the problem experienced by the client.

- Occasionally hidden personal agendas of client managers shape project objectives and evaluations, leading to a goal divergence between organisation and individual (Chelliah and Davis 2010, Chelliah 2010, Höner and Mohe 2009).

- Client satisfaction is the difference between service expectations and the service experience from the client's perspective – not the advisor (Trasorras et al. 2009, Haverila et al. 2011, Maister 2007). *"Linked to the professional arrogance ... is the tendency to assume that we know what the client wants and that by doing a good job (in our minds) we will have done a good job in the client's mind. The two are often a long way apart ..."* (Wilson 2003, page 3).

Furthermore, success in terms of service performance and outcome, and with that client satisfaction, is also contingent on the client's contributions to the process (Mattila et al. 2013, Mohe 2008, Haverila et al. 2011). As part of my own ethnographic experiences, I have observed only a few services or projects which did not require client input or collaboration, meaning that the advisor or advisory firm is briefed, goes away and comes back with a finished product or outcome. Most services and projects are dependent on a reciprocal relationship or exchange between client and advisor. Therefore, it is important for a client organisation to recognise their own role in the process and factor this into the evaluation, which of course adds to the complexity of the task (Werr and Pemer 2007, Mattila et al. 2013). Frequently, clients and client organisations do not have the skills or background to assess a service or projects technically, though this is changing (Maister 2007, Wilson 2003). More and more organisations are in the process of developing in-house expertise and professionalising the procurement of professional services (Mohe 2005).

The fact that *"clients are willing to pay higher prices if the professional service provider is able to measure delivery effectiveness and impact on their employees and business"* (Sonmez and Moorhouse 2010, page 204) should motivate advisory firms to take on this challenge. Moreover, performance dissatisfaction can adversely impact the overall client-advisor relationship and can also lead to negative word of mouth for the advisory firm (Day and Barksdale 1994, Mohe 2005, Mattila et al. 2013).

The literature reports an increase in client expectations beyond the project or service context, defined as *"going the extra mile"* (Chelliah and Davis 2010, Chelliah 2010, Levinson and McLaughlin 2011) and providing additional value-adding services such as knowledge transfer in the form of events, white papers or free-of-charge training courses (Financial Times, Managing Partners Forum and Meridian West 2012). I wonder if this, at least partially, has come about due to the lack of project evaluations in the first place. More and more firms are competing or trying to differentiate themselves on a relationship level with these additional 'free' offerings (Financial Times, Managing Partners Forum and Meridian West 2012).

As a final point, project or service interactions should be viewed as a platform or opportunity to create positive experiences, develop deep relationships and to build trust and loyalty with client contacts and client organisations (Sieg et al. 2012). Client satisfaction is, according to the literature (Bagdoniene and Jakstaite 2015, Maister 2007, Trasorras et al. 2009), at the core of all of the key relationship concepts such as trust, loyalty, retention, repeat buying and reputation measures, such as the net promoter score. Consequently, understanding and managing service delivery and outcomes should be an essential prerogative for both advisor and client (Haverila et al. 2011, Mattila et al. 2013, Day and Barksdale 2003, Sonmez and Moorhouse 2010, Trasorras et al. 2009, Mohe 2005).

7.4.2 Selection process, criteria and organisational point of view

Starting with the organisational point of view, an article from Werr and Pemer (2007) offers an account of the professional service procurement evolution in the past two to three decades; I noted the following points:

- Professional services are abstract, intangible and dependent on client-advisor interactions. This makes it difficult for clients to specify, compare and evaluate services ex-ante and post-ante.
- Many clients perceive professional services as risky to purchase due to their intangible nature and unpredictable outcomes. In order to manage this risk, clients have relied on relational or trust-based purchasing strategies.
- Until fairly recently, the purchasing of professional services was primarily within the realm of client managers and based on a dyadic, often personal, relationship between client and advisor,

with no to little wider organisational involvement such as procurement or purchasing representatives.

- It is argued that this relational approach to purchasing professional services may result in over-embeddedness, implying that client managers are sticking with their service provider even though better alternatives – cheaper, higher quality, more innovative – are available.
- In order to address this issue, organisations have started to change their purchasing strategies and installed more formalised approaches and protocols in the form of procurement policies or standards, written guidelines or preferred supplier agreements.

Mohe (2005) mentions high growth figures and, at times, uncontrolled spend on professional services as organisational drivers to rethink and redesign the purchasing strategies and processes. In addition, Mohe presents a comprehensive list of reasons why organisations have started to professionalise their procurement of services, which raises questions such as: Is a professional advisor really needed? To what extent is the selection sufficiently systematic and informed? To what degree does the client organisation manage and evaluate the services and arrangements? Mohe mentions double billings, the re-interpretation of problems to accommodate service offerings, and multiple projects addressing the same organisational problem, which are not synchronised or bundled as problem areas.

In another article, Mohe and Höner (2009) investigate the issue of goal divergence, establishing that many managers who buy professional services pursue objectives which might not always be in line with organisational objectives. They discovered that a number of mid-level managers looked out for their own or departmental interests first and allowed projects to be managed in silos. In order to mitigate goal divergences, organisations have the choice of implementing various control-based or incentive-based measures, which of course need to fit with the culture and structure of the organisation. From a relationship-marketing perspective, Chelliah and Davis (2010) uncover similar concerns and identify, based on an earlier study by Heller (2002), three motives which drive clients' psychological, informal expectations: 'super ego motives', which are somewhat aligned with a wider organisational view; 'ego motives' to further personal aspirations; and 'political motives', which include the evasion of responsibility and intra-organisational competition.

In response to all of these challenges and developments that have been identified in the literature, organisations have started to a) build up their own expertise, b) deploy purchasing strategies and measures, c) develop governance expertise and administration such as databases, and d) even set up their own in-house professional service units (Werr and Pemer 2007, Mohe 2005, Sieweke et al. 2012). Two studies (Sieweke et al. 2012, Skjølsvik 2012) refer to and discuss Baker and Faulkner's (1991) four different purchasing strategies: there is consensus that organisations are abandoning relational strategies in favour of 'fractional' (a preferred supplier for a particular service); 'transactional'; 'cherry-picking'; and 'serial' (general preferred supplier agreements) strategies. Tale Skjølsvik (2012) proposes a fourth strategy – 'multiple-firm pre-selection' – which, as an intermediary position, takes on elements of all four strategies.

Comparing the literature observations with my own findings, I would conclude that all the concepts that have been identified as part of my research were also found in the existing literature and were discussed in the context of the client decision-making process. Regarding the proposed decision-making matrix model, a focus on 'control and balance advisors and manage risks' was only mentioned to a limited degree in the literature. However, to a certain degree, senior management representing and managing the concerns of the wider organisation, or the 'super ego' to take on Heller's (2002) definition, are reflections of this phenomenon. The negative aspects I picked up as part of the organisational context or constraints, such as 'asking for external support is seen as a sign of failure in this organisation' only appear to a limited extent in the literature. Sieweke, Birkner and Mohe (2012) discuss the tensions and potential conflict that a client manager might experience due to the formalisation of purchasing, and that he or she might choose or better try to resist organisational interventions.

7.4.3 Selection process and criteria

It is important to differentiate between selection criteria and project evaluation criteria (Day and Barksdale 1994). Identification of meaningful selection criteria for professional services is challenging since they lack "search properties", which Day and Barksdale (1994, page 47) define as *"attributes that a client can verify prior to purchasing the service"* – *"you can't kick the tires or compare sticker prices"*, and therefore surrogate indicators or cues are being used (Day and Barksdale 2003), especially for softer or more subjective criteria, such as a firm's commitment to a project. The client's level of experience regarding the service to be purchased is also reflected in the selection criteria and the ensuing process; often professional service firms end up educating and also influencing 'novice buyers' (Day and Barksdale 1994, 2003). Furthermore, depending on the length of the decision-making process, the composition of the client's selection committee might change, and with that, the selection criteria and weighting of criteria might change as well (Day and Barksdale 1994).

The decision to search for, select and appoint a professional advisor usually starts with the recognition of a need or problem. Frequently, advisors are or could potentially be involved in the problem or need identification (Day and Barksdale 1994, 2003, Sieg et al. 2012). The actual selection process encompasses at least two stages: the first stage is described as a screening or qualification exercise, which determines which professional services firm is capable of providing the relevant services and concludes with a short list of candidate firms. Compensatory decision rules have often been observed during this stage, meaning that firms need to meet a minimum number or level of requirements (Day and Barksdale 2003, Sonmez and Moorhouse 2010). The second stage involves choosing one of the short-listed firms. Especially during this second stage, softer or rather subjective criteria are being applied and the focus shifts away from the wider firm and onto the individual advisors who are being presented to the client as the team delivering the planned service (Day and Barksdale 1994, 2003, Sonmez and Moorhouse 2010, Maister 2007).

Selection criteria can be grouped into a number of high-level categories. In summary, I would describe them based on the literature findings as follows (Day and Barksdale 2003, 1994, Maister 2007, Sonmez and Moorhouse 2010, Skjølsvik 2012):

- Perceived experience, expertise and competence of the advisory firm, but most importantly the project lead and team put forward by the advisory firm.
- Demonstrated knowledge, understanding of the problem and commitment to address the issue, which should be reflected in the proposed service offering.
- Satisfaction with past performances (directly or indirectly via references).
- The professional service firm's reputation, capability and capacity.
- Costs or pricing.

The last two criteria groupings are more easily evaluated, whereas the first two are probed by decision-makers during the second or final stages of the selection process. *"If all other things [are] equal, chemistry (with the proposed project lead and team) can be the deciding factor"* (Day and Barksdale 2003, page 574). This notion of a 'cultural fit' has been echoed by many researchers (Maister 2007, Skjølsvik 2012, Day and Barksdale 2003, Sonmez and Moorhouse 2010, Mohe 2008). Interestingly, Skjølsvik (2012) discovered that 'chemistry' is even more important than trust; only past experiences are more critical. However, some client organisations exercise 'turn taking' (meaning to distribute assignments to a group of advisory firms), which can influence the final selection of a professional advisor, especially if only a small number of firms are capable of providing the service (Day and Barksdale 1994). This arrangement is also reflected in my findings on the aspect 'balance the use of different advisors', although senior executives might advocate this notion based on an ethical distribution and or as a way of mitigating exposure or risk ('it's not good to be too reliant on advisors').

A slightly different selection approach is being put forward in the article by Haverila et al. (2011). They recommend concentrating on prior experiences, as these determine the likelihood of future success, and therefore the five main drivers for client satisfaction should be applied and leveraged in the selection process. The five high-level drivers, which are underpinned by an exhaustive list of factors, are 1) consultant or team characteristics, 2) project management, 3) customer focus, 4) value and 5) enterprise considerations. Past experiences or previous performances are by far the most frequently cited selection criteria and a key determinant that shapes the ongoing 'client-advisor relationship'.

Comparing the selection criteria mentioned in the literature findings to the findings of my study, the skills, experiences and expertise of the lead advisor and team are the most frequently mentioned aspects. Legacy or established relationships are mentioned less often in terms of coverage and frequency. Previous experiences, either direct or indirect, are in conjunction with fairly important criteria. The noted empirical results are in agreement with the literature findings. In contrast, a fair or competitive price featured more heavily in my study compared to the literature discussions, which usually put cost as the least important – but still important – criterion (Sonmez and Moorhouse 2010, Skjølsvik 2012, Day and Barksdale 2003, Haverila et al. 2011). This variance could be due to the research context; perhaps senior executives providing client feedback were keen to communicate the cost aspect because they felt 'Big Four' firms are more expensive and should monitor their pricing. Or, possibly, the disparity is due to semantics: fair and competitive pricing is not the same as total cost in terms of being a selection criterion.

Beyond that, a stronger research focus on who is actually making the selection decisions and the general approach that is being taken (selection mode), as well as taking note of selection behaviours, not just processes and protocols, might provide a more holistic and realistic or better naturalistic view of the decision-making process in future research.

7.4.4 Client-advisor relationship set up

The client-advisor relationship can be more than a rapport or a series of interactions as part of a project, although this is one facet of a relationship and one which can, as I mentioned previously, serve as a platform to deepen and widen the interactions between client and advisor organisations. The client-advisor relationship can (but does not have to, especially for those clients following a transactional purchasing strategy) extend and go on beyond the project dialogue. Some authors such as Skjølsvik (2012) speak of a spectrum: a transactional exchange at one end and a personal friendship at the other. Karantinou and Hogg (2009) differentiate between within-project and between-project relationships, and between relationship seekers and relationship switchers. Looking at my findings, I found that for very senior executives as well as senior lead partners, such differences did not necessarily hold true. At any given time, a number of different projects are being delivered by a particular professional services firm within the divisional remit of, for example, a CFO. This means that project messages and results will be reported up and that the CFO might occasionally be involved in project interactions to varying degrees. Consequently, there is no definite in-between project and within-project distinction for very senior stakeholders in organisations which frequently and widely use professional service firms.

Regarding a clear classification of clients as relationship seekers or switchers, as described by Karantinou and Hogg (2009), based on my findings, it is important not to rely on and make a judgement based on a single advisor's view. A senior client might, for example, have a close relationship with one advisor from one particular firm and, for various reasons, not be interested in building a close rapport with other advisors (for instance, CRO_4 in my sample group). Depending on who the researcher interviews, the former or latter advisor, he or she will gather very different data points. It would also be of interest to determine how many close relationships a 'relationship seeker' is maintaining at any given time. For example, CFO_4 spoke of having more than 20 advisor telephone numbers stored on his phone. Furthermore, I believe that there are senior managers who are neither relationship seekers nor switchers. For instance, COO_1 was looking for minimal dialogue, focusing on professional debates and fairly little personal contact (no lunches for example); at the same time, there were no indications that they were prepared to switch relationships unless absolutely necessary. Consequently, I am wondering if a refinement of this relationship seeker-switcher model (Karantinou and Hogg 2009) might offer a framework for future research.

Assuming that the client is interested in an ongoing relationship, a pro-active dialogue can facilitate and enrich the rapport and generate benefits for the client such as problem-solving and free insights, and act as catalyst for change (Sieg et al. 2012). For the advisor and advisory firm, there is of course the opportunity to develop affinity, install trust and create client loyalty, as well as possibly positive word-of-mouth, which in turn secures future sales prospects (Chelliah 2010, Karantinou and Hogg 2009, Sieg et al. 2012, Avakian et al. 2010, Bagdoniene and Jakstaite 2015). Karantinou and Hogg (2009, page 250) point out that *"loyal customers can be more accommodating, more tolerant and forgiving of mistakes (Leuthesser 1997) and more willing to provide feedback and insights on unfulfilled needs (Morgan et al. 2000)"* which is an interesting observation that should warrant careful strategic consideration by advisory firms and lead to contemplating the following questions: is a loyal client really 'the most desirable client' for a professional service firm? And should loyal clients be more elevated and rewarded than other clients in the relationship marketing approach? This is a consideration that I would like to revisit in the management implications as part of Chapter Eight.

Both clients (managers) and advisors pursue informal agendas or psychological expectations as part of a project arrangement (Chelliah and Davis 2010, Chelliah 2010, Höner and Mohe 2009). The expected outcomes for the advisor are additional business, referrals and new business, as well as a degree of self-affirmation (Chelliah and Davis 2010). Researching and confirming these psychological expectations overtly is not easy. During my own interviews, I came to recognise that some senior executives were fairly open to discussing their more personal thoughts and motivations, but others were reluctant to share this type of information. Nonetheless, as part of my analysis, I picked up some indirect psychological expectations and general personal principles such as 'need to feel important', 'self-promotion without substance is a no-go' or 'I like to stay in control and monitor advisor activities'. However, I believe that these are really the tip of an iceberg and a number of respondents did not volunteer any personal preferences at all.

The most informative lesson I extracted from the relationship literature is the confirmation that the advisor or advisory firm have indeed a very different outlook and prioritisation compared to clients. Two studies in particular quantitatively substantiated this notion (Financial Times, Managing Partners Forum and Meridian West 2012, Skjølsvik 2012). The FT research report (2012) highlighted the fact that advisors (accountants and consultants) overestimate their own performance in all five service determinants compared to clients' perceptions. Skjølsvik (2012) confirms a strong advisor emphasis on relationships as a key selection criterion, which is not reflected in the private client or buyer (procurement) comments. As a selection criterion, relationship was overall mentioned less frequently by managers (35%) compared to advisors, who assumed it to be 87%. Furthermore, clients identified past experience as a key criterion (60%) and placed less emphasis on trust (40%). In contrast, advisors attached more importance to trust (73%) (all taken from Skjølsvik 2012). In terms of important priorities that define the client-advisor relationship, the FT study (2012) uncovered the following three from an advisor's perspective: firm brand, reputation and mystique, which were markedly different from the clients' top three: the firms' specialist and sector focus, formal performance measures for fee-earners, and investment in technology and systems that will enable consistent service delivery.

In addition, a number of studies (Skjølsvik 2012, Karantinou and Hogg 2009, Day and Barksdale 1994, Mohe 2005) indicated that clients were becoming more discerning and even critical of advisors. Although embeddedness and continuity provide a number of benefits, clients are found to be increasingly aware of the drawbacks or sacrifices (Skjølsvik 2012) that come with an overly close working relationship.

In summary, these findings suggest that an advisor's perception does not necessarily match the client's view, and that relationship and trust are two concepts which the advisor perceives to be more impactful and pivotal compared to the client's viewpoint.

7.4.5 'Trusted advisor' concept

Trust is a frequently researched concept (Maister et al. 2000, Nikolova et al. 2015, Sheth and Sobel 2000, Avakian et al. 2010, Bagdoniene and Jakstaite 2015) in the context of client-advisor relationships, and it also featured in a number of aspects within the data of my research project, for example, the client expectation 'earn my trust and bat for me', personal principles such as 'need to be able to trust the advisor or firm' and 'integrity is important' but also indirectly in the selection criteria 'fair price'. There are a number of different attempts to describe the notion in the literature (Maister et al. 2000, Nikolova et al. 2015, Sheth and Sobel 2000, Avakian et al. 2010, Bagdoniene and Jakstaite 2015). One source (Mayer et al. 1995) established that trust is based on the perception of ability, benevolence and integrity; another body of research (Glückler and Armbrüster 2003) identified market reputation, directly experienced or communicated through a network of trusting acquaintances, as the foundation. Nikolova et al. (2015) recognised trust as a key aspect in a successful client-advisor relationship, and established that it is a mental as well as social process based on three social practices:

- Signalling ability and integrity, clients use references, past experiences, expertise and reputation as reference points.
- Demonstrating benevolence, clients look for cues such as listening, understanding, flexibility.
- Establishing an emotional connection, which is experienced in the form of chemistry, empathy, positive first impressions and compatible personalities.

The trust framework presented above illustrates to me how far-reaching the trust concept is and how closely the different, more tactical aspects or cues are linked to it. Based on my own empirical findings, I would deduce that trust as an aspect is difficult to grasp for a client. Many senior executives spoke of 'having to be able to trust an advisor' as a personal principle, but did not provide any concrete example of how this would or could come about. Difficulties expressing or describing the concept could possibly be due to the fact that trust is linked to a process (Nikolova et al. 2015), it evolves and changes, and therefore, more tactical aspects or cues, such as those listed above, feature in client comments. However, it is important to note that these cues or expectations, such as the selection criterion 'legacy or established relationships' can be linked back to the trust concept.

The term 'the trusted advisor' was coined and widely communicated through a book with the same title published by Maister, Galford and Green in 2000. Sheth (2000, page 6) describes a trusted advisor as someone who: "*has the best interest of the client in mind, does everything possible to make the client successful, makes the client look good, is a leader in the field, adapts his experiences to client circumstances, is open to feedback to improve performance and doesn't work with client competitors*". All of these characteristics are either directly or indirectly reflected in the advisor expectations that I have captured during my coding. Expectation aspects were the most cohesive group of codes as part of the research, and I questioned if these were a common set of expectations that over time have become socially acceptable and developed into some kind of standard set of expectations. Reading through the literature, I am more and more convinced that this ideal picture of an advisor has evolved and been formed through publications such as *The Trusted Advisor* (Maister et al. 2000) as well as informal messaging from advisors. Consequently, senior executives' stated expectations are possibly more strongly informed by these common understandings than pronounced personal expectations. Besides, the trusted advisor concept also seems to appeal to the advisors' need for self-affirmation (Chelliah and Davis 2010, Sieg et al. 2012, Levinson and McLaughlin 2011). Being referred to as 'the trusted advisor' is a badge of honour and signals an achievement; it elevates the advisor above others who just 'deliver or executive projects'. Unfortunately, the term has experienced a *"scary level"* of inflation in the past years, according to Charles Green (Green 2012). In the book *The Trusted Advisor,* Green, Maister and Galford (2000) introduced the notion by saying, *"While none of us begin our career as a trusted advisor, that is the status to which most of us aspire'* and clarified that the term was understood to apply to *'senior, wise-in-the-ways-of-the world people in high positions (Green 2012); people like Clark Clifford* (an American lawyer who serves as a political advisor), *or Felix Rohatyn* (an American investment banker who is credited for averting bankruptcy for the city of New York)*"*. Green (2012) complains about the increasingly frequent and indiscriminate use of the term, concluding his article with the following observation which speaks for itself: *"I ran across "Trusted Advisor Marketing Tip #1: How to Shock and Awe Your Clients into Lowering Sales Resistance". This takes trusted advisor inflation beyond the realms of exaggeration, well into cognitive dissonance".'*(Green 2012)

7.5 Summary of findings and first reflections

Considering the literature findings and discussions presented in the previous sections, it appears that the key aspects of the emerging substantive theory are indeed part of the discourse in the existing literature. All four foci of the matrix model that I propose – 'trust and empathy', 'embeddedness and continuity', 'competitiveness, merit and skills' and 'balance, monitor and risk management' – are aspects that have been referred to by academics and practitioners engaged in understanding the social phenomena of clients interacting with advisors. The fact that relationships and advisor selection are addressed via two distinct bodies of literature underlines my assumption that there are indeed two separate decision processes: to develop and maintain a rapport or relationship with an advisor and to select and appoint an advisor for a particular task. The literature has also offered significant insights into the 'trusted advisor' concept and the discourse related to advisor expectations, as well as the lack of objectives or tangible measures surrounding past experiences.

7.5.1 To what extent does the client-advisor relationship impact project appointment decisions?

The literature review also offered evidence and some insightful pointers regarding the question: To what extent does the 'client-advisor relationship' impact or influence the 'selection decision'? Revisiting the articles, I took note of the following influencing aspects:

- Consistent high-quality service delivery at competitive terms, and if possible, some value-add in the form of additional services, is what clients are primarily looking for. Beyond that, a more strategic and commercial dialogue with the advisor, highlighting the impact of socio-economic and political developments on the client's organisation is a secondary demand. Both demands are frequently expressed by clients, especially since they are not always met in full (Financial Times, Managing Partners Forum and Meridian West 2012).

- A positive working relationship with the delivery team, lead partner and advisory firm is widely recognised by clients as a key contributor to a successful project or service delivery. Consequently, preliminary interactions and general 'chemistry' (term frequently used in the literature to describe affinity between client and advisor) with the proposed project lead and team can be decisive and inform the selection of advisors (Day and Barksdale 2003, Maister 2007, Mohe 2008, Karantinou and Hogg 2009).

- Professional advisor embeddedness (familiarity and presence in client organisation) and continuity provide some excellent benefits for organisations, as well as easing confidentiality concerns, but come with trade-offs such as a lack of work effort and knowledge loss (Karantinou and Hogg 2009, Skjølsvik 2012).

- Procurement of professional services has become more professionalised in recent years. Possibly sparked by less positive experiences with professional service firms, clients have become more critical or possibly sceptical of advisors and have built up their own expertise, which has led to clients being more exacting and demanding when it comes to procuring professional services (Mohe 2005, Karantinou and Hogg 2009, Financial Times, Managing Partners Forum and Meridian West 2012, Werr and Pemer 2007).

- Aspects such as trust, contextual knowledge and 'chemistry', which are informed by the existing client-advisor relationship, feature in the selection process but not quite to the degree assumed by advisors (Skjølsvik 2012). Past satisfaction, which is described as an outcome of previous service delivery, has frequently been identified as the most influential selection driver (Day and Barksdale 1994, Mattila et al. 2013, Trasorras et al. 2009, Skjølsvik 2012, Haverila et al. 2011).

- It is clear that a good client-advisor relationship can contribute to a positive experience and client satisfaction, as well as being a product of an affirmative project or service experience. Furthermore, positive (primarily project or service) experiences contribute to the trust process, which forms the basis of the 'client-advisor relationship' but also features as one, albeit not always the most pivotal, selection criterion recurrently mentioned (Skjølsvik 2012, Karantinou and Hogg 2009, Day and Barksdale 2003, Nikolova et al. 2015).

7.5.2 Focus for future research

Although the research project in conjunction with the literature findings has brought some insight into the phenomena (the interactions between professional advisors and clients), there is scope for further research.

First and foremost, it is crucial to gather client viewpoints directly and not vicariously through advisor statements, since studies have found substantial differences in emphasis and perspectives. Secondly, it is important to investigate the interactions from different viewpoints: this could be the company board, senior management, operational mid-level management, and procurement on the client side, as well as the professional service firm's leadership, senior partners and service delivery-focused managers on the advisory side. I believe that perspectives and priorities differ greatly, as Kastantiou and Hogg (2009) have mentioned.

Understanding and comparing these various viewpoints, and the potentially resulting alignments or conflicts, will generate the much-needed discernment to comprehend the overarching dynamics between client and advisors and help to identify or develop suitable conceptual frameworks and theories.

My research project focuses primarily on senior executives' decision-making processes when interacting with, selecting and appointing 'Big Four' advisory firms, and therefore only offers a partial view of the entire phenomena. Therefore, the degree to which the emerging theories of this study can be transferred and applied to the wider context still needs to be tested. In Chapter Eight, I will return to these aspects in my discussions of study conclusions, implications and limitations.

Chapter 8

Conclusions, reflections and implications – inferences for client organisations, professional service firms and academia

The objective for this last Chapter Eight is to wrap up the research project with a set of final conclusions informed by the literature findings and the substantive theory, as well as inferences and implications for client organisations, professional service firms and academia, followed by a section on limitations and opportunities for further research. The chapter concludes with a number of reflections on the research journey and a contemplation of the study's contribution to the present field of knowledge.

Looking back at the research journey charted in this document so far, the first chapter describes the background and context of the study and sets out the overall aim and objectives – to investigate the interactions between professional advisors and senior executive clients and the clients' decision-making process when it comes to relating to, selecting and appointing advisors. The second chapter discusses the adopted research methodology (constructivist grounded theory) (2006, Charmaz 2009, Bryant and Charmaz 2007), and corresponding underpinning components such as theoretical sampling, saturation and sensitivity, as well as other methods and tools that were utilised. Chapters Three and Four chart the progress from exploration of the data and observed phenomena to an emerging conceptual framework, advised by naturalistic decision-making theories, and culminating in theoretical saturation. This is followed by an in-depth demonstration and discussion of the empirical findings, resulting in first theories in the ensuing Chapter Five. In Chapter Six, the empirical debate concludes with the rationalisation of the emerging theory and the presentation of substantive theoretical models. In line with the grounded theory methodology, the review of the literature in the field and a critical analysis of the substantive theories follows post-data analysis and can be found in Chapter Seven.

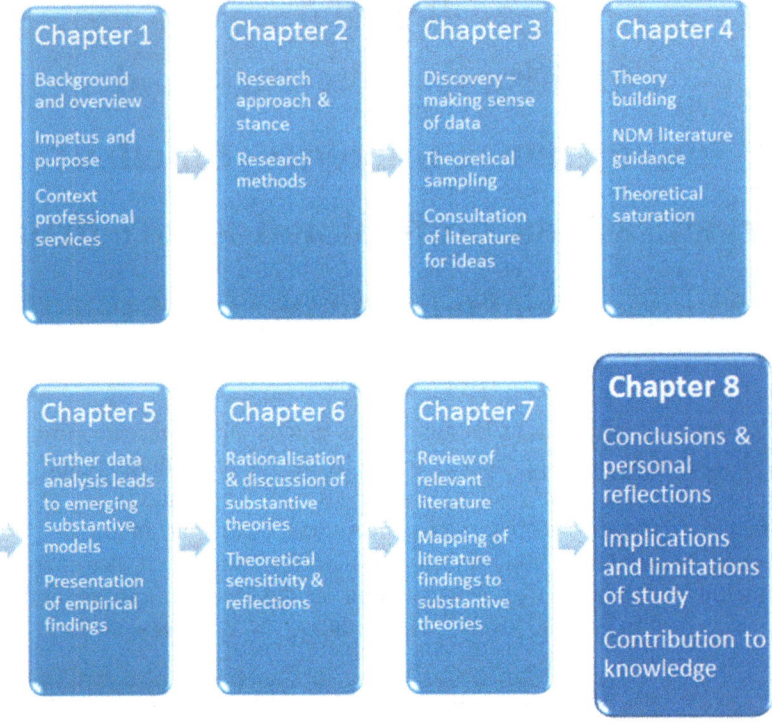

Figure 8.1 – Overview of thesis structure and content of the eighth chapter

8.1 Conclusions

Reflecting on the research progress and findings, the phenomenon that has surprised me the most is the level of changeability observed: The interactions, as well as the associated two decision-making processes, are extremely hard to grasp. The decision-making processes are not only informed by personal aspects such as preferences or expectations; situational aspects, linked to the general organisational environment (for example, procurement procedures) and the project environment (project trajectories such as objectives and triggers), feature as strongly. Therefore, if there is a slight alteration, for example, a new procurement policy is being introduced or the client has had a negative or positive experience, the decision-making configuration changes. Consequently, trying to accurately anticipate senior executives' decision-making behaviour and the resulting outcomes appeared to be almost unachievable. A decision-making behaviour or pattern observed in one situation (for example, selection of an advisor for one project), is not necessarily going to be repeated in the next situation, since there is a reasonable likelihood that some aspect will be different (e.g. project trajectories, new experiences, organisational changes).

Nonetheless, reviewing the substantive theory and reflecting on the literature findings, a number of conclusions emerge regarding the research purpose – **to investigate the interactions between professional advisors and senior executive clients with an emphasis on the decision-making process of these senior executives when it comes to relating to, selecting and appointing advisors**. A sequential rundown of the study's conclusions can be found in the following sections.

8.1.1 Senior executive and professional advisor interactions are multifaceted

The research study found that client-advisor interactions constantly shift from a more personal ongoing rapport or relationship to institutional contractually bound arrangements and collaborations between the client organisation and professional service firm, resulting in project relationships or rapport (Karantinou and Hogg 2009). There is not necessarily a temporal divide between the two, especially for senior executives who oversee a vast number of different concurrent projects and initiatives supported by professional advisors.

The interactions between professional advisors and senior executive clients appear to consist of:

- **Project-driven rapport** linked to the advisor's current, live engagements (Karantinou and Hogg 2009);
- Broader, beyond specific projects, rapport, which can involve **networking, coaching, information and knowledge exchange** on a more personal level between client and advisor **as part of a general ongoing dialogue and relationship;**
- **Assistance with a particular organisational problem**, potentially related to a live project but outside the agreed scope; or a new challenge, **which might remain part of the wider ongoing relationship** by informally elaborating the issue in various discussion formats, possibly including the support of other advisors or experts, or even leading to some small and most likely free-of-charge work for the advisor (Sieg, Fischer et al. 2012);
- **Informal conversations transmuting into an organisational need for a service or a project – at this point there is a shift,**

and in order to address the issue it turns into an organisational decision, eventually resulting in a legally binding agreement between the organisation and the advisory firm. The selection and appointment of an advisory firm to deliver the project or service will most likely require a formalised decision-making process, contingent, of course, on organisational guidelines and the personal preferences of the senior manager.

The decision to develop and maintain a rapport or relationship with the advisor beyond a project context appears to be a personal decision process, in which the senior executive determines the intensity and level of intimacy of the interactions, assuming the advisor is prepared to accommodate. On the other hand, project rapport is the result of an organisational decision process to select and appoint a professional services firm to deliver a service or project. Depending on circumstances, these two types of rapport or relationship can coincide or be sequential. However, for senior executives of companies that make extensive use of professional services, the two relationship types frequently coincide, and unless projects are of strategic importance or of a very large scale, specific-project rapport does not feature quite as heavily as part of the interactions.

8.1.2 Two distinctive decision-making processes come into play

Consequently, when it comes to senior executives, such as CFOs, COOs and CEOs, interacting with large, multi-service professional service firms, such as the 'Big Four' accountancy firms and their advisors, two distinctive decision-making processes come into play:

1. The decision process to develop and maintain a broader, ongoing personal rapport or relationship with the advisory firm and their advisor(s).
2. The decision process on behalf of the client organisation to appoint and transact with a professional services firm to deliver a particular service or project.

The first decision process – to develop and maintain an ongoing rapport or relationship – is primarily a personal decision, which is determined by a set of imperatives, being general expectations of an advisor and advisory firm, as well as personal principles and preferences. It is a continuous and affirmative decision-making process in which the physical proximity, intensity and intimacy of the rapport is likewise steered by the advisors' activities.

The second decision process – to select and appoint a professional services firm and advisor for a particular service or project – is clearly a binary decision made by the senior managers or others on behalf of the client organisation. Depending on the organisational challenge and resulting service or project need, organisational protocols as well as personal principles, the senior executive initiates a decision-making process to select and appoint a suitable advisory firm. The senior manager might opt to be personally involved and/or responsible for the selection and appointment, to delegate the decision-making to a direct report or to task a group of managers and/or procurement to take on matters. Thus, it is not necessarily the senior executive who personally makes that second decision.

8.1.3 Components of the selection and appointment process for a particular project or service

Once an organisational problem has been diagnosed and the need for intervention has been identified, as part of either an interaction between a senior manager and an advisor or a dialogue within the organisation, the process commences to instigate a project initiative, and with that the search for a suitable external partner, if required.

The trajectories of the initiative, being the triggers and objectives of the project including the organisational gaps that the professional services are tasked to fill, determine the selection process comprised of selection mode (who makes the decision), general selection approach (level of formality or structure), selection steps and protocols, as well as the selection criteria.

Organisational context, which takes into account organisational purchasing requirements or structures, and the organisational culture as regards working with professional advisors or external support, as well as the experiences and expertise of the decision-maker(s) in selecting a professional services firm, are pivotal influencers on the entire process.

8.1.3.1 Selection mode

Who will be tasked with the selection process and decision-making, and how structured or formal the process will be, is contingent on the anticipated trajectory of initiative, organisational protocols and the personal preferences or principles of the senior manager initiating the activities. For instance, on a personal level, a number of CEOs consciously and categorically step out of the selection and decision-making process and delegate it to a direct report or someone else. Some senior executives prefer to be personally involved in the decision-making in some capacity, either taking the lead or being part of a panel or group decision.

On an organisational level, purchasing protocols, for example, might call for a formal selection and decision-making process led or facilitated by a procurement manager for projects over a certain anticipated fee or budgetary threshold. Other less structured arrangements might call for a senior executive – frequently the CFO – to have final review and approval of the project plans, budget and choice of professional service firm.

8.1.3.2 Selection process

Most selection and appointment decisions involve at least two phases: a qualification or screening stage, which usually encompasses the submission of a written proposal or offer and ends with a short list of potential providers, followed by the final selection or choice from the short list, which could require a number of reiterative selection sub-phases informed by formal presentations and informal debates (Day and Barksdale 1994, 2003, Maister 2007, Sonmez and Moorhouse 2010).

8.1.3.3 Selection protocols and behaviours

In addition to formal selection practices, often installed on an organisational level and enforced by senior leadership and procurement (Werr and Pemer 2007, Mohe 2005, Höner and Mohe 2009), the study took note of informal selection behaviours and common practices.

A frequent and commonly accepted notion mentioned by senior executives is that significant projects, either from a cost or risk and exposure perspective, should go through a formal and structured tender process, whereas insignificant projects, again from a cost or functional or departmental reach perspective, would not necessarily have to go through a lengthy (and costly) formal selection process.

Some identified selection behaviours that could be described as exceptions to the existing purchasing protocols, for example 'emergencies can bypass selection processes', or described as underlying imperatives applied to the entire selection process and interpretation of selection criteria, for instance 'established relationships act as a screening mechanism', meaning that only known advisors or firms will be invited to tender or submit a proposal. A personal preference like 'select advisor or advisory firms purely on merit' or organisations trying to balance the appointment of advisors can also be observed; Day and Barksdale (1994) referred to this as turn taking in order to avoid over-reliance on one supplier.

8.1.3.4 Selection criteria

Selection criteria, for both qualification or screening and final choice, can be grouped into five high-level categories (Day and Barksdale 1994, 2003, Sonmez and Moorhouse 2010, Skjølsvik 2012, Maister 2007):

- Perceived experience, expertise and competence of the advisory firm, but most importantly the project lead and the team being put forward for the project or service.
- Demonstrated understanding and knowledge of the problem and the organisation and the advisory firm's commitment to address the issue.
- Client satisfaction with past performances, either drawn from personal experiences of the decision-maker(s) or vicariously through references and recommendations by others.
- The professional services firm's reputation, capability and capacity.
- Cost or pricing models put forward.

In the literature, the last two categories are often described as hard, or measurable, factors (Day and Barksdale 1994, 2003, Sonmez and Moorhouse 2010) and are pivotal in the first phase (qualification or screening). The first three categories listed above, are predominantly described as soft factors, and perceptions are frequently tested and confirmed by observing the potential professional service partners in formal presentations and informal exchanges as part of the second phase.

In the literature, cost recurs as the least important category (Day and Barksdale 2003, Sonmez and Moorhouse 2010), and the findings of this study also confirm that pricing has to be competitive and fair but not necessarily the lowest, nor is it in general a stand-alone final decision-making factor. However, I have observed as part of the win/loss reviews that, for certain project trajectories or types, cost is more important than for other projects or services. Therefore, further more granular investigation of these aspects would be helpful.

Due to the high level of credence and the experiential nature of professional services, it is difficult for decision-makers to form a view of the soft factors in particular, such as advisor experience and expertise (Day and Barksdale 2003, Sonmez and Moorhouse 2010). Past, especially project or service, performances and experiences, and the resulting client satisfaction are used as a proxy for future experiences (Day and Barksdale 1994, Sonmez and Moorhouse 2010). Past experiences shape the client's view and associations with a specific advisory firm or advisor. In particular, negative project experiences appear to have a detrimental impact on a professional service firm's opportunities, potentially leading to the advisory firm being excluded from future selection processes for similar projects or services. Frequently, less seasoned senior managers rely on references and recommendations from individuals whom they trust within the organisation, but more often outside of the organisation (Bagdoniene and Jakstaite 2015, Trasorras et al. 2009). For example, a senior manager of a life sciences company proactively contacted a senior manager in a telecommunications company for recommendations and advice.

Chemistry (affinity between client and advisor) is repeatedly mentioned as a final decisive factor (Day and Barksdale 2003, Skjølsvik 2012). At the end of a selection process, if all things are equal, decision-makers look at the experienced chemistry between the client and the advisory firm, predominantly the project lead and the presented team, during the meetings and presentations as the final decision-making criteria. This notion can be traced back to project experiences and performance. A positive – constructive and productive – project relationship between the client and advisor team is regularly seen as a key contributing factor for a successful project (Day and Barksdale 1994, 2003, Sonmez and Moorhouse 2010, Haverila et al. 2011). One could argue that, by looking at the team chemistry, the decision-maker is trying to gauge the potential for a successful collaboration and positive project outcomes.

8.1.4 The decision-making matrix – an alternative perspective on the selection process

Beyond the above-mentioned selection process and corresponding components, the research has identified four underlying conceptions, or leitmotifs, which determine how the selection process unfolds and how the criteria is applied and weighted. I started to refer to this construct as the decision-making matrix, in which the four foci can be somewhat in opposition with each other and the decision-maker has to find an acceptable balance of the four dimensions for the impeding decision to be made while considering the wider landscape made up of organisational context and past experiences. The matrix offers an alternative perspective on decision-making, a supplementary model to the process-oriented view, which focuses primarily on the sequential aspects or steps of the decision-making (Klein 1993).

The four domains emerging from analysis that determine the selection decision-making are 1) 'trust and empathy', 2) 'continuity and embeddedness', 3) 'control & balance advisors and manage risk' and 4) 'competitiveness, skills and merit' (a comprehensive description and discussion can be found in Chapter Six). The tension between 'continuity and embeddedness' and 'competitiveness, merit and skills' has been documented in the literature (Skjølsvik 2012, Uzzi 1997). Continuous collaboration over an extended period of time provides a number of benefits, which are often summarised as embeddedness, but also generates drawbacks such as a lack of work effort and knowledge loss (Skjølsvik 2012), which can be extended to a lack of competitiveness and new insights or skills. For some projects or services, continuity and embeddedness are deemed absolutely essential for the success of the project; for other projects, new insights, particular skills and a competitive proposition might be the way forward. The dichotomy of 'trust and empathy' and 'control or balance advisors and manage risk' is a phenomenon that has not been observed previously in the context of professional services. The research showed that a number of senior executives were fairly comfortable and inclined to trust the professional advisor they had been working with; for instance, CRO_3 mentioned that he was confident that the advisor would quote a fair price for a project which required an immediate start and therefore proceeded without validating the figures or asking for another firm to provide an alternative quote. This contrasts with another group of senior executives, who felt that they needed to monitor the advisor and advisory firm and their activities, either because they were more sceptical of the advisors' intentions, perceived that an over-reliance on an advisor or advisory firm was a risk, or pursued a general policy of turn-taking or balancing of professional service fee spend. CFOs and CEOs in particular – possibly linked to the differences in their job role – communicated that they monitored spending by advisory firms and that a balance of advisors was preferred. In a particular selection decision, reliance on one advisor might not be an appropriate approach to managing organisational risk for a large programme; alternatively, a project might be extremely sensitive and highly confidential, when trust becomes the overriding criteria. The concept of balancing and monitoring advisors and advisory firms is a feature of the organisational buying and procurement literature (Werr and Pemer 2007, Mohe 2005, Höner and Mohe 2009, Sieweke et al. 2012) but it has not been discussed against the concept of trust – a recurring concept in the marketing literature (Avakian et al. 2010, Bagdoniene and Jakstaite 2015, Trasorras et al. 2009).

Reflecting on the interview experiences as part of this study, the use of this internal matrix appears to function in the following way: As part of the selection process, the decision-maker contemplates the four foci and identifies an appropriate balance of the leitmotifs for the project decision at hand, consulting their past experiences and considering the organisational context. Therefore, the decision-maker most likely intuitively uses the matrix to guide the selection process and the evaluation of selection criteria.

8.1.5 Increasing professionalisation of professional services purchasing changes dynamics

A number of studies (Sonmez and Moorhouse 2010, Werr and Pemer 2007, Mohe 2005, Mohe 2008, Höner and Mohe 2009, Sieweke et al. 2012) report a trend towards the professionalisation of professional service purchasing, i.e. organisations are moving away from the previously prevailing relational purchasing strategy (single-firm long-term relationship approach), testing other purchasing strategies (fractional, transactional and serial) (Baker and Faulkner 1991, Skjølsvik 2012) and approaches such as preferred supplier programmes (Werr and Pemer 2007, Sieweke et al. 2012). This is alongside the development of their own expertise to administer and manage professional services more effectively or even build internal professional service units (Werr and Pemer 2007, Mohe 2005, Sieweke et al. 2012). The underlying objectives for these changes are, on the one hand, to manage costs, create better synergies and assure the best possible service quality and outcome for the organisation units (Werr and Pemer 2007, Mohe 2005, Sieweke et al. 2012). On the other hand, with these programmes and measures, organisations try to make the selection process more structured and transparent and therefore more objective, and reduce personal biases (Werr and Pemer 2007, Mohe 2005, Sieweke et al. 2012, Höner and Mohe 2009). Following this approach, the organisation effectively steps between the client manager who will most likely be receiving the services, and the professional advisor (Höner and Mohe 2009). From an individual manager's perspective, this of course creates potential for conflict, increasing avoidance strategies, and might even have an impact beyond the broader project and client-advisor relationship, especially at the mid-manager level. The study found that the majority of senior leadership – who most likely instigated and at least officially support the professionalisation – embraced the notion of control and balancing advisors. A small number of senior executives agreed in principle with professionalisation measures, but thought of or found ways to work around the system, specifically for projects of urgency or personal importance, for instance by giving office access and space to favoured advisors or by asking for leniency when bypassing procurement protocols, either because they were new to the organisation, or the project was extremely urgent. On reflection, balanced, less confrontational purchasing approaches and measures including the 'client-advisor relationship', would provide more positive and productive results for all parties involved.

8.1.6 Evaluation of professional services, a priori, intra and ex post, is the biggest challenge

According to the literature, the lack of objective evaluation criteria and measures is probably the biggest hindrance in selecting the most suitable professional service provider and offering (Haverila et al. 2011, Mattila et al. 2013, Trasorras et al. 2009, Day and Barksdale 1994, Werr and Pemer 2007, Mohe 2005). Due to the intangible and experiential nature and high credence of professional services, assessing and evaluating professional services firms' offerings in the form of proposal documents and presentations a priori is difficult. There are only a few hard factors or measures, primarily linked to advisory firms' capacity and general capabilities. Soft factors, such as team expertise, experience and competency as well as an understanding of the organisation and the problem to be addressed, are gauged via personal observational cues and perceptions and are therefore extremely subjective (Day and Barksdale 1994, 2003, Sonmez and Moorhouse 2010). As previously mentioned, many decision-makers revert to past performance and experiences as predictors of future expected experiences (Day and Barksdale 1994). However, an objective evaluation of project performances and outcomes ex post is also challenging and is infrequently practised (Mohe 2005).

A structured, unbiased and sufficiently documented assessment of a project or service performance and outcome and the resulting client satisfaction would not only improve the selection decisions but would also remove certain purchasing measures, protocols and interventions; in effect, there is less need for procurement policing and more scope for facilitation of project evaluations. Feedback to professional advisors and firms would be more informed, factual and actionable for improvements.

However, reflecting on my observations as part of this study, sending out an electronic survey to client managers at the end of project asking them a couple of quantitative questions and possibly inquiring if they would recommend the firm, as is frequently practised by professional services firms, will not suffice.

First of all, a meaningful evaluation would need to capture the trajectory of a particular project or service: the drivers (who or what has triggered the need for the service or project), the objectives and goals (to deliver something specific and or provide advice on a particular issue), as well as what the task of the professional firms would be. This research project identified a number of auxiliary objectives for the professional advisor such as 'fill a resource or knowledge gap', 'teach and empower us', 'help meet a deadline' etc. The project trajectory should inform the evaluation criteria and be included in the client organisation's expectations.

Furthermore, to conduct only an assessment towards or at the end of a project would not be adequate. Firstly, client expectations and project objectives might change during the course of the project or service (Day and Barksdale 2003, Werr and Pemer 2007). Secondly, project or service performance is an ongoing process, therefore taking note of experiences throughout provides a more accurate view. Lastly, reviewing progress and providing feedback gives both the professional advisory team and the client team opportunities to take improving or corrective actions, which hopefully would lead to an enhanced outcome.

In addition, it is important to recognise the role and contribution of the client organisation to the success of the project or services. Very few professional services or projects do not require collaboration or active participation from the client (Mattila et al. 2013, Trasorras et al. 2009). For the advisory firm, partner and project team, it is important to acknowledge that the evaluation of a service project and the ensuing satisfaction need to be viewed from the client's perspective – not the advisor's. An advisory firm might be convinced that the project has gone well and is a success from their perspective, but it might have failed client expectations, and therefore no client satisfaction can be verified (Trasorras et al. 2009, Maister 2007).

In sum, and reflecting on the research findings, I believe that meaningful and practical project or service evaluation intra and ex post will not only inform and enhance the evaluation and selection of service offerings a priori but will also increase transparency and remove subjectivity and emotional judgement, resulting in an overall improvement in the dynamics between client manager, organisation and professional service firm and advisor.

8.1.7 What is the impact of client-advisor rapport or relationship on the selection decision?

A number of studies in the literature (Trasorras et al. 2009, Haverila et al. 2011, Skjølsvik 2012), as well as the empirical data, confirm that a positive or strong client-advisor relationship does not automatically put the advisor at a competitive advantage or ensure a positive outcome in the selection process. A more nuanced view needs to be taken.

A positive or productive project relationship can contribute to a successful project or service performance and outcomes, leading frequently to client satisfaction. Satisfaction and past performances and experiences are key reference points for future selection decisions (Karantinou and Hogg 2009, Trasorras et al. 2009, Werr and Pemer 2007, Mohe 2005, 2008). The impact of the project relationship – concurrent or past – is especially pertinent if the same stakeholders are involved in the planned future project(s) and the same or similar type of project is being decided on. This is not always the case when dealing with large professional services firms. Most of the time, the senior partner who fronts the proposal will remain, but a different project manager and team might be presented occasionally due to availability constraints. A change will most likely be required to meet project expertise and competence expectations.

Good chemistry (interpersonal relationships and affinity) between the proposed professional services firm project lead and team and the client decision-makers, formed during proposal meetings and presentations, can be a decisive factor if all other aspects are equal. Good chemistry can be seen as a cue or indicator for the anticipated or projected project relationship (Day and Barksdale 1994, 2003).

The impact of the broader client-advisor relationship beyond the project is less clear and more complicated. A positive client-advisor relationship can generate opportunities and might create a personal bias. For example:

- Having an ongoing dialogue with a senior client manager provides opportunities for a professional advisor to raise and discuss potential organisational problems which might lead to the identification of an organisational need and a fee-generating project or service to address this particular need. In order to have these types of conversation, the advisor needs to have a fairly interactive, open and frequent relationship contact with the senior manager (Sieg et al. 2012).

- Offering personal support, in the form of networking, coaching and free advice and competitive or industry insights to receptive senior managers, can generate a positive view and bias toward the professional advisor, which the senior executive might or might not exercise in a selection decision (Financial Times, Managing Partners Forum and Meridian West 2012).

- Being present, visible and engaged within a client organisation, either in the form of relationship meetings or on-site project work, makes the professional advisor available and accessible for informal conversations. This also places him or her as a natural first port of call. Opportunities for the advisor can arise by simply being in the right place at the right time; relationship dialogues facilitate this presence, especially if there is no on-site project work (Sieg et al. 2012).

However, none of these aspects automatically ensures the selection and appointment of the advisor, beyond informal free-of-charge work. Gathering of organisational insights and providing informal advice contributes to the advisor's organisational knowledge and acumen, which can inform and enrich formal proposals and offerings (Skjølsvik 2012, Day and Barksdale 2003, Werr and Pemer 2007).

As part of the study, I have detected a close connection between the senior executive-professional advisor relationship and a project or service appointment decision, but only if a senior executive:

- chooses to make a direct personal decision (selection mode);
- prefers an ad hoc or intuitive selection approach;
- decides to concentrate on the foci 'trust and empathy' and/or 'continuity and embeddedness' within the decision-making matrix; and
- the organisational context is addressed and past experiences or performances with the particular advisor are positive while the project objectives are being met.

This scenario presents itself primarily in relation to free-of-charge work, confidential or sensitive advisory work and small, low-risk projects.

In summary, the impact of the wider, beyond-project client-advisor relationship is simply more indirect and subtler. Although it does not feature as a dominant evaluation or selection criterions such (Skjølsvik 2012), it creates opportunities and contributes to the overall perception of the advisor and advisory firm.

Regarding the two previously mentioned senior executive decision processes – to maintain a relationship with an advisor or advisory firm and to select and appoint an advisory firm for a particular project or service – the following conclusions can be drawn:

The research has shown that there are a number of very senior executives, chiefly senior CEOs, who are open to a broader, beyond-project relationship, but who would not, in general, get actively or directly involved in individual selection and appointment decisions. In other words, this group of senior managers subscribe to a wider client-advisor relationship as a result of the first decision process but refrain from getting involved in the selection decision process.

Conversely, a few senior executives were rather reluctant or distant in terms of engaging with the advisor or advisory firm beyond the project context; however, they were actively involved in previous selection decisions, which led to the appointment of the advisor and advisory firm.

Consequently, developing and maintaining a close 'client-advisor relationship' with a senior executive, which extends beyond project conversations, does not automatically mean that this senior manager is actively involved in the second decision-making process or willing to exert his or her influence on the decision-making process.

8.1.8 Where next with 'client-advisor relationships'?

Tying into the conclusions presented above, it is important for the advisor and advisory firm to take note of individual senior executives' expectations, preferences and constraints, and respect and respond to these as part of the 'client-advisor relationship' process. Not every senior manager who is interested in developing and maintaining a wider relationship is willing or in a position to get involved in the selection and appointment process. Nor does a senior manager's lack of interest in a wider dialogue or relationship mean that he or she is not prepared to select and appoint the advisor or advisory firm for a particular project.

A positive and close 'client-advisor relationship' beyond the realms of the project can provide occasions to create or make a positive impression and generate opportunities for the advisor, but should not be viewed exclusively as a sales channel. The impact of the wider dialogue on the final selection and appointment decision for significant fee-paying projects or services is, if at all, rather subtle and not a primary selection driver (Skjølsvik 2012). Furthermore, some senior executives are increasingly sceptical of advisor and advisory firms' motives when it comes to additional offerings and many feel uncomfortable accepting invitations or services, especially those outside of the professional context (Höner and Mohe 2009, Mohe 2005).

Instead of viewing the broader client-advisor relationship as a means to an end (appointment) primarily for the advisor, there is an opportunity to establish a construct with a meaning on its own. Both the client and advisory side reap benefits from a positive client-advisor relationship, on a personal as well as an organisational level (see Chapter Six for a full list), which extends beyond project or service successes. Revisiting and reviving the original 'trusted advisor' concept, as advocated by Maister, Green and Galford (2000), might provide the necessary guidance to recalibrate the relationship and shift to *"thinking things over versus doing things"* (Buchen 2001, page 96). In effect, there is scope for three different roles –

consultant, executive coach and trusted advisor – each focusing on a different outcome: *"consultants strive to help the organisation achieve excellence"*, *"executive coaches work hard to make the senior executive look good"* and *"trusted advisors seek to stir the senior manager to grow and develop executive stature"* (Buchen 2001, page 98). However, bringing these concepts into an equilibrium with professional service firms' ingrained DNA and general fee-and-profit outlook will be an interesting task. For reference, I have extracted a number of key differences between the roles and summarised them in the table below:

The consultant and trusted advisor: roles and differences

Consultant	Trusted advisor
Written agreements	Oral understanding
Evaluator	Observer
Problem solving	Problem posing
Conclusions	Explorations
Get on with it	Plenty of time
Power plays	Ethical considerations
Success	Integrity
Answers	Questions
Resolution	Ambiguity
Competition	'Coopetition'
Models	Stories

Note: The executive coach straddles both positions but leans more towards the role of the trusted advisor.

Table 8.1 – Consultant- Advisor differences (adapted from Buchen 2001, page 96)

8.2 Implications for professional service firms, client organisations and academia

The conclusions and findings from this study point towards three overarching implications or recommendations, which can be summarised as follows:

1. The interactions and ensuing rapport or relationship between client and advisor should be viewed and evaluated holistically

and not be seen as a means to an end in terms of sales (relationship marketing agenda), nor something that needs to be tightly controlled or even interrupted (professional purchasing agenda). Positive and constructive project relationships contribute to the service or project success and lead to greater client satisfaction. A strong wider, beyond-project relationship between client and advisor creates opportunities and has the potential to generate long-lasting benefits for both the senior executive and the advisor and their respective organisations, which can extend beyond projects and services.

2. Meaningful and practical service or project evaluation and experience management during the course of the project will provide opportunities for corrective actions and thus increase chances of success and satisfaction, whereas an assessment intra and ex post will increase transparency, remove subjectivity and reduce emotional judgement, and also enhance the evaluation and selection of service offerings a priori. This should hopefully result in an overall improvement in dynamics between senior executive, client organisation, professional services firm and advisor.

3. Instead of focusing on what people do wrong and offering suggestions for improvements (Kahneman 2011) or on what people do right in order to learn more powerful heuristics (Pliske and Klein 2003), the research project has tried to understand what people do, regardless of right or wrong, and by simply understanding the decision-making and different perspective taken, to be able to create a mutually more beneficial and respectful decision-making environment for collaboration.

In the subsequent sections, I will revisit these three points from the different standpoints and add a number of further observations taken from the research findings.

8.2.1 Implications and recommendations for professional service firms and advisors

Reflecting on the implications mentioned above and the literature and study findings, a number of recommendations can be identified regarding professional service firms' relationship management, performance and experience management and tendering for new projects or services.

8.2.1.1 Relationship management

The study's findings suggest that a more nuanced approach to relationship management is called for. Interactions between senior clients and advisors need to be seen from two angles: a) a rapport or working relationship tied to a particular service or project; and b) a wider, beyond-project relationship. These two relationships are linked to two senior executive decision- making processes: 1) to develop or maintain a general relationship or rapport with the professional service firm and advisor; and 2) to select, appoint and transact with the advisory firm for a particular service or project.

Regarding the wider, beyond-project relationship, it is pertinent for the advisor and advisory firm to take note of, understand, respect and respond to the senior executive's expectations of an advisor, his or her personal preferences and principles, and the broader landscape in which he or she is operating. Furthermore, it would be helpful to establish what type of role the senior executive would like the individual advisor to take on: act as a consultant and assist in achieving organisational excellence; be an actual trusted advisor and stimulate the manager to develop and gain executive status; or even function as an executive coach and make sure the client image is positive (Buchen 2001). The latter two roles are not so easily aligned with a marketing and sales agenda.

It is important to recognise that some senior managers do not want a frequent or intimate broader relationship, but are still happy to select, appoint and transact with a professional service firm and advisor. On the other hand, there are also a number of senior executives who are keen to develop and maintain a wider relationship with representatives of the professional services firm but are not in a position or have opted to not get involved in selection and appointment decisions. The professional service firm needs to take this into consideration.

A more deliberate approach to account and relationship management may assist and explore why the professional services firm wants to build a rapport and invest in the relationship. Concepts such as the loyal client and the net promoter score (NPS) are very popular in professional services relationship management. However, is the client who gives a high NPS actually in a position to select and appoint an advisor? And is the persistently loyal client really the most valuable client? Should the loyal client who continues to appoint and transact with a firm, although the services or project might not deliver the expected results (Karantinou and Hogg 2009), be rewarded or even passed around as a spokesperson for the advisory firm?

Based on the data I reviewed, professional service firms would benefit from taking a step back and reconsidering: Does the firm only want to invest in relationships with individuals who actually make that second decision, to select and appoint them? Should loyal clients be rewarded and challenging or difficult clients penalised? What about senior CEOs who just want to have a regular dialogue but do not want to be beleaguered with sales pitches or asked to intervene in particular tenders? And most importantly, should relationship management only act as a sales channel, or is there scope for a new relationship paradigm, which acknowledges the perpetual and reciprocal benefits for all sides – senior executive and advisor – as well as their respective organisations? How could such a new paradigm be operationalised and funded?

8.2.1.2 Performance and experience management

Positive project performance and experiences, which of course are determined by an affirmative client-advisor project relationship, appear to be critical to secure future appointments and collaborations. The clients' primary demands appear to be for consistent high quality service or project delivery (Financial Times, Managing Partners Forum and Meridian West 2012). Subsequently, it is vital that professional services firms establish if and to what degree a client is happy and satisfied with the firm's performance and project or service outcomes. As previously mentioned and based on my findings, it does not suffice that the advisor and advisory firm is convinced of the project's success - the client has to be comfortable and satisfied with the services and experiences.

Furthermore, the research shows that responding to client criticism, as well as intervening and addressing challenging situations, contributes more strongly and more memorably to a project experience than if everything has gone to plan. Thus, seeking client feedback and being responsive to client concerns is an opportunity to create positive reference points for future work prospects.

Lastly, and reflecting on my observations and the existing literature, a professional service firm proactively supporting and participating in a structured and objective assessment and evaluation, during and after completion of a project or service, might be a little uncomfortable and may delay the start of the project or alter the terms of the service arrangement. However, it would hopefully capture a positive service performance and make the project or service successes more demonstrable and factual. Consequently, professional services firms with a strong track record of excellent collaboration and a solid focus on successful outcomes for the client are able to set themselves apart from those competitors who fail to deliver. An objective evaluation of the advisory firm's contributions should appeal to an advisor; it is an acknowledgement of work well done and can act as an undisputable testimonial point for future references.

8.2.2 Implications and recommendations for client organisations and senior managers

The research highlights a number of considerations for both the client organisation as an entity and the senior managers interacting with professional advisors and firms.

8.2.2.1 Professionalisation of organisational purchasing

The installation of an organisational procurement strategy and programme should consider all stakeholders involved, be carefully aligned with the organisational culture and be communicated to all affected managers. Organisational purchasing measures, both control or incentive-based, can generate the desired outputs or fiscal results, but can also lead to avoidance or certain unwanted behaviours effectively trying to circumnavigate or manipulate procurement guidelines. The acceptance or rejection of purchasing programmes needs to be taken note of and understood by senior leadership – why do managers behave in certain ways? Could there be some detrimental and far-reaching underlying organisational causes? During the interviews, I have come across organisations that aimed to manage most projects in-house but failed to recruit and maintain the necessary pool of qualified project managers or companies that have tried to minimise external spend and only approved business-critical projects. This led to constant fire-fighting and no long-term success, not to mention the toll that it took on employees involved in the initiatives.

In light of today's drive towards cost reduction, more and more organisations are trying to contain or cut spending on external support, such as professional services, which is one of the main drivers for procurement measures and programmes (Financial Times, Managing Partners Forum and Meridian West 2012, Mohe 2005). Increasingly, companies are trying to manage and deliver projects in-house either with permanent or temporary staff on-site or off-shore; but are these arrangements sufficient and reliable enough to address organisational needs in the long term? Is an affordable but potentially patched together in-house project that fails, and then needs to be salvaged by an external party at a premium, a better deal for the organisation than a well-planned and competitively priced project from a professional service firm? What about staff turnover and potential talent shortages; project or service delays; systems or processes not functioning, and missed innovation opportunities? An effective and affective procurement strategy should not be purely financially driven but should address and deliver the wider organisational strategy.

Many purchasing programmes or measures aim to intervene or step in between the commissioning manager, the professional advisor and the firm. At the same time, a successful project or collaboration hinges on a good rapport between the client manager and professional service lead and team. Consequently, intervention from procurement must be balanced and give the commissioning manager the opportunity to gauge the chemistry within the team. Furthermore, too much or heavy-handed involvement of procurement, or even constraining the wider beyond-project/service relationship between client manager and professional advisor, would limit or deny the manager and the organisation those additional relationship benefits described in Chapter Six.

8.2.2.2 Evaluation of service or project performances and outputs

Objective evaluations of professional service performances and outputs, and keeping track of results for future reference, have the potential to generate significant benefits for the client organisation. Procurement could, for example, facilitate and administer the ongoing and post-project or service assessments, instead of focusing primarily or exclusively on purchasing controls and incentive measures. Based on my research observations, many companies have already added project or service assessments to the scope of supplier management programmes.

I would presume that a collaborative and mutually respectful approach, which includes factoring in the project or service contributions made by the client, leads to more productive outcomes and better dynamics than a confrontational approach. Some third parties offer project or service evaluation services, often determined by client feedback surveys, which contractually reduce the advisory fee by a pre-agreed amount or percentage if the feedback is below certain thresholds. Needless to say, these arrangements are not very popular or are being rejected by professional services firms, as I have observed in a number of internal discussions and also with peers working for other professional service firms. They definitely neither increase goodwill nor contribute to a sincerely positive project and beyond-project relationship. There is certainly a fine line between being a demanding and challenging client organisation and overdoing it. Warning signs should be if professional services firms are bidding less frequently, or not at all, for particular projects or services.

8.2.2.3 Senior executive – clarify personal expectations and preferences

There are only a few implications to be drawn for senior executives interacting with professional advisors, beyond the organisational comments made above. My observation is that clients who are more outspoken and clearly define, almost informally contract, the beyond-project rapport appear to be more comfortable with their client-advisor relationship. Communicating personal preferences and expectations, clarifying which role or aspects of a role – consultant, coach or advisor – the senior manager would like the professional advisor to play at a given time, would be helpful. I was surprised at how many senior executives were caught off-guard during the interviews when I asked them what their expectations and preferences were when it came to working with professional advisors. Finally, continuously providing honest and constructive feedback to the advisor or the advisory firm gives the advisor the opportunity to make changes where necessary.

8.2.3 Implications and recommendations for further academic research

In the next section, I review a number of potential opportunities for further research in addition to listing the limitations of this study.

For the most part, the literature can be aligned to a marketing (relationship) or an operations (purchasing and selection) camp, and although studies spell out ramifications for the other side, I have only found a handful of studies which take a more holistic approach to the debate (Skjølsvik 2012, Karantinou and Hogg 2009). This, of course, leads to silos of findings and knowledge, which do not factor in the interdependencies of both relationship and selection.

Hopefully, the results and conclusions of this study will shed some light on the client-advisor phenomenon, extend ideas regarding linkages between the two decision processes and interactions and provide sufficient insights to identify potential theories and models for future studies. The research also shows that a rigid process-oriented approach might not be able to pick up on all the complexities and variances of real-life decision-making. Image theory (Beach 1993a) offered a constructive and flexible alternative; additional research using this model or a similar adaptable approach might be more suitable to capture the phenomena.

Professional services are extremely diverse, ranging from health care, engineering and architecture to property, law, advertising and media. Even within each subdomain there are significant differences. Patient-doctor interactions and doctor selection are not quite the same for general practitioners compared to hospital-based specialists, nor are client-advisor interactions involving 'Big Four' accountancy firms, top strategy firms such as McKinsey, Bain and BCG, and technology consultancies and providers such as IBM, Wipro or EDS. I believe that it is pivotal to differentiate and possibly separate these different subgroups, and potentially compare and contrast the findings in order to draw insightful conclusions.

In a business context, it is essential to include professional services advisors who work for large organisations or partnerships, as such firms deliver a significant amount of services. A number of studies relied on single independent advisors or very small firms; this, of course, reduces the complexity involved and removes the brand impact but also leads to distinct conclusions. I believe it is absolutely critical to gather data directly from clients and not rely on advisors' views of clients' perspectives (Chelliah and Davis 2010, Chelliah 2010). The study from Skjølsvik (2012) has shown that the advisor community has their own perceptions of the selection process and interactions, and these do not always correlate with the clients' view, be it receiving business managers or procurement managers.

8.3 Limitations and opportunities for further research

Academic research in the field of professional services and the interactions between client and advisor has evolved in the past two decades, and there is clearly scope for further research. The research project has uncovered a number of different areas where additional academic investigations could provide valuable insights: investigations of more defined sample populations, establishing the impact of professional service firm branding, additional research into client-advisor relationships and roles and, lastly, examining the impact of purchasing measures on both clients and advisors. These are in addition to the study's limitations, which of course also offer future opportunities. Given the industry's *"closed and secretive nature"* (Karantinou and Hogg 2009, page 251), access to data, especially from a client perspective, is an issue. The study's auto-ethnographic approach, incorporating my professional role as a client feedback manager for one of the 'Big Four' firms, provided natural (by which I mean not staged) access to clients, client views and firm internal insights.

8.3.1 Limitations of the study

Following an inductive research approach and allowing for a constructivist interpretation of the data offers many benefits and embraces client and advisor perspectives, but it is also open to criticism, especially from those who prefer deductive and positivistic investigations. The rationale for selecting the constructivist grounded theory methods and using auto-ethnographic elements is discussed in Chapter Two. Beyond that, the study is marked by a number of limitations linked to the sample data, data collection and analytical methods.

The study relies on client feedback data and field observations from one of the 'Big Four' accountancy firms. There is a possibility that client responses might be different in the context of client feedback conversations with other 'Big Four' firms. In the subsequent sections, I discuss how these contextual circumstances have impacted my research, which can be viewed as limitations but also strengths.

8.3.1.1 Limitations due to sample data

Due to the client feedback positioning with the client (the senior executive is asked to provide candid feedback to a representative of the professional services firm, as explained in Chapter One), it is fair to assume that senior executives who agree to a client feedback interview are to a certain degree inclined towards developing and maintaining a rapport or relationship with the particular advisory firm. Senior managers who are not interested in a rapport or relationship would have most likely either not been nominated by the advisory partner or declined to be interviewed. Consequently, there is an inherent bias in the data towards a rapport or relationship.

The interviews involved primarily UK-based senior executives of large (FTSE 100 and equivalent) companies; only one organisation had virtual working arrangements across Europe, which means that the office locations of these three senior executives were flexible (one person was based in London, and the other two in Germany). Moreover, the researched organisations operated either in financial services or in telecommunications. The field observations, of course, included other industries, such as life sciences, consumer goods, manufacturing and energy and resources. Nonetheless, the bulk of the data can be traced back to financial services institutions, which also make up the largest client base for this particular 'Big Four' firm. In other words, the sample data is skewed towards financial services and telecommunications from an industry perspective, the UK from a geographic perspective and the FTSE 100 and equivalents from a client-size perspective. There is, therefore, a fair chance that the findings might have been different if the core sample data came from, for example, Germany or France, or if senior managers in consumer goods or of medium-sized companies had been interviewed.

In addition, during the interviews, it transpired that a number of senior executives were often a step removed from the actual selection and appointment process, primarily because they chose to delegate the decision to a direct report or a group. This has a clear bearing on the selection behaviour and criteria discussed, as it meant that senior executives either provided general observational comments or referred to past personal selection experiences.

8.3.1.2 Limitations due to data collection

The study's primary data are 21 in-depth interviews with senior executives conducted as part of the 'Big Four' firm's regular client feedback exercise. The following are limitations of this data collection method:

- As a client feedback interviewer, I was not able to pose research-specific questions, or ask the senior executive to recount a particular decision-making experience.
- In accordance with the client feedback guidelines, the interview is not structured and the interviewee is able to steer and influence the discussion. For instance, if a respondent is keen to discuss a particular project or incident for an extended period of time, the client feedback manager will not interrupt or stop them. From past experiences, we, the client feedback managers, know that this approach works particularly well with senior executives, who do not respond well to market research-type structured questions. However, this generates datasets which are more challenging to compare and contrast; for example, not every respondent will make comments about value for money or selection criteria.
- The client feedback manager introduces him or herself as a representative of the firm with a direct reporting line into the 'Big Four' firm's executive. This can trigger more 'diplomatic' responses and more carefully worded comments, or even inhibit some comments. At the same time, it allows us to deduct that the comments that were made, are well thought through and considered important enough for the firm's senior leadership.

On the upside, the client feedback data collection methods provide somewhat natural commentary from senior executives, recounting and relating to real situations and issues and not describing hypothetical scenarios. One could argue that, since the data is collected and taken out of a real-life business context, it is as naturalistic as possible.

Another aspect worth mentioning here is the role of the individual interviewer and the chemistry between the interviewer and senior manager. Senior executives are, after all, human beings who react and respond to situations and other people. There is a good possibility that individual interviews would have unfolded slightly differently and comments been different if another client feedback manager had interviewed the senior managers. As a result, I only used interviews that I personally conducted, and I discuss the rationale as part of the theoretical sampling approach described in Chapter Three.

8.3.1.3 Limitations due to analytical methods

The primary standpoint taken during the analysis is to focus on presence and coverage of aspects, for example how many senior executives mentioned a particular notion, and investigate the remaining respondents who did not mention it. Frequency featured to a limited degree in the analysis. A detailed discussion of this matter can be found in Chapter Five. In summary, I felt that frequency of aspects mentioned was too closely linked with an individual's personal communication style and that the 'voice of more vocal senior executives who repeatedly communicated their standpoints' would be given more weight than those who expressed their opinions only once but very precisely.

Overall, I tried to deliberate and balance respondents' viewpoints and consider the different macro perspectives, meaning client and advisor, but also the client organisation and professional services firm they represented. I will return to this debate in more detail in the later reflective section.

8.3.2 Opportunities for further research

The results of this research study suggest numerous opportunities for further research. These can be related to or categorised as investigations of more defined sample populations, in-depth explorations of the selection process and the impact of professional service firm branding, additional research into advisor-client relationships and roles, and the effects of purchasing programmes and protocols on senior managers' and advisors' behaviour and performances.

8.3.2.1 Investigation of more defined sample populations

It would be informative to investigate the phenomena by differentiating between the different types of professional services, such as accountancy, property services, management consultancy, legal services, engineering services and possibly health services. It would be interesting to distinguish between advice-based and delivery-based services. For the latter, the outcomes could be something more tangible like, for example, the implementation of a new IT system, the construction of a site or place, or new processes or programmes. For the former, the product is effectively the expert opinion, judgement or recommendation of a specialist in a field. There are of course situations or services which require both advice and delivery. Based on my observations, investigating how these differences on both levels impact the selection process and the relationship between client and advisor, and comparing and contrasting the findings would shed some more light on the phenomena.

Furthermore, this study has shown that there are pronounced differences between the generic functional roles of senior executives. CEOs mentioned different aspects compared to CROs, for example. Consequently, there is an opportunity to build on these findings and examine differences in selection and relationship behaviours and expectations according to clients' functional role and seniority, as well as to establish the impact of organisational context and past experiences on functional role and seniority segments.

Lastly, Skjølsvik's (2012) study hinted towards a gap between advisor and client perceptions regarding the importance of the overall relationship and relationship-driven perspectives such as trust and chemistry. It would be insightful to explore these views in juxtaposition, researching how particular clients and their advisors experience and perceive the relationship and its underlying components.

8.3.2.2 In-depth explorations of the selection process

There is definitely scope for further in-depth academic investigation into selection modes, selection behaviours and selection criteria, as well as 'connecting the dots' between the different selection components. By this, I mean tracing the selection progress and chosen paths for different projects or service trajectories. For instance, what selection processes do regulatory-driven projects, which require the professional services firm to fill a knowledge and resource gap, as well as help the client meet a deadline, follow? How are they different from operationally-driven projects, which require the professional services firm to fill a knowledge gap and teach and empower the client organisation?

Returning to the examination of the selection component, identifying by whom and how, in general terms, selections are made has not been sufficiently reflected in past studies. As part of this research project, I have addressed this notion, albeit primarily from the senior executive's perspective. Therefore, there is scope to build on this standpoint and investigate more widely. Is the selection decision the direct responsibility of a single individual or has the person been tasked by someone else to make the decision? If it is a group or panel decision, who has delegated them and how is the decision-making process being facilitated? Reflecting on the win-loss reviews and interviews, significant selection decisions, from a financial point of view, were almost exclusively made by a group of primarily middle- to upper-level managers. Frequently, the decision-making process was coordinated and facilitated by a procurement manager; occasionally a senior executive was either part of the group or acts as a final instance if no decision can be reached. There is substantial latitude for further research in terms of selection mode and group decision-making dynamics.

Moreover, future research into selection criteria should ideally distinguish between project or service trajectories as mentioned in the previous section. Even though the selection criteria might be the same or similar, the importance and weighting of each criteria or category of criteria will most likely be different. Based on my field observations, costs were mentioned as pivotal or even decisive criteria in significant long-running service contracts or large delivery programmes, whereas costs were not cited at all in short, strategic projects.

8.3.2.3 Establishing the impact of professional service firm branding

In summary, to what extent does the brand and brand perception of the professional services firm influence the selection and appointment decision, as well as informing the relationship between client and advisor?

The study established that some senior executives had a clear view or perception of a firm and its brand, while others simply lumped the organisations together into a 'Big Four' firm category; some senior executives' views and comments were primarily aimed at the individual advisors, whereas others saw the firm as an entity where individual advisors come and go, manifested in the identified gestalt construct. What happens if a senior advisor moves to another firm? Do clients follow? Does the relationship change because of the association with the new firm?

The research uncovered that in certain circumstances the brand is important. For instance, if a service or project involves presentation to the company board, a reputable professional services firm with the appropriate market position, branding and reach appears be more desirable for the decision-maker or project or service sponsor.

There has simply not been sufficient academic research involving large well-branded professional services firms. Past studies have looked at independent advisors operating as contractors or very small outfits.

8.3.2.4 Additional research in advisor-client relationships and roles

This research included senior executives who, for the most part, wanted to develop and maintain a type of rapport or relationship with an advisor, otherwise they would have not agreed to the interview in the first place. It would be of interest to research clients, regardless of their seniority, who are less keen or do not want to have a beyond-project rapport or relationship with an advisor and to explore what determines or informs this decision.

Furthermore, additional research regarding those clients who want to maintain a wider, beyond-project rapport with an advisor, and what role or combination of roles they would like such an advisor to take on (consultant, coach or personal trusted advisor), could provide an answer to the following concerns: Can one individual or a professional services firm take on more than one role at a time? Can a fee-charging professional advisor truly be a 'trusted advisor', as defined by Maister, Green & Galford (2000) and Buchen (2001)? These questions warrant further examination.

In addition, there is scope to confirm and extend the client-advisor motives and benefits outlined in Chapter Six of this document, keeping in mind a nuanced approach to the context. A senior executive would most likely have different expectations or emphasis compared to a mid-level manager in operations. Furthermore, clients will have different expectations of an accountant, lawyer, top strategy advisor or representative of a technology firm.

Finally, sharing insights is an integral aspect of the broader, beyond-project relationship. Some senior executives are less interested in this aspect, but the majority are attracted to this proposition. My observations concluded that it is a delicate balancing act, but could also serve as the foundation of a new relationship paradigm removed from a sales agenda. Additional academic research into sharing and accepting insights with professional advisors might provide the necessary data points to develop such a paradigm.

8.3.2.5 Examination of the impact of purchasing measures on senior managers and professional advisors

Whilst there has been strong academic interest in the operational purchasing debate and articles have been published, the individual managers' perspective and the professional services firms' viewpoint have featured less frequently.

Following up on research questions similar to those listed below might provide helpful information regarding the overarching operating discussion:

- 'Does a professionalised purchasing approach influence project or service performance, outcomes and client satisfaction?'
- 'How do senior executives and service or project commissioning managers view and embrace the different purchasing measures? What techniques do these managers consider and deploy if the purchasing approach stalls or hinders the start of project or service?'
- 'How do professional advisors and their respective firms respond to the different purchasing programmes and measures? Are they still willing to go the extra mile, submit proposals, provide free-of-charge work?'
- 'What happens if a strategic supplier programme fails? And do strategic supplier programmes, the becoming part of the organisations eco-system, deliver the anticipated benefits of being joined up and driving innovation?'

8.4 Reflections on research outcomes and approach taken

As part of my conclusion to this doctoral thesis, I shall reflect in this section on this rather personal research journey, the approach taken and methods employed, as well as on the proposed contributions to this field of knowledge.

8.4.1 The constructivist grounded theory approach shaped the auto-ethnographic research journey

Reflecting on the research journey, I would conclude that an inductive, grounded theory approach – in this case Charmaz's constructivist approach (2006) – with a delayed literature review allowed for an open and creative analytical process while still remaining grounded in primary interview data and analytic auto-ethnographic (Anderson 2006) observations.

Looking at the literature, there are undoubtedly opportunities for further research. However, I hope that the outcome of the present study will resonate with, and prove to be of use for, an academic as well as a professional audience. Grounded theory research is a process with no definitive endpoint (Charmaz 2006, Bryant and Charmaz 2007, Goulding 2002). I, therefore, do not view the discussed substantive theory, including the models and concepts that emerged from this research, as a final product. Rather I expect and hope that the constructs will evolve further over time.

The literature review has also shown that research into professional advisor-client interactions is still in its infancy and evolving, and is moreover somewhat fragmented due to the marketing versus organisational procurement standpoints. The large number of different stakeholder roles and perspectives, on both the client and advisor side, as well as the occasionally political nature of the exchanges, all add to the complexity. In recent years, I have observed that individuals who have not worked in or with professional services providers struggle to understand the multiple layers, viewpoints and dynamics between client and professional advisor. Likewise, gaining access to stakeholders – especially influential senior client executives – for research purposes is problematic. I believe that the situational setting of the data gathering has a significant impact on individuals' responses.

Reflecting on the research project, I am convinced that the senior executives I interviewed as part of a client feedback exercise would have offered more deliberate or ideal scenario responses to decision-making questions if I had interviewed them in an academic research setting. I believe that they would have provided a narrative of how they would ideally like to make selection decisions and interact with advisors, instead of an account of how situations actually and naturally unfolded.

The interview data I was able to analyse were compiled in a slightly removed context in which senior executives were effectively providing an account of their relationship and interactions with one particular advisory firm over a given period of time. I then applied an academic lens, determined by my research aims, to analyse the commentary. One could argue that the data is more natural, meaning less deliberate, censored or idealistic; at the same time, this set-up has prohibited me from posing particular research-driven questions.

8.4.2 I am willing to accept and reflect on my personal effect on the results

The constructivist grounded theory requires the researcher to accept the thought that conducting and writing research are not neutral acts; thus, in order to achieve a balanced and meaningful result, reflexivity is required (2006, Charmaz 2009).

On a personal level, I accept my personal role in the research: the varying degrees of rapport and chemistry between the senior executives interviewed and myself; the personal experiences and views which determined which observational data points to add and consult; the interpretation and coding of interview data; and the personal thoughts that went into the conceptual framework development and helped shape the emerging substantive theory.

At the same time, I was determined to follow Charmaz's recommendations and proactively recognise my own standpoint, adopt new perspectives and compare views (2006, Charmaz 2009) and attain the appropriate level of theoretical sensitivity to progress and evolve the research project. I started out with a strong senior executive standpoint and added the organisational perspective by comparing interviews of respondents from the same company once the conceptual framework emerged and the first findings transpired. I also looked at the data from the viewpoint of the individual advisor and the professional services firm. Discussions with my professional sponsor helped and enriched my thinking, and brought a degree of balance to my otherwise strong client focus.

In retrospect, I recognise my overarching advocacy of, or possibly empathy with, the client and client organisations, albeit working for a professional services firm I acknowledge and appreciate the other major perspective. Overall, I feel that a large proportion of the existing research, be it peer-reviewed or, especially, commercially driven, is geared towards the professional services standpoint, while an inadequate amount of research aims to give the client – the senior executive – a voice and document their pivotal perspective. I hope that with this particular study I have given the individual client a voice, while still addressing the other standpoints with the necessary attention and respect.

8.4.3 The study is unique and would be difficult to replicate

I found no comparable study in the literature. In the context of client-professional advisor interactions, comments from senior client executives and C-suite personnel of major organisations can be found in very few studies (Haverila et al. 2011, Financial Times, Managing Partners Forum and Meridian West 2012). As far as I am aware, no previous study has focused exclusively on this population. Furthermore, only one other study (Skjølsvik 2012) has brought these two aspects – client-advisor relationship and the selection and appointment of advisors – together explicitly in an academic research project.

Secondly, the client feedback interview and field work research setting provides a real-life context, meaning that the client commentary is not theoretical, hypothetical or gathered in a staged research setting. Rather it is genuine and part of the day-to-day interactions between client organisation and advisor firm.

I have worked in professional services for many years, first for a small strategy firm, then for a consulting arm of a global technology firm before joining a 'Big Four' accountancy firm in management consulting. I recognise that this makes me an integral part or tool of the research process. My personal interpretations of situations and the dataset, drawn from field work observations and past experiences, are part of the research process.

Replicating this particular study would be challenging, starting with negotiating access to senior executives, creating a similar interview setting to a client feedback exercise and finally involving an academic researcher with a similar professional background.

8.4.4 The research findings and resulting substantive theory offer considerable contributions to knowledge

Taking a step back and reflecting on the literature findings, empirical results and resulting substantive theory, I believe that this study makes a number of contributions to the existing body of knowledge:

First of all, by approaching the phenomena of interactions between senior executive clients and advisors from a broad and inductive grounded theory perspective, the study has uncovered two decision-making processes as part of the interactions between senior executive clients and professional advisors. These two decision-making processes are (a) for the executive client to develop and maintain a relationship and (b) to select and appoint an advisor for a particular service. These two processes have so far been examined in two distinct bodies of literature and two theoretical contexts. My thesis takes an integrated approach to the processes within one research context. As elaborated in Chapter Seven of this thesis, the existing literature on the first decision-making process is currently located in the marketing management literature, as part of the relationship management or marketing discourse. On the other hand, theoretical discussion around the second decision-making process is situated within the operational procurement or organisational sourcing discourse. Thus, the described constructivist grounded theory study links these two academic debates.

Secondly, by taking an inductive and holistic angle the research project not only brought the two academic perspectives together, but also the emerging empirically grounded theory allowed for both decision-processes to be mapped to one decision-making framework and model, the decision-making matrix. Furthermore, the study started to explore to what extent the decision-making processes impact or influence each other.

Theoretical contributions

The study enhances the professional advisor interaction and selection discourse, which previously focused primarily on the selection process and selection criteria. It does this by introducing one conceptual framework for the decision-making processes and bringing together 'imperatives', 'project and service trajectory', 'selection and choice actions' with a 'decision frame' which includes both past experiences and organisational context. 'Selection and choice actions' extend beyond selection criteria and include selection mode and selection behaviours, meaning informal activities in addition to more formal, organisational protocols, which have not featured significantly in the previous research. Most importantly, both decision-making processes, mentioned above, can now be mapped to one conceptual framework, and as a result, linkages between the two processes can be visualised more clearly and investigated. For instance, the framework illustrates how decision-makers' personal experiences are shaped as a result of a selection decision (project or service) and how these past experiences might inform future relationships as well as selection decision-making processes.

In addition to the above described conceptual framework mapping both decision-making processes, a further complimentary substantive theory, in the form of the decision-matrix, emerged from the research activities: During both decision-making processes, the decision-maker considers and balances the four foci of the matrix, namely 'competiveness, skills and merit', 'continuity and embeddedness', 'control and manage' and 'trust and empathy'. The resulting directive position not only impacts the evaluation and weighting of criteria, but also informs how the decision-process unfolds (e.g. selection mode and behaviour). The disparate axes capturing the foci 'competitiveness, skills and merit' and 'continuity and embeddedness' have indeed been previously discussed and documented in the literature (Uzzi 1997, Skjølsvik 2012), as outlined in detail in section 8.1.4. However, the second axis, involving the foci 'control and manage –

professional advisors' and 'trust and empathy', has so far not been juxtaposed and investigated as such academically; although control and management of advisors is a key aspect in the operational procurement or organisational sourcing debate, and the concept of trust frequently features within the context of relationship management literature.

In summary, two new substantive theories emerged from this empirical research project: the conceptual framework mapping both decision-making processes and the decision-making matrix, which bring two academic debates, relationship management and operational procurement, together and hopefully enrich the dialogue by increasing our understanding of interactions between senior clients and advisors. Moreover, the study also demonstrates that, in addition to the sequential process perspective, frequently applied in the previous decision-making research, there are additional considerations that determine how the decision-making process unfolds and which aspects are being considered plus to what degree; therefore, the two emerging theories should be seen as complementary to the established process perspective of decision-making.

Likewise, the study has shown that a multitude of aspects and conflicting notions feature in both decision-making processes. The senior executives' decision-making can be very situational (service or project trajectories vary) and highly contextual (past experiences and organisational aspects), and thus, a slight change in the decision-making set-up can or will lead to different decision-making outcomes. Consequently, it appears to be extremely difficult, even if all aspects are known and mapped, to accurately anticipate decision-making behaviours and outcomes.

Methodological contributions

In addition to these theoretical contributions to knowledge, the research also offers two methodological contributions:

First of all, the study provides a naturalistic account of the interactions between senior executives of large organisations and professional advisors in large firms, by following an analytic auto-ethnographic constructivist grounded-theory approach. In the past there has been limited adoption of such an amalgamated research approach as recommended by Simone Pettigrew (2000). Furthermore, as far as I can establish, there has been no previous application of such an approach within the context of naturalistic decision-making.

Secondly, according to Beach (2014, 1998), there has been limited empirical use of the three images (value, trajectory and strategic image) as part of image theory-based study of decision-making, especially in the field of management research. Therefore, this research study provides an insightful example of this methodology and illustrates how the three images and definitions can be successfully applied in an inductive and qualitative research approach.

In summary, I believe that the study's substantive theory and its proposed contributions to knowledge offer new insights into the phenomena of client-advisor interactions and will lead to further illuminating empirical academic research in the future.

References

Anonymous. Attack of the bean-counters; Professional services. 2015. *The Economist*, **414**(8930), pp. 55.

Abelson, R.P. and Levi, A., 1985. *Decision making and decision theory.* New York: Random House.

Agnew, H., 2015, 28. August 2015. Accounting for change. *Financial Times, UK Edition*, 9.

Anderson, L., 2006. Analytic autoethnography. *Journal of contemporary ethnography*, **35**(4), pp. 373-395.

Annells, M., 1996. Grounded theory method: Philosophical perspectives, paradigm of inquiry, and postmodernism. *Qualitative health research*, **6**(3), pp. 379-393.

Arnold, P.J., 2009. Global financial crisis: The challenge to accounting research. *Accounting, Organizations and Society*, **34**(6), pp. 803-809.

Asare, S.K., 1996. Screening of clients by audit firms. In: L.R. Beach, ed, *Decision Making in the Workplace: A Unified Perspective*. New York and London: Psychology Press, pp. 101-116.

Atkinson, P., 2006. Rescuing autoethnography. *Journal of contemporary ethnography*, **35**(4), pp. 400-404.

Atkinson, P., Delamont, S. and Coffey, A., 2004. *Key themes in qualitative research: Continuities and changes*. Walnut Creek, CA: Rowman Altamira.

Avakian, S., Clark, T. and Roberts, J., 2010. Examining the relationship between trust and culture in the consultant–client relationship. In: M.N. Saunders, D. Skinner, G. Dietz, N. Gillespie and R.J. Lewicki, eds, *Organizational Trust: A Cultural Perspective*. Cambridge: Cambridge University Press, pp. 129-153.

Bagdoniene, L. and Jakstaite, R., 2015. Trust as basis for development of relationships between professional service providers and their clients. *Economics and Management*, (14), pp. 360-366.

Baker, W.E. and Faulkner, R.R., 1991. Strategies for managing suppliers of professional services. *California management review*, **33**(4), pp. 33-45.

Bateson, J.E. and Hoffman, K.D., 1991. *Managing services marketing: Text and readings*. Boston: Dryden Press.

Bazerman, M. and Moore, D.A., 2012. *Judgment in managerial decision making*. 8th edn. New Jersey, NJ: Wiley.

Beach, L.R., 2014. *Decision making in the workplace: A unified perspective.* New York and London: Psychology Press.

Beach, L.R., 1998. *Image theory: Theoretical and empirical foundations.* Mahwah, NJ: Laurence Erlbaum Publishers.

Beach, L.R., 1997. *The psychology of decision making: people in organizations.* Thousand Oaks, CA: Sage Publications.

Beach, L.R., 1993a. Broadening the definition of decision making: The role of prechoice screening of options. *Psychological Science,* **4**(4), pp. 215-220.

Beach, L.R., 1993b. Image theory: An alternative to normative decision theory. *Advances in Consumer Research,* **20**(1), pp. 235-238.

Beach, L.R., Chi, M., Klein, G.A., Smith, P., Vicente, K. and Zsambok, C., 1997. *Naturalistic decision making and related research lines.* Mahwah, NJ: Laurence Erlbaum Associates.

Beach, L.R. and Connolly, T., 2005. *The psychology of decision making: People in organizations.* Thousand Oaks, CA: Sage Publications.

Beach, L.R. and Lipshitz, R., 1993. Why classical decision theory is an inappropriate standard for evaluating and aiding most human decision making. In: G.A. Klein, J. Orasanu, R. Calderwood and C.E. Zsambok, eds, *Decision making in action: Models and methods.* Westport, CT: Ablex Publishing, pp. 21-35.

Beach, L.R. and Mitchell, T.R., 1978. A contingency model for the selection of decision strategies. *Academy of Management Review,* **3**(3), pp. 439-449.

Berryman, J.M., 2007. Judgements during information seeking: a naturalistic approach to understanding the assessment of enough information. *Journal of Information Science,* **25**(1), pp. 196-206.

Betsch, T. and Haberstroh, S., 2014. *The routines of decision making.* New York, NY: Psychology Press.

Bettman, J.R., Luce, M.F. and Payne, J.W., 1998. Constructive consumer choice processes. *Journal of consumer research,* **25**(3), pp. 187-217.

Blaickie, N., 2007. *Approaches to social enquiry: advancing knowledge.* 2nd edn. Cambridge: Polity.

Boussebaa, M., 2015. Professional service firms, globalisation and the new imperialism. *Forthcoming in the Accounting, Auditing & Accountability Journal.*

Bowers, B. and Schatzman, L., 2009. Dimensional analysis. In: J.M. Morse, P.N. Stern, J. Corbin, B. Bowers, A.E. Clarke and K. Charmaz, eds, *Developing grounded theory: The second generation.* London and New York: Routledge, pp. 86-126.

Breckenridge, J., Jones, D., Elliott, I. and Nicol, M., 2012. Choosing a methodological path: Reflections on the constructivist turn. *Grounded Theory Review,* **11**(1), pp. 64-71.

Bryant, A., 2012. 'Grounded Theory' The Grounded Theory Method, *Grounded Theory Seminar held by Tony Bryant at Redding University* 2012.

Bryant, A., 2003. *A Constructive/ist Response to Glaser. About Barney G. Glaser: Constructivist Grounded Theory?* Published in FQS 3 (3).

Bryant, A. and Charmaz, K., 2007. *The Sage Handbook of Grounded Theory.* London: Sage Publications.

Buchen, I.H., 2001. The inner circle of the trusted advisor. *Industrial and Commercial Training,* **33**(3), pp. 94-99.

Burr, V., 1998. *Overview: Realism, relativism, social constructionism and discourse.* London: Sage Publications.

Cannon-Bowers, J.A., Salas, E. and Pruitt, J.S., 1996. Establishing the boundaries of a paradigm for decision-making research. *Human Factors: The Journal of the Human Factors and Ergonomics Society*, **38**(2), pp. 193-205.

Carter, C., Crawford, S., Muzio, D., Addison, S. and Mueller, F., 2015. The dark side of professions: the big four and tax avoidance. *Accounting, Auditing & Accountability Journal*, **28**(8), pp. 1263-1290.

Chambers, J.M., 1983. *Graphical methods for data analysis*. London: Chapman & Hall.

Charmaz, K., 2009. Shifting the grounds: Grounded theory in the 21st century. In: J.M. Morse, P.N. Stern, J. Corbin, B. Bowers, A.E. Clarke and K. Charmaz, eds, *Developing grounded theory: The second generation (developing qualitative inquiry)*. London and New York: Routledge, pp. 125-140.

Charmaz, K., 2008. Grounded theory as an emergent method. In: S.N. Hesse_Biber and P. Leavy, eds, *Handbook of Emergent Methods*. New York and London: Guildford Press, pp. 155-170.

Charmaz, K., 2006. *Constructing Grounded Theory A Practical Guide through Qualitative Analysis*. London: Sage Publications.

Charmaz, K. and Mitchell, R.G., 2001 Grounded theory in ethnography. In: P. Atkinson, S. Delamont, A. Coffey and J. Lofland, eds, *Handbook of ethnography*. London and New York: Sage Publications, pp. 160-174.

Chelliah, J., 2010. The psychodynamics of the client-consultant relationship. *International Journal of Business and information*, **5**(2), pp. 135.

Chelliah, J. and Davis, D., 2010. But do you like your (expensive management) consultant? *The Journal of business strategy*, **31**(2), pp. 34-42.

CIMA – Chartered Institute of Management Accounts, 2016-last update, External audit guidelines. Available: http://www.cimaglobal.com/Documents/ImportedDocuments/external _audit_guidelines_practical_experience_04.pdf2016].

Connolly, T. and Wagner, W.G., 1988. Decision cycles. *Advances in information processing in organizations*, **3**, pp. 183-205.

Coyle, A., 1995. Discourse analysis. In: J.J. Shaughnessy and E.B. Zechmeister, eds, *Research Methods in Psychology*. New York, NY: Sage Publications, pp. 366-386.

Crump, R., 2013. Competition commission aims to break big four dominance. *Accountancy Age*, **22**.

Curle, D., 2015, April 8, 2015. Why Size Matters: Big Four Accounting Firms Poised to Move In. *Thomson Reuters*.

Czerniawska, F., 2006. *The trusted firm: How consulting firms build successful client relationships*. Chichester: Wiley.

Czerniawska, F., 1999. *Management consultancy in the 21st century*. West Lafayette, IN: Purdue University Press.

Dastani, M., Hulstijn, J. and Van der Torre, L., 2005. How to decide what to do? *European Journal of Operational Research*, **160**(3), pp. 762-784.

Davis, C.A., 1999. *Reflexive Ethnography: A Guide to Researching Selves and Others.* 2nd edn. Milton Park and New York: Routledge.

Day, E. and Barksdale, H.C., 2003. Selecting a professional service provider from the short list. *Journal of Business & Industrial Marketing,* **18**(6/7), pp. 564-579.

Day, E. and Barksdale, H.C., 1994. Organizational purchasing of professional services: The process of selecting providers. *Journal of Business & Industrial Marketing,* **9**(3), pp. 44-51.

Dellve, L. and Wikstroem, E., 2009. Managing complex workplace stress in health care organizations: leaders' perceived legitimacy conflicts. *Journal of nursing management,* **17**(8), pp. 931-941.

Denscombe, M., 2010. *Ground Rules for Social Research: Guidelines for good practice.* 2nd edn. Maidenhead: Open University Press McGraw-Hill Education.

Denzin, N.K., 1997. *Interpretive ethnography: Ethnographic practices for the 21st century.* Thousand Oaks, CA: Sage Publications.

Dillon, S.M., 1998. *Descriptive decision making: Comparing theory with practice.* Department of Management Systems, University of Waikato, New Zealand.

Dip, C., 2009. Demystifying theoretical sampling in grounded theory research. *The Grounded Theory Review,* **8**(2), pp. 113-124.

Easterby-Smith, M., 2008. *Management research.* 3 edn. Los Angeles and London: Sage Publications.

Edwards, W., 1954. The theory of decision making. *Psychological bulletin,* **51**(4), pp. 380.

Eisenhardt, K.M., 1989. Building Theories from Case Study Research. *Academy of Management Review,* **14**(4), pp. 532-550.

Financial Times, Managing Partners Forum and Meridian West, 2012. *Effective Client-Adviser Relationships 2012.* London Financial Times.

Fischer, A., Sieg, J.H., Wallin, M.W. and Krogh, G.V., 2014. What motivates professional service firm employees to nurture client dialogues? *The Service Industries Journal,* **34**(5), pp. 399-421.

Friendly, M., 1991. Statistical Graphics for Multivariate Data, *SAS SUGI 16 Conference, Apr, 1991.*

Gigerenzer, G. and Gaissmaier, W., 2011. Heuristic decision making. *Annual Review of Psychology,* **62**, pp. 451-482.

Gillis, P., Petty, R. and Suddaby, R., 2014. The transnational regulation of accounting: insights, gaps and an agenda for future research. *Accounting, Auditing & Accountability Journal,* **27**(6), pp. 894-902.

Glaser, B.G., 2007. Naturalist inquiry and grounded theory. *Historical Social Research/Historische Sozialforschung.Supplement,* **5**(1), pp. 114-132.

Glaser, B.G. and Strauss, A.L., 2009. *The discovery of grounded theory: Strategies for qualitative research.* New Brunswick, NJ: Transaction Publishers.

Glaser, B. and Strauss, A., 1967. *Discovery of grounded theory.* Mill Valley, CA: Sociology Press.

Glückler, J. and Armbrüster, T., 2003. Bridging uncertainty in management consulting: The mechanisms of trust and networked reputation. *Organization Studies*, **24**(2), pp. 269-297.

Gordon, S.E. and Gill, R.T., 1997. Cognitive task analysis. In: C.E. Zsambok and G.A. Klein, eds, *Naturalistic decision making*. New York: Psychology Press, pp. 131-140.

Gore, J., Banks, A., Millward, L. and Kyriakidou, O., 2006. Naturalistic decision making and organizations: Reviewing pragmatic science. *Organization Studies*, **27**(7), pp. 925-942.

Goulding, C., 2002. *Grounded Theory: A practical guide for management, business and market researchers.* London: Sage Publications.

Goulding, C., 1998. Grounded theory: the missing methodology on the interpretivist agenda. *Qualitative Market Research: An International Journal*, **1**(1), pp. 50-57.

Green, C.H., 2012. *Truth Inflation: Not-so Trusted Advisors.* Forbes.

Greenwood, R., Morris, T., Fairclough, S. and Boussebaa, M., 2010. The organizational design of transnational professional service firms. *Organizational dynamics*, **39**(2), pp. 173-183.

Halliday, T. and Carruthers, B., 2009. *Bankrupt: global lawmaking and systemic financial crisis.* Stanford, CA: Stanford University Press.

Hammond, K.R., 1988. Judgment and decision making in dynamic tasks. *Information and decision technologies*, **14**(1), pp. 3-14.

Hanson, W.E., Creswell, J.W., Clark, V.L.P., Petska, K.S. and Creswell, J.D., 2005. Mixed methods research designs in counseling psychology. *Journal of counseling psychology*, **52**(2), pp. 224-235.

Haraway, D., 1991. *Simians, cyborgs, and women: The reinvention of women.* London: Routledge.

Haverila, M., Bateman, E.R. and Naumann, E.R., 2011. The drivers of customer satisfaction in strategic consulting engagements: a global study. *Management Decision*, **49**(8), pp. 1354-1370.

Heller, F., 2002. What next? More critique of consultants, gurus and managers. In: T. Clark and R. Fincham, eds, *Critical consulting: New perspectives on the management advice industry.* Malden. MA: Blackwell Publishers, pp. 260-270.

Holloway, I. and Wheeler, S., 1996. *Qualitative research in nursing and healthcare.* 3rd edn. Chichester: Wiley-Blackwell.

Höner, D. and Mohe, M., 2009. Behind clients' doors: What hinders client firms from "professionally" dealing with consultancy? *Scandinavian Journal of Management*, **25**(3), pp. 299-312.

Jennings, D. and Wattam, S., 1998. *Decision making: an integrated approach.* 2nd edn. London and Washington, DC: Financial Times Pitman Pub.

Jensen, M.C. and Meckling, W.H., 1979. Theory of the firm: Managerial behavior, agency costs, and ownership structure. *Economics social institutions.* Netherlands: Springer, pp. 163-231.

Josselson, R. and Lieblich, A., 2003. A framework for narrative research proposals in psychology. In: R. Josselson, A. Lieblich and D.P. McAdams, eds, *Up close and personal: The teaching and learning of narrative research*. Washington, DC: American Psychological Association, pp. 259-274.

Kahneman, D., 2011. *Thinking, fast and slow.* New York, NY: Macmillan.

Kamyabi, Y. and Devi, S., 2012. The impact of advisory services on Iranian SME performance: An empirical investigation of the role of professional accountants. *S African Journal of Business management,* **43**(2), pp. 61-72.

Karantinou, K.M. and Hogg, M.K., 2009. An empirical investigation of relationship development in professional business services. *Journal of services marketing,* **23**(4), pp. 249-260.

Kelle, U., 2007. "Emergence" vs. "Forcing" of Empirical Data? A Crucial Problem of "Grounded Theory" Reconsidered. *Historical Social Research/Historische Sozialforschung.Supplement,* **19**, pp. 133-156.

Kipping, M. and Wright, C., 2012. Consultants in context: Global dominance, societal effect, and the capitalist system. In: M. Kipping and T. Clark, eds, *The Oxford handbook of management consulting.* Oxford: Oxford University Press, pp. 165-185.

Klein, G.A., 2008. Naturalistic Decision Making. *Human Factors: The Journal of the Human Factors and Ergonomics Society,* **50**(3), pp. 456-460.

Klein, G.A., 1993. *A recognition-primed decision (RPD) model of rapid decision making.* Westport, CT: Ablex Publishing.

Klein, G.A., Ross, K.G., Moon, B.M., Klein, D.E., Hoffman, R.R. and Hollnagel, E., 2003. Macrocognition. *Intelligent Systems, IEEE,* **18**(3), pp. 81-85.

Kokot, P., 2015. Let's talk about sex (ism): Cross-national perspectives on women partners' narratives on equality and sexism at work in Germany and the UK. *Critical Perspectives on Accounting,* **27**, pp. 73-85.

Krippendorff, K., 2012. *Content analysis: An introduction to its methodology.* 3rd edn. Thousand Oaks, CA: Sage Publications.

Krippendorff, K., 2004. Reliability in content analysis. *Human Communication Research,* **30**(3), pp. 411-433.

Kvale, S., 1987. Validity in the qualitative research interview. *Psykologisk Skriftserie Aarhus,* **12**(1), pp. 68.

Lee, N., Saunders, J. and Goulding, C., 2005. Grounded theory, ethnography and phenomenology: A comparative analysis of three qualitative strategies for marketing research. *European journal of Marketing,* **39**(3/4), pp. 294-308.

Leuthesser, L., 1997. Supplier relational behavior: An empirical assessment. *Industrial marketing management,* **26**(3), pp. 245-254.

Levinson, J.C. and McLaughlin, M.W., 2011. *Guerrilla marketing for consultants: Breakthrough tactics for winning profitable clients.* Hoboken, NJ: Wiley.

Lincoln, Y.S. and Guba, E.G., 1985. *Naturalistic Inquiry.* London: Sage Publications.

Lipshitz, R., 1988. *Decision making as argument driven action.* Boston, MA: Center for Applied Social Science, Boston University.

Lipshitz, R., Klein, G.A. and Carroll, J.S., 2006. Introduction to the special issue. Naturalistic decision making and organizational decision making: Exploring the intersections. *Organization Studies*, **27**(7), pp. 917-923.

Lipshitz, R., Klein, G.A., Orasanu, J. and Salas, E., 2001. Taking stock of naturalistic decision making. *Journal of Behavioral Decision Making*, **14**(5), pp. 331-352.

Lowendahl, B.R., 1992. *Global strategies for professional business service firms*, University of Pennsylvania.

Lowendahl, B. and Revang, O., 1998. Challenges to existing strategy theory in a postindustrial society. *Strategic Management Journal*, **19**(8), pp. 755-773.

Luhmann, N., 2005. Communication barriers in management consulting. *Advances in Organization Studies*, **14**, pp. 351-373.

Luhmann, N., 1986. The autopoiesis of social systems. In: F. Geyer and J. van der Zouwen, eds, *Sociocybernetic Paradoxes: Observation, Control and Evolution of Self.* London: Sage Publications, pp. 172-192.

Maister, D.H., 2007. *Managing the professional service firm.* New York and London: Simon and Schuster.

Maister, D.H., Green, C.H. and Galford, R.M., 2000. *The trusted advisor.* New York and London: Simon and Schuster.

Martin, P. and Barnard, A., 2013. The experience of women in male-dominated occupations: A constructivist grounded theory inquiry. *SA Journal of Industrial Psychology*, **39**(2), pp. 01-12.

Mattila, J., Brolin, P. and Tukiainen, S., 2013. Understanding the reciprocal nature of client-consultant relationship in management consulting, *Proceedings of IFKAD-ISSN* 2013, pp. 787X.

Mayer, R.C., Davis, J.H. and Schoorman, F.D., 1995. An integrative model of organizational trust. *Academy of management review*, **20**(3), pp. 709-734.

McColl-Kennedy, J.R., Patterson, P., Brady, M.K., Cheung, L. and Nguyen, D., 2015. To give or not to give professional services to non-paying clients: Professionals' giving backstory. *Journal of Service Management*, **26**(3), pp. 426-459.

McKenna, C.D., 2006. *The world's newest profession: Management consulting in the twentieth century.* Cambridge: Cambridge University Press.

Meso, P., Troutt, M.D. and Rudnicka, J., 2002. A review of naturalistic decision making research with some implications for knowledge management. *Journal of Knowledge Management*, **6**(1), pp. 63-73.

Millar, C., Hind, P., Stoughton, A.M. and Ludema, J., 2012. The driving forces of sustainability. *Journal of Organizational Change Management*, **25**(4), pp. 501-517.

Miller, G.A., Galanter, E. and Pribram, K.H., 1965. *Plans and the structure of behavior.* New York, NY: Henry Holt Publishing.

Mills, J., Bonner, A. and Francis, K., 2006. Adopting a constructivist approach to grounded theory: Implications for research design. *International journal of nursing practice*, **12**(1), pp. 8-13.

Mintzberg, H., Raisinghani, D. and Theoret, A., 1976. The structure of" unstructured" decision processes. *Administrative Science Quarterly*, **21**(2), pp. 246-275.

Mohe, M., 2008. Bridging the cultural gap in management consulting research. *International Journal of Cross Cultural Management*, **8**(1), pp. 41-57.

Mohe, M., 2005. Generic strategies for managing consultants: Insights from clients' companies in Germany. *Journal of Change Management*, **5**(3), pp. 357-365.

Mohe, M. and Seidl, D., 2009. Theorising the client–consultant relationship from the perspective of social-systems theory. *Organization*, **18**, pp. 3.

Montgomery, H., 1989. From cognition to action: The search for dominance in decision making. In: H. Montgomery and O. Svenson, eds, *Process and structure in human decision making*. Oxford: Wiley, pp. 23-49.

Montgomery, H. and Svenson, O., 1989. A think-aloud study of dominance structuring in decision processes. In: H. Montgomery and O. Svenson, eds, *Process and structure in human decision making*. Oxford: Wiley, pp. 135-150.

Nathaniel, A.K., Posted on Jun 11, 2007. *Book Review: Glaser, B.G. (2007). Doing Formal Grounded Theory: A Proposal.*

Nikolova, N., Möllering, G. and Reihlen, M., 2015. Trusting as a 'Leap of Faith': Trust-building practices in client–consultant relationships. *Scandinavian Journal of Management*, **31**(2), pp. 232-245.

Novicevic, M.M., Clayton, R.W. and Williams, W.A., 2011. Barnard's model of decision making: a historical predecessor of image theory. *Journal of Management History*, **17**(4), pp. 420-434.

Noy, C., 2003. *The write of passage: Reflections on writing a dissertation in narrative methodology.* Forum Qualitative Sozialforschung/Forum: Qualitative Social Research.

Nyaupane, G.P. and Poudel, S., 2012. Application of appreciative inquiry in tourism research in rural communities. *Tourism management*, **33**(4), pp. 978-987.

Orasanu, J. and Connolly, T., 1993. The reinvention of decision making. In: G.A. Klein, J. Orasanu, R. Calderwood and C.E. Zsambok, eds, *Decision making in action: Models and methods*. Westport, CT: Ablex Publishing, pp. 3-20.

Parker, I., 1997. Discourse analysis and psychoanalysis. *British Journal of Social Psychology*, **36**(4), pp. 479-495.

Pennebaker, J.W., Francis, M.E. and Booth, R.J., 2001. *Linguistic inquiry and word count: LIWC 2001.* Lawrence Erlbaum Associates.

Pennebaker, J.W. and King, L.A., 1999. Linguistic styles: language use as an individual difference. *Journal of personality and social psychology*, **77**(6), pp. 1296.

Pennington, N. and Hastie, R., 1988. Explanation-based decision making: Effects of memory structure on judgment. *Journal of Experimental Psychology: Learning, Memory, and Cognition*, **14**(3), pp. 521-533.

Pettigrew, S.F., 2000. Ethnography and grounded theory: a happy marriage? *Advances in Consumer Research,* **27**(1), pp. 256-260.

Philp, W.R. and Martin, C.P., 2009. A philosophical approach to time in military knowledge management. *Journal of Knowledge Management,* **13**(1), pp. 171-183.

Pliske, R. and Klein, G.A., 2003. The naturalistic decision-making perspective. In: S.L. Schneider and J. Shanteau, eds, *Emerging perspectives on judgment and decision research.* Cambridge and New York: Cambridge University Press, pp. 559-585.

Pong, C. and McMeeking, K.P., 2007. Competition in the UK accounting services market. *Managerial Auditing Journal,* **22**(2), pp. 197-217.

Prince, C. and Salas, E., 1998. Situation assessment for routine flight and decision making. *International Journal of Cognitive Ergonomics,* **1**(4), pp. 315-324.

Rasmussen, J., 1997. Merging paradigms- Decision making, management, and cognitive control. In: R.H. Flin, ed, *Decision making under stress-Emerging themes and applications.* Gower Technical, pp. 67-81.

Rasmussen, J., 1986. A framework for cognitive task analysis in systems design. In: E. Hollnagel, G. Mancini and D.D. Woods, eds, *Intelligent decision support in process environments.* Berlin: Springer, pp. 175-196.

Rindfleisch, A. and Heide, J.B., 1997. Transaction cost analysis: Past, present, and future applications. *Journal of Marketing,* **61**(4), pp. 30-54.

Rusly, F., Yih-Tong Sun, P. and L. Corner, J., 2014. The impact of change readiness on the knowledge sharing process for professional service firms. *Journal of Knowledge Management,* **18**(4), pp. 687-709.

Sassen, S., 2001. *The global city: New York, London, Tokyo.* Princeton, NJ: Princeton University Press.

Savage, L., 1954. *The foundations of statistics.* New York: Wiley.

Schwartz, B., Ward, A., Monterosso, J., Lyubomirsky, S., White, K. and Lehman, D.R., 2002. Maximizing versus satisficing: happiness is a matter of choice. *Journal of personality and social psychology,* **83**(5), pp. 1178.

Seidel, S. and Urquhart, C., 2013. On emergence and forcing in information systems grounded theory studies: The case of Strauss and Corbin. *Journal of Information Technology,* **28**(3), pp. 237-260.

Shao, W., 2006. *Consumer Decision-Making: An Empirical Exploration of Multi-Phased Decision Processes,* Griffith University Australia.

Sheth, J. and Sobel, A., 2000. *Clients for life.* Simon and Schuster.

Sieg, J.H., Fischer, A., Wallin, M.W. and Krogh, G.V., 2012. Proactive diagnosis: how professional service firms sustain client dialogue. *Journal of Service Management,* **23**(2), pp. 253-278.

Sieweke, J., Birkner, S. and Mohe, M., 2012. Preferred supplier programs for consulting services: An exploratory study of German client companies. *Journal of Purchasing and Supply Management,* **18**(3), pp. 123-136.

Simon, H.A., 1955. A behavioral model of rational choice. *The quarterly journal of economics,* **69**(1), pp. 99-118.

Skjølsvik, T., 2012. *Beyond the 'trusted advisor': The impact of client-professional relationships on the client's selection of professional service firms*, Handelshøyskolen BI.

Sonmez, M. and Moorhouse, A., 2010. Purchasing professional services: which decision criteria? *Management Decision*, **48**(2), pp. 189-206.

Statistica - The Statistics Portal, 2015-last update, Revenue of the Big Four accounting/audit firms worldwide in 2014. Available: http://www.statista.com/statistics/250479/big-four-accounting-firms-global-revenue/ September, 2015].

Stock, J.R. and Zinszer, P.H., 1987. The industrial purchase decision for professional services. *Journal of Business Research*, **15**(1), pp. 1-16.

Straus, A. and Corbin, J., 1998. *Basics of qualitative research: Techniques and procedures for developing grounded theory.* Thousand Oaks, CA: Sage Publications.

Strauss, A. and Corbin, J., 1994. Grounded theory methodology: an overview. In: N. Denzin and Y.S. Lincoln, eds, *Handbook of Qualitative Research*. Thousand Oaks, CA: Sage Publications.

Suddaby, R., Cooper, D.J. and Greenwood, R., 2007. Transnational regulation of professional services: Governance dynamics of field level organizational change. *Accounting, Organizations and Society*, **32**(4), pp. 333-362.

Svenson, O., 1979. Process descriptions of decision making. *Organizational behavior and human performance*, **23**(1), pp. 86-112.

Thaler, R.H., Sunstein, C.R. and Bals, J.P., 2014. Choice architecture. In: E. Shafir, ed, *The Behavioral Foundations of Public Policy*. Oxford and Princeton: Princeton University Press, pp. 428-438.

Trasorras, R., Weinstein, A. and Abratt, R., 2009. Value, satisfaction, loyalty and retention in professional services. *Marketing Intelligence & Planning*, **27**(5), pp. 615-632.

Tversky, A. and Kahneman, D., 1981. The framing of decisions and the psychology of choice. *Science (New York, N.Y.)*, **211**(4481), pp. 453-458.

Uzzi, B., 1997. Social structure and competition in interfirm networks: The paradox of embeddedness. *Administrative Science Quarterly*, **42**(1), pp. 35-67.

Van Rooij, S.W. and Merkebu, J., 2015. Measuring the Business Impact of Employee Learning: A View from the Professional Services Sector. *Human Resource Development Quarterly*, **26**(3), pp. 275-297.

Von Neumann, J. and Morgenstern, O., 1947. *Theory of games and economic behavior.* 2d rev edn. Princeton, NJ: Princeton University Press.

Warner, J., 2011, 31 Mar 2011. Dereliction of the Big Four blamed for financial crisis. *The Telegraph*.

Werr, A. and Pemer, F., 2007. Purchasing management consulting services—From management autonomy to purchasing involvement. *Journal of Purchasing and Supply Management*, **13**(2), pp. 98-112.

Wertheimer, M. and Riezler, K., 1944. Gestalt theory. *Social Research*, **11**(1), pp. 78-99.

Wikipedia, 2016-last update, Gestalt Psychology. Available: https://en.wikipedia.org/wiki/Gestalt_psychologyFebruary, 2016].

Willig, C., 2003. Discourse analysis. In: J.A. Smith, ed, *Qualitative psychology: A practical guide to research methods.* London: Sage Publications, pp. 159-183.

Wilson, G., 2003. *Managing the Professional Service Firm - Summary of David Maister's book.* The Confident Website.

Yates, J.F., 2003. *Decision management.* San Francisco, CA: Jossey-Bass.

Yates, J.F., 2001. Naturalistic Decision Making. In: E. Salas and G.A. Klein, eds, *Linking expertise and naturalistic decision making.* New York and London: Psychology Press, pp. 9-32.

Yates, J.F. and Potworwski, G.A., 2012. Evidence-based decision management. In: D.M. Rousseau, ed, *The Oxford handbook of evidence-based management.* Oxford: Oxford University Press, pp. 716-790.

Appendix A

Final coding framework, code definitions and classifications

Final coding framework

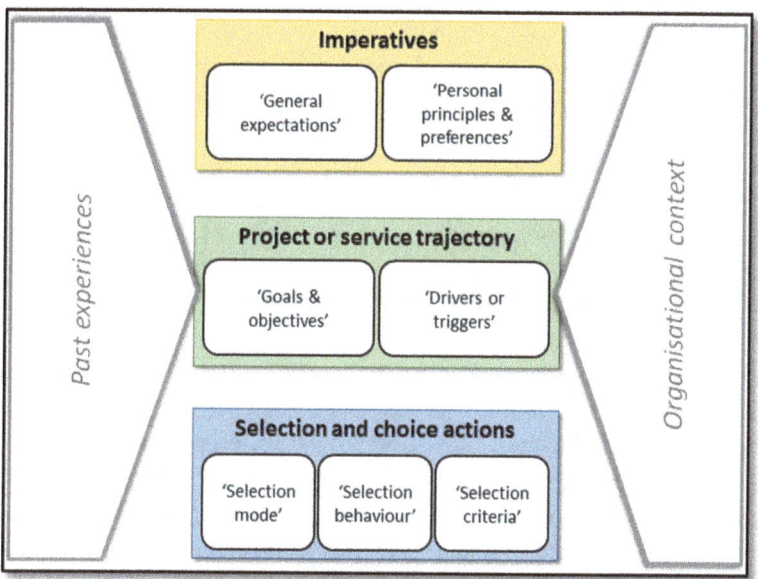

Figure A.1 – Final coding framework (code categories)

Code definitions by framework component

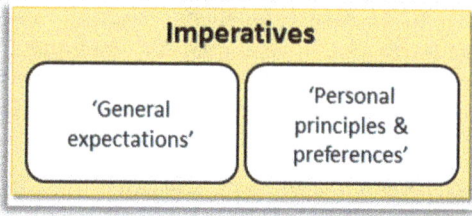

Imperatives

Imperatives – also referred to as values in the image theory literature; often defined as strongly held broad-based principles –for personal or organisational behaviour, serve as a gold standard criteria for adoption or rejection. *Within the context of this research project, the following definition has been applied:*

What is the senior executive stakeholder looking for in an advisor or advisory firm? What are the primary reasons for engaging with an external partner? What is the gold standard that will determine if he/she will choose to engage or build a rapport with and advisor? *These value image nodes are primarily based on the response to the question: 'how would the ideal advisor relationship look like or what are your general expectations of a professional advisor such as a Big 4 firm?'*

General expectations

General expectations of an advisor or an advisory firm as part of the day-to-day interactions (relationship) and engagements (projects): key qualities, attributes and characteristics or primary reasons for working with an external advisor:

VI1.1_Demonstrate empathy – advisor or firm should understand me and the organisation and act on that knowledge. The advisor should be able to listen, understand and show empathy for me as well as the organisation, and apply this understanding in his or her actions.

VI1.2_Earn my trust and bat for me - invest in the relationship and put me and the organisation first. The advisor needs to be willing to put me and organisation first, to minimise self-interest (not cover their bases and leave client exposed) and invest in the relationship (free advice or research) meaning earn my trust so that I the client can rely on the advisor.

VI1.3_Be pro-active - advice, flag and challenge as required - don't sell. The advisor needs to be able to challenge and be comfortable being challenged by client, the challenge should not undermine relationships; advisor needs to be able to have mature and informed conversations with the client and also be pro-active in bringing appropriate ideas to the client.

VI1.4_Right interpersonal skills and chemistry. The advisor needs to have the right interpersonal skills such as tact, and not be arrogant or shy; there has to be overall good chemistry between the client and the advisor.

VI1.5_Be embedded and hold a presence within the organisation. The advisor should be embedded – know what's going on the organisation, what the key issues are etc. – as well as be well-connected in the organisation. Having a presence or a name in the client organisation helps generate traction with peers and seniors.

VI1.6_Be able to solve problems pragmatically and collaboratively. The advisor should be able to diagnose and solve problems pragmatically. Advisor should provide the right balance between theory, hands-on knowledge and a pragmatic way forward. The advisor should not impose a solution; clients expect or prefer to be part of the process of defining a solution together with the advisor.

VI1.7_Be realistic, transparent and honest - stick to agreements. The advisor should be realistic about the value that he/she is able to deliver; they must not overpromise. The advisor should also be transparent about his/her activities and plans and should stick to agreed fees or costs.

VI1.8_Provide an external view, benchmarks and insights. The advisor should provide benchmarks, an external view – how does the client and organisation stack up to the external world, what are other firms doing – to provide helpful insights from the outside.

VI1.9_Help me or us understand and manage regulatory bodies. The advisor should be able to help me and the organisation understand and manage my relationship with regulatory bodies.

VI1.10_Provide and assure required competence, skills and expertise. The advisor should be able to address and deliver the tasks at hand in terms of size, complexities and required expertise; he or she should also make sure the right team – ideally the A-team – is available to support and deliver the job.

VI1.11_Step in and help out - be responsive, accessible and available. The advisor should be available for ad hoc questions, be around and physically present, be clear on who within the advisory firm should be contacted for what (contact strategy).

Personal principles and preferences

Respondent's personal principles and preferences in regards to an advisor or advisory firms, as well as more generic statements made. Definitions try to reflect or paraphrase statements of respondents:

VI2.1_Advisor is more important than the firm. 'For me the advisor is more important than the firm'.

VI2.2_Need to feel important or be a priority. 'I need to feel important or a priority to the advisor, he/she needs to be attentive to my needs and tickle my ego.'

VI2.3_Need to be able to trust the advisor or firm. 'I need to be able to trust the advisor or the advisory firm.'

VI2.4_Advisors are in business to make money. 'Advisors and firms are in business to make money, I understand and respect that. They need to make their margin or income and I am comfortable with that.'

VI2.5_Quality has its price. 'Quality has its price, you get what you pay for. If you skimp on the fees or select a cheaper aka less skilled supplier, it will come back to haunt you in the long-term.'

VI2.6_It is difficult to differentiate between firms. 'It is really difficult to differentiate between the firms, they all seem to blur together and within their category (Big 4) they are interchangeable.'

VI2.7_Don't like getting caught up in details. 'I don't like getting caught up in details; prefer big picture thinking and discussions.'

VI2.8_Bias towards previous Big 4 employer. 'I have a bias towards my previous 'Big Four' employer, either positive or negative.'

VI2.9_Self promotion without substance is a no go. 'Self-promotion without substance is a no go; I don't like meetings with empty content or advisors pretending/ presenting aspects incoherently or cannot deliver.'

VI2.10_I like to stay in control - monitor advisor activities. 'I like to stay in control and monitor advisor activities; I want to know which projects are going on where within my patch and I want regular updates.'

VI2.11_Growing through the ranks. 'It is quite helpful having grown through the ranks together with different advisors, it has created a bond and trust between me and the individuals.'

VI2.12_Thrive on challenge. 'I like or thrive on being challenged, I believe it brings out the best for me and the organisation.'

VI2.13_Don't like scare mongering. 'I don't like intimidation techniques and scare mongering in order to get me to sign up to external support/projects from advisors.'

VI2.14_Appreciate additional offerings. 'I appreciate additional offerings such as professional events, training, even access to facilities or even social events provided by advisory firms. I don't have any issue making use of these.'

VI2.15_I DON'T need to see the advisor frequently. 'I don't need to or prefer to see the advisor frequently or regularly to have or maintain a good relationship; occasional or ad hoc contact is sufficient.'

VI2.16_I DO like to meet the advisor regularly. 'I DO like or prefer to meet the advisor frequently or regularly for update and discussions.'

VI2.17_I LIKE to engage with the advisor socially. 'I like to engage with the advisor socially beyond the context of work, meet up for lunch or dinner to have a casual chat or offline discussion.'

VI2.18_I DON'T like to engage with the advisor socially. 'I DON'T like to engage with the advisor socially; I don't have any time for that or don't see the benefit in doing so. Meetings with fixed agendas work better for me.'

VI2.19_The end result matters. 'For me only the end result is what really matters, costs or issues are brushed aside or fade in the background once the project is completed and the benefits delivered.'

VI2.20_Integrity is important. 'I do take issue with integrity, conflicts of interest and even hospitality. I feel uncomfortable to cross some thresholds around hospitality.

Project or service trajectory (also benefits sought)

This is also referred to as **'trajectory'** in the image theory literature; often defined as the decision-maker's goal agenda, what he/she wants to achieve, vision of ideal or desired future. Within the context of this research project, the following definition has been applied:

Why does the senior executive stakeholder formally transact with a professional advisor? What is the respondent trying or has tried to achieve by engaging an advisor or advisory firm on behalf of the organisation? What are the objectives or goals of an engagement/interaction with an advisor or advisory firm? *These trajectory image nodes are primarily based on respondents' commentary and reflection on recent projects and engagements with advisors; what were the objectives and triggers for transacting or more formally engaging with a professional advisor.*

Goals and objectives

Primary objectives and goals (meaning those that can be deducted from respondent's commentary) which the client is looking to address by working with an advisor and or an advisory firm. What outcomes or outputs are being targeted as part of a transaction with the advisor?

TI1.1_Deliver positive results and tangible outputs. Deliver positive results or a tangible output: For advisor to execute and deliver desired outputs and outcomes via a project or an engagement. Results could be cost savings, growth agendas, outputs to appease regulators, meet KPIs, installation of systems, processes and organisational structures.

TI1.2_Provide guidance and advice (billable). Provide guidance and advice: For the advisor to diagnose, coach, counsel, validate, progress or facilitate a discussion. Provide intellectual input to further respondent's plans either as part of a larger project or engagement or on its own.

TI1.3_ProBono or free advice. Respondent is looking to receive free advice or free-of-charge work which goes beyond an informal conversation, this interaction might or might not lead to a significant billable project for the advisor.

TI1.4_Be part of organisational eco-system. Expectation of the advisor firm to join and integrate into the organisational eco-system, be part of the larger process - a preferred partner with agreed upon remit and responsibilities.

TI1.5_Guarantee for success. Provide assurance that the project or initiative is going to be success via the input (either advice or delivery) from the advisor and advisory firm.

TI1.6_Fill a resource gap. Fill a resource gap – provide flexible access to premium resources that are not available to respondent otherwise.

TI1.7_Fill knowledge gaps. Fill knowledge gaps – provide expertise, experience and benchmarking which is not available or accessible within the organisation and general networks.

TI1.8_Teach or empower us. Teach or empower us – assure knowledge transfer, don't just bring in the resources and knowledge to deliver an initiative; teach internal staff to either be part of the project or manage after the project is completed.

TI1.9_Help meet a deadline. Help the respondent and the organisation meet a deadline – time pressure, external assistance is needed to execute on time.

TI1.10_Tailored approach. A tailored approach – work with the respondent and the organisation to develop a tailored approach that meets their needs not an off-the self-solution.

TI1.11_Sharing pain and responsibilities. Advisor and the firm should have some skin in the game, share some of the risk and live up to the commitment and responsibilities agreed as part of the agreement. Take on some of the burden of the initiative.

Drivers or triggers

What or who is the primary impetus, driver or trigger or origin of the trajectory image? Who or what called for a project/transaction with an advisor or advisory firm based on respondent's commentary?

TI2.1_Regulation. Meeting or responding to demands of regulatory bodies, such as a section 166 or implementing change requests from regulators.

TI2.2_Request from board or superior. Addressing or responding to request made by the board or a superior, an initiative that originated via someone higher up in the food chain.

TI2.3_Operational response. Keeping up with general organisational and external demands, initiative was formed/developed by respondent or with his/her input.

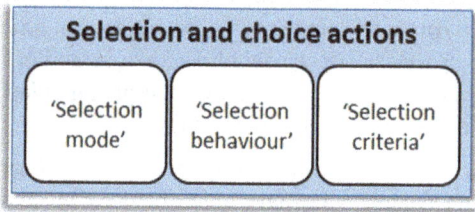

Selection and choice actions

– also referred to as **'strategic actions'** in the image theory literature; often defined as plans and tactics to progress towards the goal (being the trajectory image) and how these goals are being achieved. Within the context of this research project, the following definition has been applied:

How does the senior executive stakeholder go about identifying and selecting the appropriate advisor to help him/her execute or realise trajectory images being plans and initiatives? What steps do the respondent and with him/her the organisation undertake to identify and select a partner? Which selection criteria and selection behaviour are being eluded to by the respondent? *The strategic image nodes are primarily based on respondents' recalling selection situations and describing key criteria for appointing advisors (question).*

Selection mode

Description of the different decision-making modes discussed as part of the selection process, exploring as to who is making the decisions and in general how are the decisions made, for example rational or structured approach versus a more intuitive or automatic approach.

SI0.1_Delegate always or most of the time selection. Respondent delegates always or most of the time the selection or appointment of an advisor to one of his/her direct reports.

SI0.2_Delegate for some initiatives, for others direct personal involvement. Respondent indicates that for certain initiatives he/she do get involved directly in the decision-making or selection process, but for others choose to delegate the selection to a direct report.

SI0.3_Selection is a group decision with some or limited senior involvement. Selection and appointment of an advisor is a group decision and there is some senior involvement, either as a final sounding board or just another vote as part of the group.

SI0.4_Personally drive the selection of advisors. Respondent states that he/she personally or possibly in a collective drive or shape the selection and appointment decision.

SI0.5_Follow a rational approach to selecting an advisor or firm. Respondent discuss that he/she/they follow a structured or more rational approach by either consulting with others, applying rules or analysing data points before making a selection decision.

SI0.6_Follow an ad hoc or intuitive approach to selecting an advisor or firm. Respondents discuss automatic decision-making or mimicking of decision-making without greatly considering rules or conducting an analysis.

Selection behaviour

What steps does the senior executive stakeholder and the organisation undertake to identify and select an advisor or advisory firm? What type of behaviour is being discussed that leads to appointments?

SI1.1_Large projects should go out to tender. A formal or informal rule in the organisation or for the respondent is that larger projects (most frequently from a cost perspective) should go through a formal tender process.

SI1.2_Small pieces of work don't need to go to tender. Small projects (in terms of costs and maybe also visibility) don't necessarily need to go to tender and appointments can progress directly without a formal process.

SI1.3_Continuity creates efficiency and better results. A natural choice is to continue with or fall back on existing arrangements if it is an option; it takes less time for advisors to get up to speed and be fully functioning, it is less disruptive to the business.

SI1.4_Preference to pro-actively contact advisors. Respondent or organisation prefers to contact the advisor when they are ready to transact with the advisory firm, they determine when there is a need for support, a project.

SI1.5_Balance advisors - avoid overreliance. Respondent or the organisation overall takes a balanced approach to transacting with advisors; the general notion is to split transactions across a number of firms in order to avoid overreliance and manage risks.

SI1.6_Emergencies can bypass selection processes. In case an engagement is urgent, almost an emergency, then a formal selection process can be forgone and the advisor is appointed without a formal tender exercise.

SI1.7_Physical proximity leads to a pole position. Physical proximity, meaning the advisor is already on site delivering another project and easily accessible for informal discussions, as well as general embeddedness, meaning the advisor is frequently in the client office, puts them at an advantage. Consequently, advisor has the ability to be involved in initial discussions which might lead to an engagement.

SI1.8_Established relationships serve as a screening mechanism. Respondent mentions that he/she draws on a select number of advisors when there is a need to transact. Selection of the advisor is determined by past experiences in certain fields which are deemed the advisors' area of expertise.

SI1.9_Project extension or expansion. No formal selection takes place when a project extends or expands in scope.

SI1.10_Fire fighting, no time to plan. Respondent or organisation is constantly fire-fighting and therefore has no time to plan ahead in regards to engagements and initiatives, this means he/she is only reacting to changes and trying to keep up with issues.

SI1.11_Cost focus leads to DIY. Due to organisational cost constraints, respondents are encouraged or forced to manage initiatives with internal resources.

SI1.12_Select advisor or advisory firm purely on merit. 'Personally, I prefer or try to select an advisor or advisory firm purely on merit.'

SI1.13_Not in a position to spend more money on advisors. 'I am not in a position to spend more or any money on advisors even though I might like to or I think it would be appropriate to do so.'

SI1.14_Big projects are painful and should be avoided. 'Personally or based on past experience, I believe big project are painful and should avoided and either broken down or passed on to someone else to manage.'

SI1.15_Not good to be too reliant on advisors for everything. 'It's not good to be too reliant on advisors, some things need to be done in-house or owned by teams within the organisation.'

SI1.16_Clear picture of each advisory firm or advisor. 'I have a clear picture what each advisory firm or advisor is good at; I put them into different boxes depending on skills, working styles observed and general experiences I had with individuals and firms.'

SI1.17_Limited exchange with my peers in terms of advisor engagement. 'I have a limited dialogue with my peers in terms of engaging with advisors; I don't know how they structure their projects/terms and conditions etc.'

Selection criteria

What are the key criteria mentioned during interviews in regards to selecting and ultimately appointing an advisor or advisory firm?

SI2.1_Skills and experiences of individuals. Relevant skills, competencies and experiences of individuals or the team presented.

SI2.2_Proposed team. The overall team presented or offered to the respondent or decision-makers; is it the A-team in terms of skills and experiences; team dynamics and general presence.

SI2.3_Strong bid performance (presentation, Q&A). Strong or more convincing bid performance, either presentations or Q&As. Engagement and interaction leaves a positive impression with decision-makers.

SI2.4_Reputation and house style. Based on past experiences, respondent feels that a firm has a reputation and a type of house style, these would link to particular strengths which makes a better or more fitting choice for certain engagements.

SI2.5_Brand and reputational factors are NOT or LESS important. General branding and reputational factors are NOT or LESS important for the respondents when selecting a firm (e.g. it has to be Big 4 firm but which is not critical).

SI2.6_Clearance of conflicts of interests (e.g. audit relationships). Arrangements such as internal audit or other engagements (audit relationship with a JV etc.) might hinder or are perceived as an inhibitor for certain engagements (or just the hassle of getting clearance).

SI2.7_Relevant experiences - track record. Track record or relevant experiences of having delivered successfully something similar in terms of scope, reach and complexities to another client.

SI2.8_Internal insights or knowledge. Provide someone (team or individual) who knows the organisation, the environment the respondent and the organisation operates in and their challenges. The team will be familiar with the set-up and can get up to speed more quickly.

SI2.9_Proposition and approach. Meaning the actually content or ideas that are being presented as part of the proposal, to what degree will the proposition deliver organisational goals and objectives.

SI2.10_Legacy or established relationships. Joint history or legacy between the respondent organisation and the firm or advisor; established relationships with the client organisations and the respondent.

SI2.11_Hunger and drive. Hunger and drive to secure respondents business displayed by advisor as well as the team either during presentations or other more informal interactions.

SI2.12_Fair or competitive price. Overall price or fee structure proposed to respondent; this could be actual costs as well as structuring and taking on risk elements. Investments and other free-of-charge work are included in considerations.

SI2.13_Previous performance or experiences. Positive or poor performances or respondents' general experiences with the firm or advisor in the past are used being mentioned explicitly as a reference point or factor in the decision-making.

SI2.14_Minimum threshold. Benchmark or threshold of a minimum tender performance before firm can progress or truly be considered; needs to tick a certain number of boxes at a certain level before consideration is given.

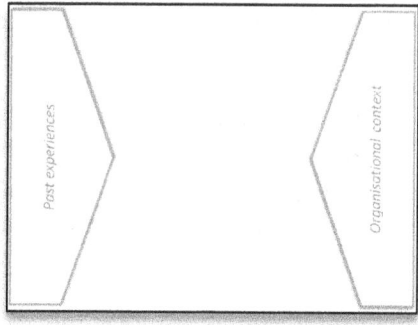

Decision frame (additional influencers)

– also referred to as **'experiences'** in the image theory literature; often defined as a respondent's store of knowledge meaning past experiences, learned experiences or observed experiences/information when applying the images and in order to come to a decision. Within the context of this research project, the following definition has been applied:

Senior executive stakeholders' store of knowledge (past experiences, learned experiences or observed experiences/information) as well as organisational context (meaning formal and informal guidelines and constraints with regards to working with external advisors) that the respondent relies on to help him/her apply the images and come to a decision; past experiences and context influences all three images especially the trajectory and strategic image.

Organisational context or constraints

Organisational principles, preferences and protocols (formal as well as informal) with regards to engaging and appointing advisors or advisory firm.

DF1.1_We tend to, prefer or are not allowed to use consultants or external advisors. As an organisation we tend to frown upon the use of external advisors, we don't allow the use of external advice or as an organisation we have a mantra to rely as little on external advice. As an organisation we don't tend to or are allowed to use consultants or external advisors. As an organisation we should rely less on external support.

DF1.2_Asking for external support is seen as a sign of failure in this organisation. Asking an external advisor or firm for help indicates that we have failed to manage or resolve the problem in house; it is viewed negatively within the wider organisation.

DF1.3_We know how to manage and get the most out of advisors and external support. We have strong organisational standards or procedures on how to select, structure and work with external suppliers. As an organisation we are very good at managing external support and or assuring synergies and or value for money. As an organisation we try and own and manage our own initiatives, we like to be in control.

DF1.4_We like to monitor and balance our external support and use of advisors. As an organisation we are keen to balance our relationships with advisory firms, overreliance on one firm is not good. We monitor spending by advisory firm.

DF1.5_We are NOT very organised in terms of managing advisors - everything is last minute, no processes and no transparency. As an organisation we tend to call in advisors in the last minute when a project is about to fail. We have no strong organisational standards or procedures on how to select, structure and work with external suppliers.

DF1.6_Increased focus on costs limits use of external advisors and external support. An overall trend, primarily driven by cost cutting, is to reduce external support and therefore we cannot appoint advisors as we may would do in other circumstances.

Past experiences

Personal experiences or knowledge base of working with advisors or advisory firms (historic PEL and recent PER), broken down into two subgroups on a temporal divide – fairly recent experiences discussed in the interview which will or will not inform future actions as such, and historic or legacy experiences which have been stored in clients memory and mentioned during interview.

PEL1.1_Clear association with ADVISOR (capabilities, offerings - strengths or weaknesses). Client has a clear view stored in their experience memory as to what an advisor, so an individual strengths and weaknesses, and calls upon those experiences for future references.

PEL1.2_Clear association with ADVISORY FIRM (capabilities, offerings - strengths or weaknesses). Client has a clear view stored in their experience memory as to what an advisory firm overall is capable off (often referred to as a house style or strength of a firm) and calls upon those experiences for future references.

PEL1.3_Legacy or established relationship with the ADVISORY FIRM. Client is discussing having an existing relationship, rapport or joint history with the advisory firm and these experiences do influence or shape the executives' decision-making.

PEL1.4_Legacy or established relationship with the ADVISOR. Client is discussing having an existing relationship, rapport or joint history with the individual advisor not necessarily the firm and these experiences do influence or shape the executives' decision-making.

PEL1.5_Past experiences shape association. Respondent more or less explicitly states that past experiences either with the advisor or the advisory firm will inform future views and decision-making.

PEL1.6_Historic NEGATIVE hands-on experiences with the ADVISOR. Past as in historic negative experiences made with the advisor such as a failing project or not managing issues do influence or shape the executives' decision-making.

PEL1.7_ Historic NEGATIVE hands-on experiences with the ADVISORY FIRM. Past as in historic negative experiences made with the advisory firm such as a failing project or not managing issues do influence or shape the executives' decision-making.

PEL1.8_Historic POSITIVE hands-on experiences with the ADVISOR. Past as in historic positive experiences made with an advisor such as a successful project, a good initiative to progress, responding to personal requests do influence or shape the executive's decision-making.

PEL1.9_Historic POSITIVE hands-on experiences with the ADVISORY FIRM. Past as in historic positive experiences made with an advisory firm such as a successful project, a good initiative to progress, responding to personal requests do influence or shape the executive's decision-making.

PER1.1_Value for money achieved. Recent engagement delivered value for money for the client, he/she felt they received the appropriate value in return for the money spent on the advisory engagement.

PER1.2_Value for money questionable. Recent engagement did not quite or not at all deliver value for money for the client, he/she felt that the advisory engagement did either not deliver the value promised or could not deliver any value at all (Section 166 - regulatory work) for the client as such.

PER1.3_Positive outcome or experience, achieved benefits or objectives. Respondent discusses a recent advisory engagement, the outcome or experience was positive, the project achieved the desired benefits and or objectives.

PER1.4_Overall or on balance positive outcome or experience, some minor aspects did not go so well. Respondent discusses a recent advisory engagement, the outcome or experience on balance positive there were some minor issues or challenges but all in all the project achieved all or most of the desired benefits and or objectives.

PER1.5_Negative outcome or experiences, wrong advisor. Respondent discusses a recent negative experience and concludes that the wrong advisor (or team) was selected for the job (skills and capabilities).

PER1.6_Negative outcome or experience, possibly wrong firm. Respondent discusses a recent negative experience and concludes that the wrong advisory firm was selected for the job (skills and capabilities).

PER1.7_Client lesson learned, clarify objectives or services to be received up front. Respondent discusses lessons learned from a recent engagement, he/she establishes that as a client he/she or the organisation should have been much clearer and pro-active in drawing up the construct of the engagement and be more up front with what should be delivered.

PER1.8_Client lesson learned, advisors overstays welcome or overcomplicates next phase. Respondent discusses lessons learned from a recent engagement, the advisor either tried to overstay or extend a project beyond what the respondent desired or overcomplicate the next phase of the engagement (in order to secure the piece of work in a non-compete set-up).

PER1.9_Client lesson learned, overreliance - we put too much into the hands of the advisor. Respondent discusses recent experiences with an advisor and concludes that too much was put in the hands of the advisor and as organisation there was too much reliance on the advisory firm to deliver and not ownership or coordination from him/her or the organisation overall.

Interview (source) classifications

The following classifications were assigned to each transcript during the research project:

- **Account classification:** 'Big Four' internal account classification given to the company at the time of interview, for example: key or strategic account.
- **Buying role:** General buying role assigned to the senior executive as defined by the account team or partners working with client (extracted from briefing interviews), for example: buyer, sponsor, influencer/occasional buyer.
- **Career path:** General background information about the interviewee, has the person spent significant time working for a professional service firm, only worked for this one organisation (lifer) or held various corporate roles.
- **Dominant selection mode observed:** Based on coding the results in regards to selection mode and observational memos, the researcher assigned a dominant or preferred selection mode, for example delegation, hybrid, group decision or primary direct.
- **Education:** Level of education of interviewee based on public information (e.g. company websites or databases).
- **Gender**
- **Level in organisation:** This could be board level (chairman etc.), group level (if there is one), c-suite and head of department/area reporting into the C-suite.

- **Nationality:** Based on public information (e.g. company websites or databases)
- **Organisational legacy:** Description of the legacy or background of the organisation senior executive is currently working for, for example, is it well established, meaning that it has been around for many years with little change; has it been spun off from other firms, or is it the result of multiple mergers or acquisitions.
- **Generic role:** Generic role in the organisation based on functional focus and responsibilities to allow for comparison amongst respondents.
- **Satisfaction rating:** Overall satisfaction rating stated by respondent at the end of interview, averaged out by CF manager if there are two ratings; these are the ratings presented to senior management.
- **Satisfaction rating response:** Captures how the respondents communicated the overall satisfaction rating – numerically or verbally or a combination of the two– plus if the individual provided an unprompted explanation of the rating given.
- **Supplier management:** To what extent is a procurement or supplier management with appropriate processes and protocols in place in the client organisation, based on client commentary and insights from procurement interviews (if these took place).
- **Tenure:** How long has the respondent worked for the company, based on public information, partner briefings and interview commentary.
- **Value for money response:** Documents how senior executives responded to the value for money question (if it came up in the course of the interview); some individuals diverted into a general debate or a pricing discussion, others provided an intuitive judgement and discussion.

Appendix B

Example of senior executive profiles utilised as part of the analysis

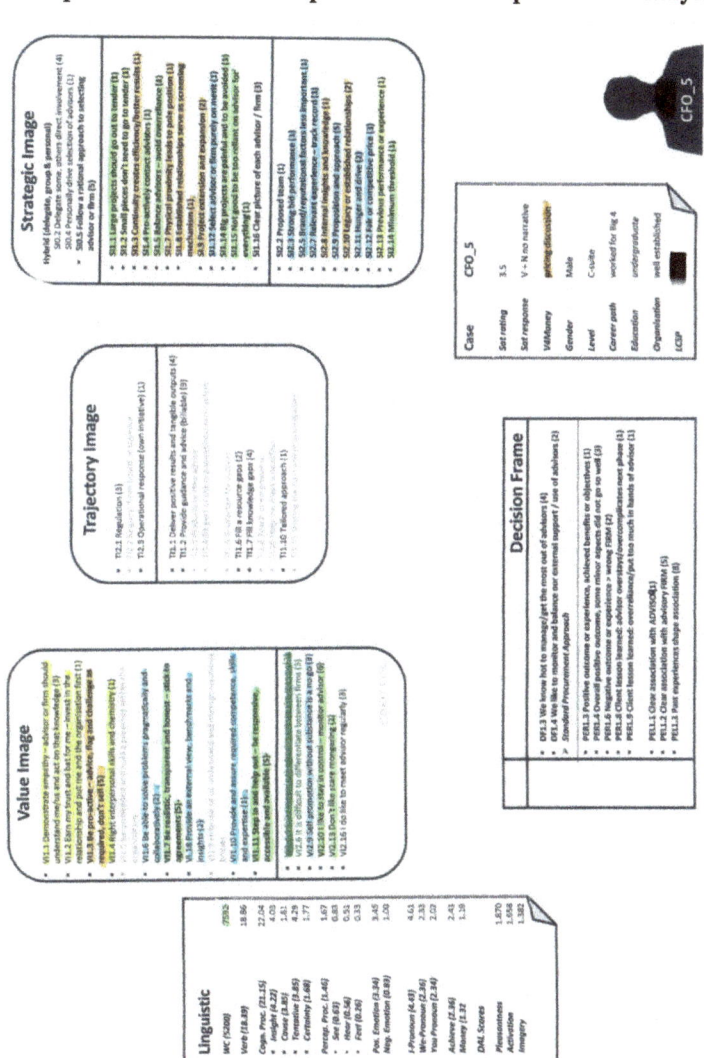

Index